Policing the empire

GOVERNMENT, AUTHORITY AND CONTROL, 1830–1940

edited by

David M. Anderson
and David Killingray

**MANCHESTER
UNIVERSITY PRESS**

Manchester and New York

Distributed exclusively in the USA and Canada
by ST. MARTIN'S PRESS

Whilst copyright in the volume as a whole is vested in Manchester University Press, copyright in individual chapters belongs to their respective authors, and no chapter may be reproduced wholly or in part without the express permission in writing of both author and publisher.

Published by MANCHESTER UNIVERSITY PRESS
OXFORD ROAD, MANCHESTER M13 9PL, UK
and ROOM 400, 175 FIFTH AVENUE, NEW YORK, NY 10010, USA

Distributed exclusively in the USA and Canada
by ST. MARTIN'S PRESS, INC.
175 FIFTH AVENUE, NEW YORK, NY 10010, USA

A catalogue record for this book is available from the British Library

Library of Congress cataloging in publication data
Policing the empire: government, authority, and control, 1830–1940 /
   edited by David M. Anderson and David Killingray.
      p.   cm. – (Studies in imperialism)
   Includes index.
   ISBN 0-7190-3035-8
   1. Law enforcement – Great Britain – Colonies – History. 2. Great Britain – Colonies – Administration – History. I. Anderson, David M. II. Killingray, David.   III. Series: Studies in imperialism (Manchester, England)
   HV8195.A2P637 1991
   363.2'09171'241 – dc20   91-9688

ISBN 0 7190 3035 8 *hardback*

Printed in Great Britain
by Bell & Bain Limited, Glasgow

⸺STUDIES IN⸺
IMPERIALISM

general editor John M. MacKenzie

Established in the belief that imperialism as a cultural phenomenon had as significant an effect on the dominant as on the subordinate societies, Studies in Imperialism seeks to develop the new socio-cultural approach which has emerged through cross-disciplinary work on popular culture, media studies, art history, the study of education and religion, sports history, and children's literature. The cultural emphasis embraces studies of migration and race, while the older political, and constitutional, economic and military concerns will never be far away. It will incorporate comparative work on European and American empire-building, with the chronological focus primarily, though not exclusively, on the nineteenth and twentieth centuries, when these cultural exchanges were most powerfully at work.

STUDIES IN IMPERIALISM

CONTENTS

[v]

CONTENTS

TABLES

ILLUSTRATIONS

GENERAL EDITOR'S INTRODUCTION

Although colonial police forces were significant agents of imperial and settler power, until recently they have received too little attention from historians. Consequently they have been the subject of generalisations and oft-repeated assertions – for example their alleged common descent from the Royal Irish Constabulary – that are only now being challenged. The contributors to this volume examine a number of colonial police forces across the full spectrum of empire and examine them in their widest social, legal, administrative and anthropological contexts. While they uncover the complexities of colonial policing, this is not to say that an unconnected diversity rules. They establish interactive influences between metropolis and periphery and, more significantly, many inter-imperial linkages as well.

The volume is thus representative of the 'new imperial history'. The authors of the various essays consider examples of policing in territories as diverse as Canada, Australia, New Zealand and South Africa as well as in India, Caribbean islands and African colonies. They establish patterns of urban, rural and frontier policing, the range of practice from the paramilitary to the civil and the dynamic of change from one to the other, and the role of indigenous auxiliaries, operating within a strict and often complex hierarchy, in many forces. We confront a number of paradoxes in these studies. Although colonial police forces seem at first sight to be a principal element of coercion within the imperial system, they were often considered to be the 'cinderellas' of colonial expenditure, undermanned, poorly trained, and behindhand in their professional practices. Their relationship with administrations was never simple and there were sometimes conflicting interpretations of their duties. In choosing auxiliaries they contributed to martial race theory, but reputation and reality were often at variance. And, as always in imperial history, activities on the ground invariably diverged both from intention and from common perception. Moreover, the power structures of colonial territories were so complex that policing tactics might move from suppression to support according to the needs of the moment.

This volume, and its companion on the policing of nationalism and decolonisation, arose from a conference in London which brought together scholars from a number of Commonwealth and other countries with interests in policing and legal history. I trust that readers will derive as much interest and excitement from the comparative approach as was enjoyed by the participants in that conference.

J.M. MacKenzie

ACKNOWLEDGEMENTS

The majority of the papers presented in this volume were initially prepared for a conference on the theme 'Policing the Empire', held at Birkbeck College, University of London, in May 1988. Of the twenty-seven papers delivered at that conference, nine are published here, along with a further four chapters (those by Finnane, Robb, Willis and Nasson). The editors are grateful to all those who attended the conference and contributed their ideas and comments to the discussion. Particular thanks must go to those who chaired panels – David Arnold, Clive Emsley, John Lonsdale, Andrew Porter, Peter Robb, Jim Sturgis and Richard Rathbone – and to Ann Myles for invaluable secretarial and administrative assistance.

D.M.A.
D.K.

CONTRIBUTORS

David M. Anderson is Lecturer in History at Birkbeck College, University of London. He is co-editor of the *Journal of African History* and has edited (with Richard Grove) *Conservation in Africa: people, policies and practice* (Cambridge, 1987) and (with Douglas H. Johnson) *The Ecology of Survival: case studies from northeast African history* (London, 1988). He is working on a history of crime, prosecution and punishment in British Africa.

Mark Finnane teaches history at Griffith University, Nathan, Queensland. He has written a number of articles on the history of policing in Australia and is the editor of *Policing in Australia: historical perspectives* (Kensington, New South Wales, 1987).

Albert Grundlingh is Lecturer in History at the University of South Africa, Pretoria. His most recent book is *Fighting their own War: South African Blacks in the First World War* (Johannesburg, 1987).

Richard Hawkins was born in Wembley, the great-grandson of the first Metropolitan Policeman to be stationed in the area. He is a graduate of the University of Cambridge. His research has focused mainly on the history of nineteenth-century Ireland, and since 1973 he has been secretary to the multi-volume *A New History of Ireland* publication project, based at the Royal Irish Academy, Dublin.

Richard S. Hill studied at the University of Canterbury, Christchurch, and at Churchill College, University of Cambridge. He is author of the two-part work *Policing the Colonial Frontier: the theory and practice of social and racial control in New Zealand* (Wellington, 1986), which constitutes the first volume of the History of Policing in New Zealand series. His present position is Senior Policy Adviser, Treaty of Waitangi Policy Unit.

Douglas H. Johnson has a Ph.D. from the University of California at Los Angeles, and has published extensively on the history of the Nuer peoples of the southern Sudan. He is co-editor, with David Anderson, of *The Ecology of Survival: case studies from northeast African history* (London, 1988), and is compiling the Sudan volume of the British Documents on the End of Empire series. His monograph *Nuer Prophets* is soon to be published.

Howard Johnson taught at the College of the Bahamas, Nassau, until moving to his present post as Professor of History at the University of Delaware in 1989. He has published numerous articles on the nineteenth and twentieth-century history of the Caribbean and is editor of *After the Crossing: immigrants and minorities in Caribbean Creole society* (London, 1988).

[xi]

CONTRIBUTORS

David Killingray is Reader in History at Goldsmiths' College, University of London. He has co-authored (with Anthony Clayton) *Khaki and Blue: military and police in British colonial Africa* (Athens, Ohio, 1989), co-edited (with Richard Rathbone) *Africa and the Second World War* (London, 1986) and is co-editor of the journal *African Affairs*. He is in the course of writing a book on Africa and the first world war.

William R. Morrison is Professor of History, Centre for Northern Studies, Lakehead University, Ontario. He is the author of *Showing the Flag: the Mounted Police and Canadian sovereignty in the north, 1894–1925* (Vancouver, 1985) and co-author (with K. S. Coates) of *Canada's Colonies: a history of the Yukon and North West Territories* (Toronto, 1985).

Bill Nasson studied at the University of Cambridge, and is now Senior Lecturer in the Department of Economic History at the University of Cape Town. He has published on South African social history, education and politics. His most recent book is *Abraham Esau's War: a black South African's war in the Cape, 1899–1902* (Cambridge, 1990).

Peter Robb teaches the history of South Asia at the School of Oriental and African Studies, University of London, where he is also Chairman of the Centre of South Asian Studies. His publications include *The Government of India and Reform* (Oxford, 1976) and *The Emergence of British Policy towards Indian Politics* (New Delhi, 1990). His current research concerns colonial policy and agrarian conditions in Bihar, India.

James L. Sturgis is Lecturer in History and co-Director of the Centre of Canadian Studies at Birkbeck College, University of London. He has written extensively on nineteenth-century Canadian and imperial history, and is researching the history of alcohol prohibition in the British Empire.

Justin Willis gained his Ph.D. from the School of Oriental and African Studies, University of London, in 1989. His research interests focus upon the social, cultural and linguistic history of eastern Africa in the nineteenth and early twentieth centuries. He holds the post of Assistant Director at the British Institute in Eastern Africa, Nairobi.

CHAPTER ONE

Consent, coercion and colonial control: policing the empire, 1830–1940

David M. Anderson and David Killingray

From the Victorian period to the present, images of the policeman have played a prominent role in the literature of empire, shaping popular perceptions of colonial policing. Such distinguished authors as Rudyard Kipling, George Orwell, Graham Greene and Paul Scott have provided us with characterisations of the policeman's lot in the far-flung outposts of empire, although not surprisingly perhaps, they do not offer a consensus as to the nature and experience of colonial policing. Kipling's unorthodox policeman, Strickland, breaks many of the rules of British society in India but is very much a 'protector of the people', knowledgeable about local cultures, sensitive to indigenous sensibilities and capable of remaining aloof from yet melding with 'the native crowd'.[1] Contrast this with Paul Scott's portrayal of Captain Merrick in *The Raj Quartet*: alien, alienating and alienated, a man at odds not just with the colonial peoples whom he must police but also with the wider European community of which he is a part.[2] Leaving aside the propaganda of the glories of empire in its heyday as viewed by Kipling, and the unpleasantness of its nadir as seen by Scott, perhaps the petty corruption first surrounding and finally embroiling Greene's Inspector Scobie in West Africa and the sense of the mind-numbing futility of the colonial service conveyed in Orwell's *Burmese Days* come closest to reflecting the realities of colonial policing.[3]

Whilst these, and other writers of fiction, have seized upon the colonial policeman as a vehicle for exploring the complexities and ambiguities of imperial power and control, colonial policing seems to have held less fascination for the historians of empire. The neglect is both surprising and puzzling. It is true that archival sources on the history of policing are fragmented and incomplete for many colonies. On the other hand, the study of the exercise of power and the establishment and maintenance of authority lie at the very heart of the historiography of empire: as the most visible public symbol of colonial rule, in daily contact with the

[1]

Contact with the

population and enforcing the codes of law that upheld colonial authority, the colonial policeman – be he a European officer or a local native recruit – stood at the cutting edge of colonial rule. The blending of military and civilian roles in colonial police services tended to reinforce the position of the policeman as the colonial state's first line of contact with the majority of the populace. The centrality of policing in the wider social and political history of colonialism appears undeniable. Yet Sir Charles Jeffries' *The Colonial Police*,[4] published in 1952, still remains the only work of synthesis and, despite its many limitations, continues to mark the starting point of any discussion. Alongside this account by a former civil servant in the Colonial Office there is, of course, a wide range of published personal career biographies and reminiscences of former colonial policemen. This colourful genre merits serious study in its own right, and although such accounts tend to present a somewhat lopsided and often idiosyncratic picture, they have frequently proved a valuable source for the historian.[5] Aside from these essentially anecdotal personal reflections, the historical study of colonial policing has remained an underdeveloped field.

In recent years this deficiency has begun to be made good with the completion of a number of research theses and scholarly publications dealing with the history of policing within individual colonies and territories. Some of these have been institutional histories of particular police forces, but most have been driven by the wider concerns of social history, and have been firmly rooted in the local history of the colonial experience. By examining policing as part of broader social, political and economic processes writers such as Arnold (for India), Haldane (for Australia) and McCracken (for central Africa) have added a colonial dimension to English and European writing on the social history of crime and the role of the state in seeking to prevent crime and maintain social order.[6] That colonial dimension has emerged as distinct from its English counterpart, and at the same time highly differentiated in its various parts: it is apparent that the colonial experience did not mirror that of England, and was not even consistent from one colony of another. Most fundamentally, the collective impact of this work has raised serious questions about Jeffries's oft quoted assertion that Irish and Metropolitan models of policing determined developments in the colonies.[7] The colonial reality was clearly much more complex.

This volume marks the first attempt to draw together the various parts of this emergent 'new history' of colonial policing. The thirteen essays gathered here share a wide range of common themes, yet the collection does not offer a singular approach to the history of policing: no such consensus has yet emerged. The value of the collection lies in the range and diversity of cases, and the opportunity for comparison

[2]

that they afford. Comparative studies in this field seem particularly worthwhile and appropriate, for the questions addressed are relevant both to an understanding of the broader pattern of imperial history and to the reconstruction of the social and political history of specific colonial societies.

England, Ireland and the empire: models or muddle?

With the establishment of the Metropolitan Police in London during the later months of 1829, legislation to create similar police forces in the provincial boroughs in 1835, and the obligation laid upon every local authority in 1856 to set up and maintain its own police force, the modern era of British policing can be said to have begun. Although historians have disagreed as to the immediate impact of these directives, there can be no doubt that the emergence of the 'New Police' marked a significant shift in British efforts to deal with the problems of crime and social order.[8]

The extent to which these developments were reflected throughout the parts of the British Empire was to be gradual and partial. The conventional, and now long accepted, wisdom is that the development of policing in the colonies in the mid-nineteenth century was founded not upon the New Police in England but upon the principles of the Royal Irish Constabulary and, later, its successor in the north, the Royal Ulster Constabulary. Descriptions are legion of various colonial forces in this period which refer to 'the Irish model' or 'the Ulster model' by way of explaining the organisation, structure and functions of the force. Sir John Macdonald said that he used the RIC as a model in creating the North West Mounted Police in Canada in 1873, although the RIC was not a mounted force.[9] Killingray (chapter 7) reminds us that in the Gold Coast in 1865 Colonel Conran similarly styled his locally recruited policemen in the mould of the force he had known in his native Ireland, while Finnane and Hill (chapters 3 and 4) state that in Australia and New Zealand Irish 'models' were commonly invoked by senior commanders and governors in the reorganisation of police forces until the late nineteenth century. More substantively, Phoenix Park, and subsequently Newtownards, became important training centres for colonial police officers. The apparent explanatory power of the export of such 'models' has impressed itself upon many historians of policing in the British Isles. Stanley Palmer's magisterial study of crime and policing in England and Ireland in the mid-nineteenth century, for example, draws heavily upon Jeffries, and upon sources cited by Jeffries, to assert that the colonies adopted English and Irish models of policing – an English model for urban policing and an Irish model for rural policing. 'Both were exported,' states Palmer, 'but the Irish dominated the colonies.'[10]

[3]

But what was meant by such references to 'the Irish model'? And how do such statements stand up when tested against the actual practice of imperial policing? As Richard Hawkins asserts in this volume, such 'models' were exceedingly difficult to define precisely. In most cases the reference to an Irish element in the structure and organisation of a colonial force served to highlight three distinctions not found in the English (or Scottish) police of the nineteenth or twentieth centuries: the police were to some extent – and this varied from force to force – organised along military lines (which meant they were armed), were housed in barracks rather than living among the community they served, and were directed and centrally controlled as a national or territorial force. One or other of these distinctions applied to all police forces throughout the empire until the last quarter of the nineteenth century, and persisted in many parts of the African and south-east Asian colonies much longer.

Yet, as Hawkins points out and subsequent chapters reiterate, no colonial force was quite like the Irish or Ulster constabularies, whatever claims may have been made for the influence of any model. Nor was the distinction between forms of urban and rural policing as sharp as Palmer's neat categorisation would imply. The gulf between the rhetoric of theory and the reality of practice in colonial policing was in many respects striking. Most obviously, whereas Ireland was heavily policed, the colonies were not. Single European officers frequently presided over huge tracts of territory and large, if scattered, populations, with only a handful of locally recruited and often untrained constables under their charge. Less obviously, although many forces in colonial Africa adopted an RIC structure of command and organisation, they did not follow RIC practices in training, method or development.[11] Moreover, some colonial forces claimed to be organised on the basis of English models, whilst others were deliberately hybrid. Hong Kong's first police force, established by Sir Charles May in the 1840s, was modelled on the Metropolitan Police.[12] With centrally controlled forces, which functioned mainly in rural areas (as Peter Robb here describes), Indian policing drew heavily on the style and practice of both the Met and the RIC (rather in the manner Palmer supposes was commonplace elsewhere in the empire).[13]

In short, the assertion that colonial police forces followed one or another model tells us precious little about their history and development, and may indeed obscure more than it reveals. Especially in the early stages of the establishment of colonial control, or in the process of its extension over outlying territories, in function and form the colonial police were often indistinguishable from a military garrison. Troublesome frontiers, unruly peoples and 'unsettled' territories required

[4]

military force to guard, extend and uphold the authority of the Crown and what was often new and alien law. Simply in terms of the small numbers of policemen involved in this task, the policing of the empire – the maintenance of 'the thin blue line' – was a conjuring trick of enormous proportions. Of course, it was achieved by police forces which were armed (unlike the police in England), often mercenary bodies, with the army and other quasi-military forces in close attendance to aid the civil power, and bolstered by many other forms of institutional and informal structures of authority, from the District Commissioner and Resident Magistrate to the estate or plantation manager and the labour recruiter. The powerful coalition of interests these forces represented was more overt and direct in its combined actions and attitudes in the colonies than in England, especially in those territories where the element of race played a significant role in establishing and maintaining the hierarchies of authority. It would be wrong, therefore, to assume that policing the empire was much the same as policing Limerick, or London, or Leicestershire.

Government, authority and control

The administrative and legal systems within which the colonial police worked and the laws which they sought to enforce were often significant-ly different in many respects from those which prevailed in England. To assume that a common system of law bound the empire together is to assume too much: English law was transplanted in the colonies, but that transplantation bred several mutant strains. Colonial legislative codes were invariably hybrids, formed of parts from other colonies as well as from England, these being moulded by the local political and social environments into which they were placed. Examples of this abound: legal codes were taken from the Caribbean islands to Nigeria, where they operated alongside Islamic codes and customary practices in local courts; in East Africa, Indian legal codes dominated the statutes until the 1930s.[14] This all had profound implications for the forms and methods of policing, as Anderson (for Kenya) and Robb (for nineteenth-century India) each demonstrates in this volume. Legal and adminis-trative categories that would be distinct and separate in England were often confused and overlapping in the colonies, especially on the frontier of settlement and control: administrator and magistrate might be one and the same official, the operation of the criminal law a *de facto* mixture of local customs and legislative codes neither of which was likely to be familiar to the police recruit. Colonial policing evolved as part of these hybrid legal and administrative systems, and so the practices of policing in each colony came to acquire certain distinctive features.

Yet a general pattern to the development of colonial policing can be discerned, albeit one that displays a different temporal frame from place to place. Like their counterparts in England, the colonial police of the nineteenth century had more to do with the protection of property and of the propertied classes, and with the maintenance of social order (and the *pax britannica*), than with the prevention or detection of crime. As patterns of authority, of accountability and of consent, control and coercion evolved in each colony the general trend was towards a greater concentration of police time upon crime. Colonial governments aspired to move towards more distinctly civilian forms of policing. This was true everywhere, but within individual colonies the process could be uneven. Resources were limited, and choices had to be made: not all areas of the colony could be effectively policed. The choices were inevitably political, and it is impossible to divorce the changing practices and functions of policing from the evolving politics of the colonial state.

The frontier, marking the temporary limit of conquest, administration or settlement, was an inevitable feature of colonial life. All colonies initially required a frontier style of policing. In the Australian territories nineteenth-century policing tended to follow a commercial frontier, defined by the gradual extension of settler pastoralist farming and by discoveries of gold and other minerals.[15] In early colonial Africa the demands of commerce dictated that customs posts, factories and trade routes should be policed, but police garrisons were also deployed to bolster the authority of political allies.[16] As the frontiers of colonial administration pushed onwards, policing extended but became more varied in its forms and practices: in Canada, Sturgis shows, new forms of urban policing were being employed towards the end of the century in the major cities to combat what were perceived as emergent social problems, whilst Morrison's study of the Yukon in the same period shows that a paramilitary police force continued to operate in this outlying region, where the writ of government still depended more upon coercion than consent.

As settled administration was established over the economic and political centres of each colony, governments commonly sought to isolate the problems of the frontier, leaving such troublesome and backward regions as militarised zones and concentrating policing in the settled areas. The frontier became an area apart, which required special forms of administration and which could not be expected to develop at the same pace as the rest of the colony. The frontier districts of north-west and north-east India, the Northern Frontier District of Kenya, and the Northern Territories of the Gold Coast all continued with a military style of policing long after it had been given up in other areas of the

[6]

colony. In such regions the colonial state made no pretence of seeking to police communities by consent.

The initial and often continuing role of the colonial police force as an arm of the conquest state was reflected in patterns of recruitment. Men of the 'right quality' were hard to find, and recruits to the local police had to be cut from whatever cloth was available: rank-and-file ex-servicemen, vagabonds and adventurers dominated in Australia, Canada and New Zealand,[17] and added to this motley crew in the African colonies were former slaves and refugees of various sorts, along with a substantial number of men who may have been compelled into service by one device or another.[18] The standard of recruits to the ranks of European inspectors and of 'native' constables improved in time but only rarely came up to the expectations of Colonial Office inspectorates.

The uncertain legitimacy of the colonial state in the eyes of many of its subjects added to the problems of recruiting reliable constables from among the local population. Like the military, the police actively sought recruits from areas peripheral to the colony: the trustworthy stranger to police other strangers was the man required.[19] In some colonies specifically favoured ethnic groups originating from other colonies dominated the police – for example, Indians in Mauritius, Trinidad and Fiji, Chinese and Indians in Malaya, and Sikhs recruited from India for the Hong Kong police. As Howard Johnson indicates, the martial races notion was strongly apparent in the West Indies during the nineteenth century, allied to a firm belief in the importance of policing with 'other-islanders'. Thus Barbadians were employed to police Trinidad, deeply unpopular though they were.[20] These patterns suggest the tenuous nature of colonial control and reveal the significance of imperial prejudices about the attributes of different races and cultures.

In colonial Africa the West Indies, the Pacific, south-east Asia and in India[21] race was a crucial element in policing. The structure of recruitment and command in these colonies was based upon race. Gazetted officers were for the most part white, or different in race from those of the rank and file they commanded, and were therefore commonly recruited from outside the colony. Changes to this pattern were slow in coming, and although there were greater opportunities for the advancement of locally recruited men in south Asia, the structure of most forces retained a markedly racial division until at least the end of the 1930s.[22] African, Asian and West Indian constables tended to work in a world where those with white skins generally policed themselves: it was a bold 'native' constable indeed who would, of his own initiative, have sought to police a member of the white ruling class.

By contrast, for the European police recruit to any part of the dependent empire from the mid-nineteenth to the mid-twentieth century the power and authority of empire, underscored by a clear sense of racial superiority, were profoundly manifest. After limited training, the recruit was soon invested by his race and his rank into a position of considerable authority. The young colonial policeman had greater latitude in his daily work than his English or Irish counterpart; his power over those under his command was significantly greater; he could expect responsibility at a younger age and with less experience. Many colonial forces earned an unenviable reputation for excess and high-handedness, and whilst this was commonly attributed to the over-zealousness of 'native' constables the European inspectors cannot escape criticism. Even as the quality of European recruits to forces in the dependent empire improved after 1920 the rough image of the early days lingered on.[23]

Failings in discipline within the ranks of the colonial police were undoubtedly less acute than the poor standards of service to be encountered in the many other policing authorities that were to be found in every colony. In all colonies the colonial police were augmented by other uniformed bodies which also performed a policing role. Most operated as distinct authorities, each with differing functions – water police, district watchmen, 'boss boys' in the mines, company security guards, forest guards, cattle and sheep patrols, game guards and so on. Each was subject to the control of the colonial administration or of commerce, and all were perceived to be part of the structure of the colonial state (whether directly so or not). The most important of these groups were the tribal or Native Authority police forces, which were responsible for the policing of the countryside in large parts of colonial Africa and India.[24] These bodies commonly incorporated local structures of authority – chiefs and headmen and other 'native' appointees of the state – and were often under the command of the local district administrator. Minimally trained, poorly equipped, and often comprising numbers of former soldiers whose suitability for a civilian policing role might be highly questionable, the Native Authority police had a low reputation almost everywhere. In every sense viewed by the imperial power as a second-rate force performing second-grade tasks, their existence was often justified as being a valued element of indirect rule. In fact the reason for their employment was more financial than ideological. Other than as a cheap means of maintaining a presence in the colonial countryside, their merits were dubious. Inefficient, unreliable, corrupt, and too often operating simply as a coercive force at the disposal of the local chief, the Native Authority police did little to enhance the reputation of colonial policing, though their actions often bolstered the authority of the colonial chief.[25]

Coercion and consent

Police commanders in the colonies of Africa and south-east Asia, where the majority populations were not of European descent, were little concerned even in the twentieth century with any notion of policing by consent. In his perceptive analysis of policing in Madras, David Arnold argues that the police, although often inefficient, first and foremost served the interests of the state and were little accountable to representative bodies or the community.[26] Increasingly the police took over the internal security role of the military, expanding to become the main coercive arm of the state in combating the growing weight of nationalist opposition. Throughout the period of the Raj the police were identified with the interests of the propertied classes, but they paid scant regard to any ideal of the need to cultivate a community of consent. Similarly, in all parts of colonial Africa the ideology of colonial trusteeship and the practice of indirect rule (in its many varied forms) did little to make the police accountable and indeed tended to ingrain the coercive character of policing: in the Sudan, as Douglas Johnson shows, policing never lost its military element, whilst in many other African colonies the gradual trend towards the prevention and detection of crime in police work was not matched by any move towards policing by consent. But with the European settler populations in Canada, Australia and New Zealand the themes of consent and accountability did develop over the nineteenth century as these societies assumed an increasing degree of political responsibility. The difference between the development of policing ideologies and practices in the 'Old Empire' of white settlement and the 'New Empire' of colonial Africa during the twentieth century was marked.

Through their coercive internal security role the colonial police in India, in Arnold's words, serve as a metaphor for the colonial regime as a whole.[27] As Finnane argues here for colonial Queensland – a case surely applicable elsewhere – policing played a vital role in the construction of the colonial social order. In Australia, as in India, the police were among the first institutions established by the colonial state, and quickly became one of the state's major bureaucracies. Senior colonial officials were inclined to give the police a prominent role in the forging as well as the regulation of a new society: magistrates and policemen were the primary 'instruments of civilisation', in the view of Governor Maclean on the Gold Coast.[28] In similar vein, Grundlingh (chapter 10) reminds us that the South African constabulary were presented as 'the standard bearers of a new and better order' by the British administration seeking to establish its authority over the countryside in the wake of the South African war. Policing lay very much at the centre of the ideologies of imperial rule that informed social construction as well as political domination.

It was a view held by the ruling classes in nineteenth-century Britain that social regulation would help to 'civilise' the industrial and rural classes. The idea was exported to the colonies, to be applied to the white lower class of settlers and, with greater paternal vigour and force, to native peoples. The 'dangerous classes' of industrial Britain needed close policing, as did those identified as dangerous classes, both white and native, throughout the empire.[29] This colonial *mentalité* was most visibly evident towards the end of the nineteenth century in an urban context – in the towns of Australia and Canada, as well as in those of India and Africa – where we see the emergence of forms of policing that closely resemble those then prevalent in England. Constables in colonial towns walked a beat, or patrolled in twos and threes, covering the commercial and upper and middle-class residential areas of the town. Much urban policing was concerned with minor offences – petty theft, assault, public nuisances and civil cases, and (increasingly) traffic offences. Protection of property and the propertied classes was self-evidently the principal aim of urban policing, and increasingly the colonial police forces adopted modern techniques and procedures in the prevention and detection of urban crime: fingerprinting, forensic testing, detective work and intelligence gathering all became part of the weaponry of colonial urban policing by the early 1900s.[30]

It was also in the towns that the colonial police most directly enforced the moral and political imperatives of the state. The urban social ills of vice, vagrancy and liquor were as much the enemy of the ruling classes of the colonial world as they were of their late Victorian and Edwardian counterparts in England.[31] Whether the East End of London was policed with any more consent in the 1890s than were the poorer areas of Bombay, Durban or Melbourne is to be doubted. However, the demands of the colonial political economy were not always the same as those of the metropole, and this had an impact on the ruling classes' expectations of the policing of the city. First, legislative controls in these areas frequently gave colonial police greater powers than would be acceptable in London. This was especially so in Africa and India, where the question of policing by consent may have been desirable but was in fact largely immaterial. For example, Nasson and Willis show that pass laws in Cape Town and their equivalent in Mombasa allowed the police to regulate the population of the city closely through the policing of labour registration. In deciding how rigorously to enforce such legislation the police were making an essentially political choice, and were accordingly subject to political pressures. Their reluctance to become involved in the policing of labour registration stemmed partly from the constraints imposed by limited resources, but also from an awareness of the difficulties of policing such laws *without* a degree of public consent. Second, social morality took on a different guise where matters of race were concerned. It is interesting to contrast the political struggles over liquor prohibition in Hamilton – essentially a 'white' city – described here by Sturgis, with the motivation behind the enforcement of liquor laws in Mombasa in the same period. In Hamilton the policing of liquor laws was a matter of contestation on grounds of social morality, and the regulation of liquor consumption required a large degree of public consent. In Mombasa, as Willis makes clear, agitation for the regulation of liquor consumption was directly tied to the regulation of African labour, and the police were urged to act in order to protect the supply of *labour* rather than to prevent the supply of liquor.[32]

While the metropolitan and county forces in England moved closer to the ideals of consensual policing during the twentieth century, this trend was not mirrored in the dependent empire. Colonial rule in India and Africa simply would not permit such a development: the policing of labour disputes, and then of political agitation linked to nationalist or other anti-government activities, pushed the colonial police into a prominent internal security role. They continued to carry arms, and to be viewed as an important element in the defence of the colonial state: coercion was a necessary element of control, consensus at best a dim and distant goal.

This was not, of course, how the Colonial Office liked to see things. The evolution of a 'civilised' colonial society might be measured by the style of policing required, and from time to time the Colonial Office expressed concern at the failure of colonial forces to keep pace with reforms in Britain. For the most part it was prepared to allow for 'local conditions', but by the late 1930s pressure was growing within the CO for the implementation of reforms aimed at regularising policing in the colonies and introducing practices more akin to those then in vogue in England and Wales. The senior officers from the Home Office who advised the Colonial Office in this period frequently expressed astonishment at the nature of policing in the empire, shocked by the absence of 'modern methods', by the inappropriateness of the structures of command and deployment, and by the low success rates in arrests and prosecutions. That the standards of colonial forces were not up to those of the Metropolitan Police or the county constabularies was apparent, but this had more to do with improvements in policing in Britain than with any decline in the colonies. The gap in performance between English and colonial police by the 1930s reflected the great gap in resources directed at policing. To some extent the colonial police were always a 'Cinderella service', conditions of work and terms of pay rarely keeping pace with local civil servants' and invariably running well behind conditions in England. But the shortcomings of the colonial police service were perhaps especially acute during the 1930s, when economic depression caused retrenchment in all arms of the colonial administration, with reductions in expenditure and manpower.[33]

More effective reform came in the late 1940s. Good policing, on the British model, came to be thought of as one of the benefits or empire in this phase: but there were contradictions implicit in the intention of policy and the practice of colonial government. In the 1940s the colonial police invariably served the political interests of the colonial state more overtly than ever before, and were nowhere in any real sense accountable to the community. The colonial police were able to carry out their duties more efficiently and with greater reliability, but the nature of those duties remained coercive rather than consensual. The improved policing of the 1940s was to a large extent directed at strengthening the ability of the colonial state to coerce an increasing number of industrial, agrarian and political opponents more effectively.[34]

Imperial linkage: making the connections

We began by questioning the validity of the models of policing that have been used to describe and explain the origins and development of the colonial police. The chapters which follow do not completely reject the influence of Irish or English policing in the colonies, but instead set that influence in perspective by giving greater emphasis to the local context in which policing evolved. From the range of cases assembled here a number of related themes emerge as significant – the importance of the conquest phase; the existence of frontier zones; the continuing paramilitary role of the police; their status in the colonial social system; the type and quality of recruit attracted to the service; colonial attitudes towards race; and the political aspect of colonial policing. It is doubtful whether one could reconstruct a 'colonial model' of policing from these elements, but it is clear that the realities of policing the empire were simply too varied and complex to be held within the models of nineteenth-century policing that emerged in England or Ireland.

The work of the sociologist Michael Brogden has recently turned on its head the conventional wisdom that the British Isles exported models of policing to the colonies, by suggesting that, far from British practice informing and directing the empire, it was imperial experience that informed Britain. According to Brogden, colonial methods of policing disturbances – labour disputes, riots and political protests – have been employed with increasing frequency in Britain since the early twentieth century. The interface between the colonial and the British forces can also be measured by the high number of officers who returned from service in the colonies to take up senior appointments in the Metropolitan and county constabularies.[35] Seen in this light, colonial service was itself an important element in the profile of British policing.

While this brings an important corrective to the study of the relationship between British and colonial policing, it is more helpful to the historian of policing in Britain than the historian of colonial policing. From a colonial perspective Brogden's view needs further, and important, modification: the empire was a system in which ideas flowed not only outward from the metropole and back again but between the various colonies themselves. In some very real senses imperial policing was part of a single system – bounded by shared institutions and common expectations. Ideas and practices from one colony were borrowed and applied in another; this was especially true both of administrative practice and of legislation. But the most important aspect of imperial linkage in colonial policing was the movement of personnel from one colony to another. The pool of experience that senior officers in the colonial police were able to draw upon was likely to have been a significant element in defining the character and development of policing. By examining these imperial linkages and by comparing the experience of the colonies we may yet learn a great deal more about the policing of the empire.

Notes

1 Strickland first makes an appearance in 'Miss Youghal's Sais', published in the *Civil and Military Gazette*, 25 April 1887. He subsequently features in four other Kipling short stories, Rudyard Kipling, *Plain Tales from the Hills* (London, 1888), and as a minor character in *Kim* (London, 1901).
2 Paul Scott, *The Jewel in the Crown* (London, 1966); *The Day of the Scorpion* (London, 1968); *The Towers of Silence* (London, 1971); *A Division of the Spoils* (London, 1975).
3 Graham Greene, *The Heart of the Matter* (London, 1948); George Orwell, *Burmese Days* (New York, 1934; London, 1935).
4 Sir Charles Jeffries, *The Colonial Police* (London, 1952).
5 See, for example, M. Wynne (ed.), *On Honourable Terms: the memoirs of some Indian police officers, 1915–48* (London, 1985); C. Harwich, *Red Dust: Memories of the Uganda Police, 1935–55* (London, 1961); L. van Onselen, *A Rhapsody in Blue* (Cape Town, 1960).
6 David Arnold, *Police Power and Colonial Rule: Madras, 1859–1947* (Delhi, 1986); R. Haldane, *The People's Force: a history of the Victoria Police* (Carlton, Victoria, 1986); John McCracken, 'Coercion and control in Nyasaland: aspects of the history of a colonial police force', *Journal of African History*, 27 (1986), pp. 127–48. The thrust of this approach is well described and justified by Eric H. Monkkonen, 'From cop history to social history: the significance of the police in American history', *Journal of Social History*, 15 (1982).
7 Jeffries, *The Colonial Police*, passim.
8 C. Emsley, *Crime and Society in England, 1750–1900* (Harlow, 1987), pp. 171–93. See also C. Steedman, *Policing the Victorian Community: the formation of English provincial police forces, 1856–80* (London, 1984); David Philips, *Crime and Authority*

in *Victorian England: the Black Country, 1835–60* (London, 1977), chapter 3; J.J. Tobias, *Crime and Police in England, 1700–1900* (Dublin, 1979), chapters 4 and 5.

9 S.W. Horrall, 'Sir John A. MacDonald and the Mounted Police Force for the North West Territories', *Canadian Historical Review*, 53, ii (1972).

10 Stanley Palmer, *Police and Protest in England and Ireland, 1780–1850* (Cambridge, 1988), pp. 711–15.

11 David Killingray, 'The maintenance of law and order in British colonial Africa', *African Affairs*, 85 (1986), pp. 411–37.

12 Norman Miners, 'The localization of the Hong Kong police force, 1842–1947', *Journal of Imperial and Commonwealth History*, 18, 3 (1990), pp. 296–315.

13 See also Arnold, *Police Power*, and Sir P. Griffiths, *To Guard my People: the history of the Indian Police* (London and Bombay, 1971).

14 For West Africa see T. O. Elias, *The Nigerian Legal System* (2nd edn, London, 1963); for East Africa, Y. P. Ghai and J. P. W. B. McAuslan, *Public Law and Political Change in Kenya: a study of the legal framework of government from colonial times to the present* (Oxford, 1970), and H. F. Morris and J. S. Read, *Indirect Rule and the Search for Justice: essays in East African legal history* (Oxford, 1972).

15 For example, M. Finnane (ed.), *Policing in Australia: historical perspectives* (Kensington, N.S.W., 1987), and L. E. Skinner, *Police of the Pastoral Frontier* (St Lucia, 1975). For New Zealand, see Richard S. Hill, *Policing the Colonial Frontier: the theory and practice of coercive social and racial control in New Zealand* (2 vols., Wellington, 1986).

16 W. H. Gillespie, *The Gold Coast Police, 1844–1938* (Accra, 1955); T. N. Tamuno, *The Police in Modern Nigeria, 1861–1965* (Ibadan, 1970); W. R. Shirley, *History of the Nigerian Police* (Lagos, 1955).

17 See, for Australia, Robert Clyne, *Colonial Blue: a history of the South Australia Police Force, 1836–1916* (Adelaide, 1987), and R. B. Walker, 'The New South Wales Police Force, 1862–1900', *Journal of Australian Studies*, 15 (1984), pp. 25–39; for Canada, H. Boritch, 'Conflict, compromise and administrative convenience: the police organisation in nineteenth century Toronto', *Canadian Journal of Law and Society*, 3 (1988), pp. 141–74; and, for New Zealand, Hill, *Policing the Colonial Frontier*.

18 See Killingray, 'The maintenance of law and order', p. 423.

19 For India see David Arnold, *Police Power and Colonial Rule*, pp. 59 ff.; for Africa, A. H. M. Kirk-Greene, '*Damnosa hereditas*: ethnic ranking and martial race imperatives in Africa', *Ethnic and Racial Studies*, 2, 2 (1979).

20 Howard Johnson, 'Barbadian immigrants in Trinidad, 1870–97', *Caribbean Studies*, 13 (1973), pp. 2–18; see also his 'Social control and the colonial state: the reorganisation of the police force in the Bahamas, 1888–93', *Slavery and Abolition*, 7 (1986), pp. 46–58.

21 One might also add nineteenth-century Australia and New Zealand to the list. See R. Evans *et al.*, *Exclusion, Exploitation and Extermination: race relations in colonial Queensland* (Sydney, 1975); Marie H. Fels, *Good Men and True: the aboriginal police of the Port Philip district, 1837–53* (Melbourne, 1988); Richard S. Hill, 'Maori policing in nineteenth century New Zealand', *Archifacts*, 2 (1985).

22 Jeffries, *The Colonial Police*, Part II.

23 For commentaries on the quality of European and African recruits to the Kenya Police see W. R. Foran, *The Kenya Police, 1887–1960* (London, 1962), and J. B. Wolff, 'Asian and African recruitment in the Kenya Police, 1920–50', *International Journal of African Historical Studies*, 6 (1973), pp. 401–12. On the general training of colonial police, see Jeffries, *The Colonial Police*, p. 171, and Anthony Clayton and David Killingray, *Khaki and Blue: military and police in British colonial Africa* (Athens, Ohio, 1989), pp. 7–12.

24 On Native Authority police see, for example, K. Rotimi, 'The Native Administration police forces of western Nigeria, 1905–1951', *Odu*, 30 (July 1986); Tamuno, *The Police in Modern Nigeria*, chs. 3 and 4.

25 For examples of the failings of the Native Authority police see chapter 9 and Killingray, 'Maintenance of law and order', pp. 416–18 and 426–9.

26 Arnold, *Police Power*, pp. 232–4.

27 Arnold, *Police Power*, p. 2.

28 See G. E. Metcalfe, *Maclean of the Gold Coast: the life and times of Sir George Maclean, 1801–1847* (London, 1962), chapter 8.

29 P. T. Smith, *Policing Victorian London: political policing, public order and the London Metropolitan Police* (Westport, Conn., 1985), and, for an analysis of a specific dimension of this, R. Storch, 'The policeman as domestic missionary', *Journal of Social History*, 9 (1976), pp. 481–95.

30 Evidence of this is to be found in the various 'official' histories of colonial police services. See, C. Marlow, *A History of the Malawi Police Force* (Lilongwe, 1971), and Foran, *The Kenya Police*.

31 For examples see Haldane, *The People's Force*, and Charles van Onselen, *Studies in the Social and Economic History of the Witswatersrand, 1886–1914*, (2 vols., Harlow, 1982). American models played a role in the development of colonial urban policing in this period as much as did experience drawn from England. See Eric H. Monkkonen, *Police in Urban America, 1860–1920* (Cambridge, 1981), and James F. Richardson, *Urban Police in the United States* (London, 1974).

32 This, of course, reflects the extent to which colonial police became entwined with the requirements of colonial capital. There are parallels in the use of police in England to deal with labour disputes in the early twentieth century. On this general area see Jane Morgan, *Conflict and Order: The police and labour disputes in England and Wales, 1900–39* (Oxford, 1987), and Roger Geary, *Policing Industrial Disputes, 1893 to 1985* (Cambridge, 1987).

33 E.g. *Report on the Northern Rhodesia Police by Sir Herbert Dowbiggin* (Lusaka, 1937), p. 79.

34 These points are pursued in greater depth in a companion volume, David M. Anderson and David Killingray (eds.), *Policing and Decolonisation: politics, nationalism and the police, 1917–65* (Manchester, 1991).

35 Mike Brogden, 'An Act to Colonise the Internal Lands of the Island: empire and the origins of the professional police', *International Journal of the Sociology of Law*, 15 (1987), pp. 179–208, and 'The emergence of the police: the colonial dimension', *British Journal of Criminology*, 27 (1987), pp. 4–14.

PART I

Policing the colonies of settlement, 1830–1900

CHAPTER TWO

The 'Irish model' and the empire: a case for reassessment

Richard Hawkins

I

The fact is that the really effective influence upon the development of colonial police forces during the nineteenth century was not that of the police of Great Britain, but that of the Royal Irish Constabulary ... Into the merits or demerits of this system, as applied to Ireland, it is not for me to enter; but it is clear enough that from the point of view of the colonies there was much attraction in an arrangement which provided what we should now call a 'paramilitary' organisation or gendarmerie armed and trained to operate as an agent of the ... government in a country where the population was predominantly rural, communications were poor, social conditions were largely primitive, and the recourse to violence by members of the public who were 'agin the government' was not infrequent. It was natural that such a force, rather than one organised on the lines of the purely civilian and localised forces of Great Britain, should have been taken as a suitable model for adaptation to colonial conditions.
[Sir Charles Jeffries, *The Colonial Police*, London, 1952, pp. 30–1]

This passage is still invariably the starting point of any attempt to set the police history of Ireland in an imperial context. The present volume indicates the scope of work done since 1952 in colonial police history. In Irish police history – never an overworked field – Galen Broeker's pioneering study *Rural Disorder and Police Reform in Ireland, 1812–36* appeared in 1970; Kevin Boyle's work on police before 1800, a few years later; and most recently Stanley Palmer's indispensable *Police and Protest in England and Ireland, 1780–1850* marks an epoch in the historiography of police in the 'British archipelago' by the breadth of its research, by its comparative approach, and by its taking a first step in the quantitative analysis of police service records; the path thus opened for further work is already being followed.

The picture presented by Sir Charles Jeffries is still intact. Broeker devoted half his very brief epilogue to quoting or paraphrasing Jeffries; Palmer, with the aim of bringing out the full extent of Ireland's contribution to police development, finds the Irish 'model', 'pattern', 'example' or 'influence' at work throughout the British Empire, in Canada and Australasia as well as in the colonies Jeffries considered.[1] Yet anyone who surveys the police forces of the empire, at whatever period, expecting to find so many replicas of the Irish constabulary, will be disappointed and indeed bewildered.[2] The assertion that someone familiar with Irish police routine could walk into a police station anywhere in the empire with a confident expectation of what would be happening there at any given time is still current, and is not unfounded; but the more closely one looks at some forces the less they seem to resemble an 'Irish model'. From 1907, when all officers of colonial police forces had to undergo instruction at the Dublin depot, the RIC undoubtedly held primacy among the police forces of the empire; but has there perhaps been a tendency to read the pattern set up in 1907 back into the previous forty or sixty years? A force may be government-controlled, equipped, drilled, and distributed in paramilitary fashion; it may include personnel with Irish service, and at its setting up the example of the Irish force may have been explicitly considered; but to say that it was 'modelled' on the Irish constabulary may still be misleading. Familiar-sounding designations of rank such as 'inspector-general' (itself, of course, a term much older than the Irish constabulary), 'sub-inspector' or 'head constable' may be found, but without denoting the same functions as in Ireland; it is worth remembering that in Ireland itself the terms 'county inspector', 'sub-inspector' and even 'constable' do not mean the same in one period as in another.

To evaluate the precise role of the 'Irish model' in colonial police forces is at present probably beyond the powers of any one scholar. Each colony needs to be examined for the extent to which Ireland was drawn upon for example, advice or (where applicable) personnel. In this last respect, the single most important contribution that can be made in Britain is the analysis of the 90,000 service careers comprising the class of Royal Irish Constabulary records at Kew;[3] even this indispensable work, however, while it yields much useful information on those who proceeded direct from Ireland to colonial service, will not pick up those who broke their journey in a British force or in some other occupation. To find conspicuous dissimilarities between the police of Ireland and forces elsewhere is of course not difficult. The North West Mounted Police may have resembled the Irish constabulary in being armed and government-controlled, but the disparities in equipment, structure, operating conditions, purpose and relationship to society are so marked that 'model' is hardly applicable. The police of the British West Indies in the 1880s may have been influenced by RIC example – they were stiffened by small numbers of trained men recruited direct from the RIC, not to mention the presence of a Governor who had been an RIC

The Royal Irish Constabulary depot, Phoenix Park, August 1909: senior officers of the RIC with colonial police officers. Further details in the list of illustrations

officer, Resident Magistrate and 'Special RM' in Ireland – but the practice favoured in the West Indies of recruiting police largely from among Barbadans (paralleled elsewhere in the empire by drawing upon 'loyal aliens', 'martial races' and other distinct ethnic groups) was fundamentally opposed to the practice in recruiting the rank and file of police in Ireland after 1836.[4] The police of Australia are 'Irish' rather than 'English' in structure, in that within each state there is only one force; and within their history the withdrawal of powers from the local justices of the peace, and the extension to the police of numerous general administrative duties, are strongly reminiscent of events in Ireland; but, given the number of Irishmen, and even of former Irish policemen, who went to Australasia, the visible influence of the Irish constabulary seems curiously small. W.G. Cahill, on becoming commissioner of the Queensland force in 1899, 'made several changes in administration on the lines obtaining in the R.I.C.', but one would like to know how much this owed to the short period he served in the ranks in Ireland many years earlier, before coming to Queensland at the age of twenty-four.[5]

Kenya serves as an example of the 'constabulary influence' working at one remove, by way of the Indian system. Here again is an armed and drilled police force, centrally controlled, its officers from 1907 schooled at Phoenix Park to the extent that the commanding officer complained in 1911 of having to spend too much time on 'the unteaching of what has been learnt by Dublin'. Yet the same CO had criticised the general state of the force two years previously in terms that show a marked absence of some of the RIC's most salient characteristics: there was insufficient selection and training of men, no depot and no uniform training system, no set code of regulations, and no *esprit de corps*; most units were under unqualified administrative officers. Even his complaint about the Dublin training for officers makes it clear that it was unsuitable not for its 'Irishness' but because it was a very thorough training for European policing without reference to African circumstances. The fact that the force included European and Asian officers, and Asian and African NCOs and men, had of course no parallel in Irish practice.[6]

In any assessment of the 'Irish model' the position of India is crucial: the system established by the Indian Police Act of 1861 was the dominant influence on police development in the Far East and British Africa. In turn, it derived from the success of the police organised in Sind by Sir Charles Napier after his conquest in 1843; and Napier, it is generally affirmed, formed his police 'on the model of the Royal Irish Constabulary'.[7] The more closely one looks at descriptions of the force, and at the writings and biographies of Napier, the harder it becomes to accept this. The Sind police consisted of three classes: urban (further subdivided into two strata), rural (which did not completely supersede the existing village police) and mounted, all distinguished by function as well as distribution. The rank structure included lieutenant, captain and 'captain-chief of police'; the Sind recruits were stiffened with Pathans and Rajputs. The system operated alongside, but carefully separated from, the fiscal and administrative division of Sind into collectorates. 'Perhaps only the English,' remarks one historian of Indian police, 'could have invented an arrangement so open to criticism by theorists and politicians – but it worked.'[8] Not the words one would apply to the Irish constabulary, whose formation marked a major step in rationalising Irish administration. Along with these surface differences, however, go some basic similarities; the police, while capable of serving as soldiers, were to be 'a separate and self-contained organisation under their own superior officers, whose sole duty and responsibility was to supervise them...', and Napier hoped that 'the police, by mixing with the people, would acquire great local knowledge ... which would make them especially useful in collecting the revenue, defeating conspiracies, and as guides in case of war'.[9] Charles Napier had an active and imaginative interest in questions of government, society and peace-keeping, and a particular concern for the problems of Ireland. It is inconceivable that he was not aware of the Irish police experiments, and it is not unlikely that he may have been influenced by their example. Although in 1843 the Irish constabulary, in its full-blown form, had existed for only seven relatively tranquil years and had not yet been severely tried, the principles behind it had long been current, the need for development in this direction had long been asserted, and opinion was already forming by 1843 that the new institution was not merely viable but beneficial. Napier could well have decided to apply the same ideas in Sind; but there seems to be no direct evidence that he based his force 'on the model' of the Irish one. In his brother's substantial *Administration of Scinde* and *Life and Opinions*[10] there is no mention of the Irish example even as a precedent. One might ascribe this to William Napier's reluctance to admit that Charles's achievement owed anything to the work of another; but the lack of any obvious structural resemblance between the forces of Sind and Ireland is suggestive. The chief similarity of principle – Napier's insistence on separate organisations, so that troops should not be scattered in penny packets, the civil authorities should not be dependent on the army, and the police should be outside the control of local authorities – could have come as easily, and more directly, from Napier's practical experience in northern England and elsewhere as from the Irish example. A modern study of Napier's work in Sind mentions the Irish example only to cite Napier himself as tracing the origin of his ideas to his administration of Cephalonia in 1822–28.[11]

Sind is an extreme example of the difficulty, and importance, of defining 'model'. The Irish constabulary system is a coherent but complex one, with several different aspects; when it is spoken of as a 'model' one of the first necessities is to ascertain which aspect, or combination of aspects, is being considered. The 'Irish model' is defined often by contrast: for instance, within the context of the 'British archipelago' the contrast is with the local and civil English (or, sometimes, London Metropolitan Police) model, tending to obscure the common ground shared by Irish and London police of being 'ruler-directed' forces; or the Irish system is held up as a model for rural conditions, obscuring its role in towns of up to 380,000 population, where it operated on similar lines to the Metropolitan Police. It may be seen as a merely repressive or coercive force with a reactive policy to crime; this would have distressed the first Inspector General, James Shaw Kennedy, who in the original 1837 rule book laid great stress on the prevention of crime and on the discharge of police duties 'with the utmost forbearance, mildness, urbanity, and perfect civility towards *all* classes of her majesty's subjects'.[12] Kennedy must, however, have known that a 'repressive' image was already current, and it was this that the 1839 commissioners of inquiry into a police for the counties of England and Wales had in mind when they wrote:

> The Irish constabulary force is in its origination and action essentially inapplicable to England and Wales. It partakes more of the character of a military and repressive force, and is consequently required to act in greater numbers than the description of force which we consider the most applicable, as a preventive force.[13]

militarism compared to ideal model

They nevertheless went on to make recommendations that embodied what were or would be some of the Irish force's main characteristics: a national force, capable of dealing with widespread problems; a 'disposable body' or reserve task force of 300–400 men; the men to be thoroughly trained, unconnected with the district in which they acted, subject to periodic changes of district, and 'under general rules and principles, and in subordination to general directions from one general and responsible executive authority'.[14] Fourteen years later the visible success of the system in Ireland evoked more positive approval from the witnesses before the 1853 select committee on British police: many witnesses recommended a national force; the chief of the Hampshire police favoured drilling constables in the use of arms and proposed 'to ingraft the discipline of the Irish constabulary upon the system of doing duty in this country',[15] while the Chief Constable of Essex wanted a 'uniform constabulary' throughout England and Wales, limited in strength to one per thousand of population (thus avoiding the objection of 1839 to the 'greater numbers' needed by the Irish system), but also doing various administrative duties for the government, acting as coastguards and public prosecutors, and, at need, forming 'an efficient and respectable defensive force of 14,000 men'.[16]

The 1853 evidence also provided a striking example of the ambiguity of the term 'Irish model': a West Country JP confirmed that 'the Gloucestershire police is founded on the model of the Irish police', meaning only that the constables were not distributed singly in each parish but grouped at stations under a sergeant or superintendent.[17] This was certainly a characteristic of the Irish system, and its presence in Gloucestershire no doubt derived from Chief Constable Lefroy, a former Irish police officer; but this underlines the danger of reading more into the term 'model' than is intended. Often, one might suggest, 'precedent' would be a better word than 'model', with its associations of deliberate replication; for in some cases to say that the X constabulary was 'modelled on' that of Ireland appears to mean no more than that both are in some sense the same sort of thing, the Irish example being better known and earlier established.[18] The success of the Irish system validated further attempts on similar lines elsewhere; it served as a precedent to be cited, an example to be considered, and a standard to be striven for; the extent to which it was actually copied in any given instance, however, remains to be established, and has too often been taken for granted. A full evaluation of the 'Irish model' may need to go beyond the context of Britain and its empire. As was generally recognised at the time of its development, the Irish constabulary was an example of a gendarmerie, a system common in continental Europe. Comparisons in police development could usefully be made between the colonies of Britain and those of countries where gendarmeries were the prevalent systems.

II

The duties of the constabulary are multifarious and onerous, and are becoming, every day, more and more so. In fact, whatever is to be done is expected to be performed by it. The constabulary is now the great machine by which almost every measure is worked, and there is no doubt that it is becoming gradually of greater political importance; therefore, the greater care should be taken not to make its members politicians ... [Mr and Mrs S. C. Hall, *Ireland*, London, 1841–43, I, p. 420].

Everything in Ireland, from the muzzling of a dog to the suppression of a rebellion, is done by the Irish constabulary. [H. A. Blake, 'The Irish police', *Nineteenth Century*, IX, 1881, p. 390].

As Jeffries points out, the Irish constabulary system was well adapted to imposing order by means of its own resources under conditions where little assistance could be expected from society; but it had not been suddenly called into existence with the main purpose of enforcing British rule. The system set up by the Constabulary Act of 1836 cannot be isolated from its antecedents. It was the culmination of fifty years of gradual progress away from the local institutions of law enforcement and the ideal of the 'self-policing community' imported from England; fifty years of gradual transfer of executive power from an incomplete, fragmented, diffuse and local system in the hands of the landed, Protestant, and 'loyal' sections of Irish society to one that was comprehensive, uniform, centralised and controlled direct from Dublin Castle. The shortcomings of the old system had been manifest in the late eighteenth century, evoking from the Irish parliament the timid and incomplete Police Acts of 1786, 1787 and 1792. The union of parliaments in 1801 transformed the context by making it unnecessary for a police system to be based directly on Irish society, reflecting its internal stresses. A 'remedial' system could be devised outside Ireland and imposed with the resources of the imperial government, which in the last resort was more interested in the tranquillity of Ireland than in maintaining the position of any social group. The paradox here was that the attempt to solve the problems of Ireland, and make the union with Britain a more positive achievement, produced a divergence between the institutions of the two countries. In the sense of being the passive object of legislation which, however well meant, originated elsewhere, Ireland was in no less 'colonial' a position after the union than before, despite a parliamentary representation that became in the course of the nineteenth century larger than its shrinking population warranted. The 'colonial' status of Ireland was not ignored in political discourse; and when in the 1880s the difficulties of governing Ireland were greatly increased by mass agrarian agitation and the efforts of Irish MPs in and out of Parliament, there were, as well as those who saw the solution in home rule for Ireland, others who felt that it might lie in out-and-out colonial rule.[19]

Detaching the police system from the divisions of Irish society had been necessary both for the sake of efficiency and, as the Halls put it, 'to exhibit the law as acting for the protection of every class of the community'.[20] It had of course a negative side, shown in a chronically uneasy relationship between the constabulary and the unpaid justices of the peace. The police attitude was guarded: the JPs were to be given due respect, necessary information and such obedience as the law required, but no influence or patronage, still less control, over policemen, and they were not to be given access to the standing rules and regulations, a copy of which was in each of the 1,400–1,500 police barracks in Ireland. The JPs in turn complained of the aloofness, military inflexibility and lack of initiative of the police. Over twenty-five years after the 1836 Act, Nassau Senior found Lord Rosse (the celebrated astronomer) wishing to return to a force of about 2,000 men, 'a real police, named by the magistrates and under their orders, ... resembling the old police, living among the people, and knowing their habits – the servants of the *civil power* [my italics] instead of being its rivals'.[21]

The constabulary was further deliberately separated from community influence by regulations that a man could not serve in a county in which he had family connections, should not be in employment or in the liquor trade (later extended to cover any kind of business or the holding of land) and should not vote. At its most negative, this separation could reach the point embodied in the police's frequent self-description as 'Ishmaels', and in the comment of a former RIC officer in 1881:

> Not one in five hundred of the community, be he gentleman or peasant, looks upon the commission of crime as a matter affecting anybody but the government. It is entirely a matter for the police, and neither the desire for security nor the temptation of a large reward will induce any person to offer assistance.[22]

This should not be seen as an opposition to 'the whole system of law'[23] (in general, Irish society in the nineteenth century showed a keen appetite for litigation); but by the 1880s the constabulary found its resources overtaxed by nationwide agitation, regardless of the level of actual crime, and virtually unable to secure substantial assistance from the public.

Separation from society went hand in hand with centralisation (though it should be remembered that the separate 'revenue police', of 1,200–1,500 men, were not superseded till 1855, or the independent town forces of Belfast and Derry until 1865 and 1870). The 1836 Act firmly established what John Tobias has called the 'two ... key features in the transplantation of the system [to the colonies]'[24] – the control of the force by its own officers, headed by the inspector-general, and his direct subordination to the central government. This brought into being throughout Ireland a network of between 8,000 and 14,000 literate government employees, whose usefulness as an administrative tool was quickly recognised at a time when government intervention in society was expanding, more rapidly in Ireland than in Britain. The smallest unit of the system was the sub-district, with four to six men in a 'barrack' (usually a rented house); eight to a dozen sub-districts made up a district, under an officer with a head constable; each county, in turn, under its county inspector, comprised on average six to eight districts. While the density of distribution varied greatly from one period and one part of Ireland to another, the general strength of police relative to population was roughly one to 400 or 500 – twice as much as in Britain and more than in many colonies. For police duties alone this strength would have been hard to justify and was often criticised, but the constabulary were by degrees loaded with added responsibilities which by the early twentieth century included taking the census (omitted in 1921, a conspicuous gap in Irish population statistics); enumerating emigrants; collecting agricultural statistics; preventing the spread of animal diseases; making returns of fines and penalties; enforcing the fishery Acts, spirits Acts, town improvement Acts, Acts for the protection of animals and children and the licensing of dogs; executing warrants; acting as auctioneers for sales of distress, and as inspectors of weights and measures: preventing smuggling and illicit distillation; and performing odd jobs and confidential enquiries for various departments. This range of duties was perhaps exceeded only in some Australian forces, which have been described as 'social service organisations rather than law enforcement agencies'.[25]

Centralisation could take law enforcement out of politics when the issues were those of class conflict, sectarian conflict and faction, but clearly could not when the issues focused on control of the central government. The Home Rule movement from the 1870s directed political attention not merely to the conduct of executive officials and the manner of enforcing the law, but to the need to make the police of Ireland responsible to Irish elected representatives. In the Home Rule Bills of 1886 and 1892 it was envisaged that the RIC and Dublin Metropolitan Police would be gradually replaced by county and borough forces under local authorities. However, in the Bills of 1912–13 and the Act of 1914 (4 and 5 Geo. V, c. 90) it was instead provided that the constabulary should come under Irish government control after six years. By this time opinion in Britain was setting in the direction of increased centralisation. When the Irish Convention met in 1917–18 to consider methods of implementing Home Rule, the Inspector General presented a cogent case for the centralised system (including the point that the work of many government departments would suffer without the help they received from the police).[26] Although subsequent changes were more radical than anything he then envisaged, the centralised police system has in effect survived intact in both parts of Ireland, and has even been accentuated by the absorption of the Dublin force into the Gárda Síochána in 1925.

Centralisation had its own administrative problems. In normal times it distributed forces to meet temporary needs more efficiently than local control could do, but the crisis of the early 1880s produced a dual overload on the system. The Inspector-General's office, handling all transfers of men between counties, was literally swamped with detail, 'as if a general, in command of 11,000 men in the face of a vigilant enemy, were ordered to do all the regimental work of the battalions, and elaborate

[27]

his tactics in the intervals of escape from the fiddle-faddle of the orderly room'.[27] Second, the constant stream of emergencies prevented any coherent pattern of manpower use to fit regional needs. A scheme of regional control was set up at the end of 1881 under a group of active executive officials whose personal qualities gave the system most of what success it had. Although extended to the whole of Ireland in 1885 and continued to 1899, the 'divisional' system was never fully integrated with the police command structure, nor did it reconcile the status of police officers and magistrates. A more radical proposal of the same period would have given the government-appointed Resident Magistrates a status something like that of a prefect in France or 'a petty governor in the smallest colonies';[28] but whatever administrative advantages this might have had, there was no prospect of achieving it. The 1880s were a time of hectic and more or less successful experimentation, in which officials with empire experience played a notable role: for instance, Clifford Lloyd, RM, formerly of the Burma police; Henry Brackenbury, organiser of the Cyprus police, who gave brief but important service in setting up a police-and-crime department in 1882; and E. G. Jenkinson, his successor, a former Indian civil servant.

III

An army of occupation on which is imposed the performance of certain civil duties. [C. D. Clifford Lloyd, *Ireland under the Land League*, Edinburgh and London, 1892, p. 51]

They are bad soldiers, because they have never been trained to act in bodies; they are bad constables, because they have never acted alone. [Francis Trench, 26 October 1858[29]]

The 'semi-military' character of the Irish constabulary (that adjective was most used during its existence) set it firmly apart from the police of Great Britain, affected all aspects of its work, and made it more adaptable to colonial conditions. 'Semi-' might seem a needless qualification. Constabulary uniform followed the main trends in military fashion, with a deliberate resemblance to the Rifle Brigade; furniture, clothing and weapons were supplied through the War Office; the normal weapon at most times was a carbine with sword bayonet, but revolvers, shotguns, repeater rifles and (in the final years) grenades and automatic weapons were issued for special duties; the force had a strong *esprit de corps* and a band comparable with any in the army; it contributed a special unit of mounted orderlies to the Crimean campaign; the system of ranks was assimilable to the army's; the recruitment of officers and their relationship to other ranks resembled army conditions more than those of British police forces, a practice justified partly by the military aspect of the force and partly by the social attitudes of Ireland;[30] and many of the commanding officers came direct from previous army service.

As a large armed force the constabulary was naturally moulded by army practice; but it was armed not for a military role but for the internal security work for which the army had previously been the best, although by no means an ideal, source of strength. It was essential that the civil power should not have to rely on military assistance. However, it was inevitable that the idea of using the constabulary for a military role should crop up – for instance, in 1848, when the emergency was too brief for the idea to be much developed.[31] In 1859, however, international crisis led to the re-equipment of the constabulary with Minié rifles and a new drill book to enable it to be handled *en masse* like soldiers. If this had ever been applied in earnest, the police would in effect have been absorbed into the army, rather than acting in its place. Their militarisation was not tested in battle but produced in the early 1860s many complaints that their efficiency as police had been impaired, and the report of the 1866 committee of inquiry included a strong recommendation by Sir Richard Mayne, former head of the London Metropolitan Police, that the constabulary 'should as far as possible be divested of a military character'.[32] Next year, however, the Fenian risings were put down, largely by small bodies of constabulary under their own officers, earning the change of title to 'Royal Irish Constabulary'; shortly afterwards the long rifles were replaced by carbines. This pattern of events was repeated in milder form over the next forty years of agrarian and political agitation: the force was not obliged to become more military, but it was deterred from becoming less so. In 1895 the Under-secretary for Ireland (another former constabulary officer) suggested rearming with a full-size rifle. This was not done, but in 1900, when the second Boer war had inflamed European feeling, a scheme of mobilising the RIC for military use was drafted, and it must have been wished that the 1895 plan had been adopted, for the RIC with carbines could hardly have faced a European army.[33] Within twelve years it was clear that even in an internal role the RIC might have to face large organised bodies better armed than itself. When war broke out in 1914 the police role if Ireland were invaded was considered, revealing that after eighty years as an armed force the constabulary still lacked an unambiguous legal standing as a defence organisation.[34] In that period the gap between a gendarmerie and a true military force had widened. The constabulary could have played a part alongside regular troops in 1859, but hardly in 1914, and still less later. For this reason it is not in the same category as those colonial forces that performed both a military and a police role, or (as with the South African Constabulary) began with a miliary role and developed police functions later, or (as in New Zealand) eventually divided into separate military and police forces. Unfortunately the RIC, unlike the unarmed Dublin Metropolitan Police, could not stand aside, however ill prepared it might be, from a shooting war if one occurred.

Religious dissension was a major problem for the Irish administration, as for colonial governments, not merely in intercommunal violence but as an aggravation of other social divisions. Moreover, at the time of the Act of Union the state tended to be identified with the Protestant interest. It never completely lost this association, but attempts were made to achieve a practically neutral state, all the more necessary because of a concurrent rise in sectarian animosity. Police reform is some index of success in this attempt. The statutes of 1787–92 had required constables to be Protestant; this was not so in later measures, but the means of appointment had a marked effect on the religious composition of police forces. JPs would naturally appoint constables whom they had reason to trust, and in this context it is noteworthy that the proportion of Catholics in the 'county constabulary' of 1822–36 was as high as 32 per cent in 1824 and 36 per cent in 1833. The real change came in 1836, when local control of appointments ended and a determined effort to avoid religious distinctions seems to have been made. As early as 1841 53 per cent of the constabulary were Catholic, and from 1861 the census returns made it possible to compare religious groups in the police with those in the population. Between 1861 and 1911 the proportion of Catholics fell from nearly 78 per cent of the population to nearly 74 per cent, while in the police it rose from 68 per cent to 78 per cent; thus, from being clearly underpresented in 1861, they were slightly over-represented in 1911. Members of the Church of Ireland remained visibly overrepresented: their share of the population rose slightly, from 12 per cent in 1861 to 13 per cent in 1911, while in the police it fell from 27 per cent to 16 per cent. Other denominations had about half the representation in the police that their numbers in the population would suggest, but the numbers were in any case small and diminishing; by 1917 there was marked difficulty in attracting Protestant recruits.[35] The chronic predominance of Protestants among constabulary officers reflected not so much positive discrimination as the effect of recruiting most officers by direct entry. As the proportion of officers promoted from head constables was increased, the proportion of Catholic officers also increased.

IV

The constabulary system developed in Ireland so thoroughly in response to local circumstances that one might easily be sceptical of its having any real common ground with forces in other parts of the world. The nebulous assumption of common ground in terms of a protean 'Irish model' has not been helpful, but the real work of substantiating the links between Irish and colonial policing is there to be tackled in all its prospective detail.

In 1905 the Inspector General of the RIC drafted a 'memorandum on Irish police duties' for West Indian reference.[36] He considered (predictably enough) the RIC's high standards of discipline and training, the use of batons and procedure in cases of riot, but in mentioning the great usefulness of bicycles he added, 'Bicycles are not supplied to the Royal Irish Constabulary. Every man who chooses to do so purchases his own machine, and is paid an allowance for its use on the public service.' This communicates with a peculiar immediacy something of the atmosphere of the RIC at the time, and, whatever was done in the West Indies about bicycles, it is on this level that the links with colonial policing need to be explored.

Notes

1 G. Broeker, *Rural Disorder and Police Reform in Ireland 1812–36* (London and Toronto, 1970), pp. 241–2; S. H. Palmer, *Police and Protest in England and Ireland, 1780–1850* (Cambridge, 1988), pp. 542–5.
2 In this chapter, 'Irish constabulary' refers to the centralised force established by 6 Will. IV, c. 13 (20 May 1836), and renamed Royal Irish Constabulary on 12 September 1867. 'Police', when used for the period 1836–1922, means the same, except in the analysis of religious allegiances, where it includes all police in Ireland at the censal dates.
3 PRO, HO 184. The analysis of this material is being undertaken by Dr W. J. Lowe of Chicago State University and Dr Elizabeth Malcolm of the University of Liverpool.
4 Below, chapter 5.
5 G. M. O'Brien, *The Australian Police Forces* (Melbourne, 1960), pp. 5, 40, 62–3.
6 W. R. Foran, *The Kenya Police, 1887–1960* (London, 1962), pp. 38–9.
7 J. C. Curry, *The Indian Police* (London, 1932), p. 31; Jeffries, *Colonial Police*, pp. 31–2; J. Cramer, *The World's Police* (London, 1964), p. 138; Sir P. Griffiths, *To Guard my People: the history of the Indian police* (London and Bombay, 1971), p. 428.
8 Griffiths, *To Guard my People*, pp. 67–71.
9 Curry, *Indian Police*, p. 31; H. T. Lambrick, *Sir Charles Napier and Sind* (Oxford, 1952), p. 184.
10 Sir W. F. P. Napier, *History of General Sir Charles Napier's Administration of Scinde* (London, 1851); *The Life and Opinions of General Sir Chalres James Napier, G.C.B.* (4 vols., London, 1857).
11 Lambrick, *Napier and Sind*, p. 184; Napier, *Life and Opinions*, I, pp. 306, 388–91.
12 J. S. Kennedy, *Standing Rules and Regulations for the Government and Guidance of the Constabulary Force of Ireland* (Dublin, 1837), pp. 2–4.
13 *First Report of the Commissioners appointed to Inquire as to the best Means of Establishing an Efficient Constabulary Force in the Counties of England and Wales*, pp. 160–1 [169], HC 1839, XIX, pp. 166–7.

14 *Ibid.*, pp. 166–7, 186 (Ms. pp. 172–3, 189).
15 *First Report from the Select Committee on Police; with the Minutes of Evidence,* p. 18, HC 1852–53 (603), XXXVI, p. 22.
16 *Second Report ... ; together with the Proceedings of the Committee, Minutes of Evidence, and Appendix,* pp. 153–4, HC 1852–53 (715), XXXVI, pp. 325–6.
17 *First Report from Select Committee,* p. 128 (Ms. p. 132).
18 In some cases 'modelled on' may prove to have been used as loosely as 'calculated to', which can mean simply 'suitable' or 'likely to', with no implication of intention.
19 E.g. Goldwin Smith, 'The administration of Ireland', *Contemporary Review,* July 1885, p. 6.
20 Hall, *Ireland,* I, p. 124.
21 N. W. Senior, *Journals, Conversations and Essays relating to Ireland* (2 vols., London, 1868), II, p. 266.
22 Blake, 'Irish police', p. 392.
23 J. J. Tobias, 'The British colonial police: an alternative police style', in P. J. Stead (ed.), *Pioneers in Policing* (Montclair, N. J., and Maidenhead, 1977), pp. 242–3.
24 *Ibid.*, pp. 246–8.
25 O'Brien, *Australian Police Forces,* pp. 9, 40–1, 62–3; Blake, 'Irish police', p. 390; Treasury Blue Notes, PRO, T 165/49 (1922–23), 'Constabulary of Ireland', p. 3. The annual Blue Notes give the clearest and most comprehensive accounts available of the administrative history of Irish police under the Union. The role of the police in 'internal colonisation' is outlined by W. E. Vaughan in W. E. Vaughan (ed.), *A New History of Ireland,* V, *Ireland under the Union,* I, *1801–70,* (Oxford, 1989), pp. 765–72.
26 *Report of the Proceedings of the Irish Convention,* pp. 123–6 [Cd 9019], HC 1918, X, pp. 819–22.
27 Blake, 'Irish police', p. 396.
28 BL Ad. Ms. 46049, ff. 117–18.
29 Quoted in Senior, *Journals,* II, p. 91. An odd echo of Trench's remark occurs in Herbert Spencer's 'Policemen are soldiers who act alone; soldiers are policemen who act in unison', quoted in Foran, *Kenya Police,* p. 1.
30 *Constabulary, Ireland. Report of Commissioners,* pp. 13–14 [3658], HC 1866, XXXIV, pp. 179–80; *Royal Irish Constabulary. Report of the Committee of Inquiry; 1883,* p. 17 [C. 3577], HC 1883, XXXII, p. 273.
31 PRO, T 165/9 (1891–92), p. 6. 'The O'Brien rebellion spoiled them. They were so much praised on that occasion for their soldierly conduct, that they have ever since fancied themselves soldiers instead of constables' (Francis Trench, quoted in Senior, *Journals,* II, p. 91).
32 *Constabulary, Ireland. Report,* p. 32; for a reply by the current inspector-general to the complaints see H. Brownring, *Examination of some recent Allegations concerning the Constabulary Force of Ireland* (Dublin, 1864).
33 PRO, CO 904/174/1.
34 PRO, CO 904/174/2. The law officers held that the RIC might not be entitled to combatant rights under the Hague Convention; the War Office held that they would. Similar problems arose in Northern Ireland in 1940–41, when the Home Guard was organised for local reasons as part of the Ulster Special Constabulary. They were solved by attesting the Home Guardsmen for military service; J. W. Blake, *Northern Ireland in the Second World War* (Belfast, 1956), pp. 178–87, and Ken Miller, ' "But they turned out black": on account of the formation of the Ulster Home Guard and some of the consequent legal–political problems', *Retrospect* (1983), pp. 21–3.
35 *Report of Irish Conventions,* p. 126.
36 PRO, CO. 884/9, p. 76. I am indebted to Mr W. Chamberlain for this reference.

CHAPTER THREE

The varieties of policing: colonial Queensland, 1860–1900

Mark Finnane

Queensland, a colony whose name signifies its founding at the high point of the Victorian age, was separated from New South Wales in 1859. It was, therefore, the youngest of the Australasian colonies in constitutional terms and its history to federation in 1901 was marked by this fact. The earliest days of British settlement from the 1820s saw it used as a convict outpost, at Moreton Bay, close to the later site of the capital, Brisbane. From the beginning its history, like that of New South Wales, Tasmania (Van Dieman's Land) and Western Australia, the colony bore the mark of the convict taint. In Queensland, however, this gave way more quickly than in the other colonies to the imperatives of free settler economic development. By the time of separation and self-government in 1859 the convict days were past. The government of the colony for the remainder of the colonial period passed to the hands of a semi-autonomous parliament based in Brisbane, in the very south-east of this extensive colony of 667,000 square miles, with 3,200 miles of coastline.

Queensland differed from most of the other colonies in a number of respects; two important differences were distance and late settlement. Even more than those in the largest colony, Western Australia, Queensland settlers were spread over an enormous geographical area by the 1890s. Population was relatively more decentralised than in other colonies, with a number of coastal ports serving the inland pastoral and mining regions. And extensive settlement took place after self-government rather than before as in the denser and older colonies of the south-east.

The organisation of policing in Queensland was almost contiguous with the arrival of self-government. Typically in Australia the police forces developed first on a local model, with constabularies responsible for the small colonial towns, subject to the direction of local magistrates. Special forces for rural policing in particular developed from the 1830s to the 1850s, the Mounted Police of New South Wales being such a force, the Field Police of Tasmania another. Dissatisfaction with the poor administration of these various forces, and their inadequate handling of urban disorder and goldfield disturbances, led in the 1850s to increased attention to the desirability of centralisation. This was achieved in Victolia in 1853, Western Australia in 1862, New South Wales in 1862 and Queensland in 1864. Other police models were pursued in South Australia, the only non-convict colony (Victoria having been part of New South Wales until formal separation in 1851): its police were under close government direction from 1838. Tasmania provided the only Australian example of a police organisation comparable in form to the English, with municipal police forces replacing the magistrate-controlled constabularies from 1857. Only in 1899 were the Tasmanian police consolidated in a body under the characteristic Australian governance of a Commissioner subject to the direction of the responsible Minister of government. For the most part, however, the strongly centripetal characteristics of colonial self-government, combined with the weakness of local government, facilitated the consolidation of the constabularies into police forces in the Australian colonies from mid-century.[1]

The organisation of the colonial forces for the most part followed a similar pattern. Headed by a Commissioner, the force was administered from the capital city of the colony. Recruiting was centralised, with cadet or 'supernumary' constables spending an initial period in the police depot for drill training and elementary instruction in their duties before assignment to police stations often in remote rural regions. Recruits tended initially to be drawn from an ex-military background or from other police forces, especially British and Irish. As in Ireland, the arming of police distinguished local constabularies from their English counterparts. In rural areas, especially, police frequently inhabited barracks. Patrol duty on horseback was a regular requirement of rural policing, monitored by diary recording and inspection by the powerful second rank of officers, the inspectors. These patrols could be very extensive, not to say taxing: Dalby magistrate Philip Pinnock reported in 1869 that two constables in that district had recently completed a 700 mile patrol in the course of a month, executing warrants and serving summonses.[2] In the cities and towns, beat duty was the dominant form of police work, though the extent of its monitoring by senior police varied between the different colonial forces. Discussion of its organisation during the 1899 Queensland Royal Commission suggested colonial dissent from strict timekeeping on beat duty on the English model: for some that smacked of the constable being an 'automaton'.[3]

In spite of all they shared, the colonial forces had distinctive histories. The argument of this chapter is that the Queensland force faced a unique set of circumstances in the Australian context, deriving from the specific

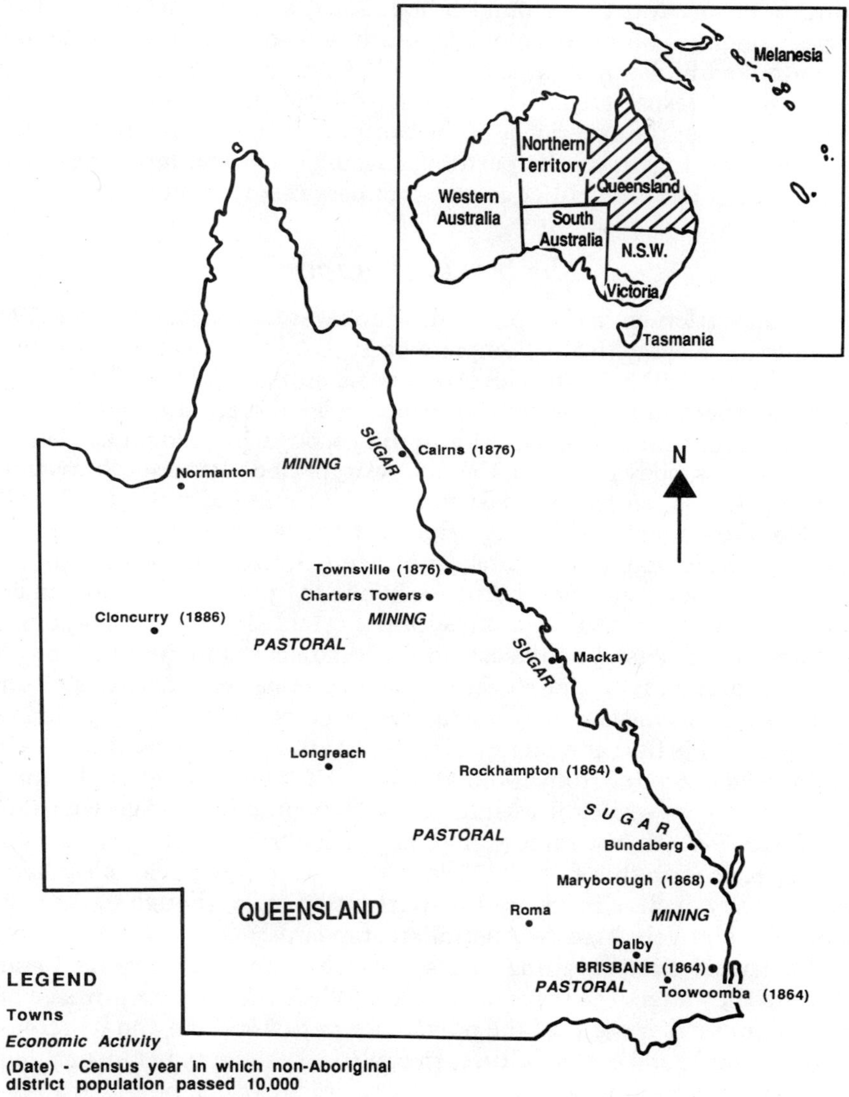
Melanesia
Northern Territory
Western Australia
Queensland
South Australia
N.S.W.
Victoria
Tasmania
N
SUGAR
Cairns (1876)
MINING
Normanton
Townsville (1876)
Charters Towers
Cloncurry (1886)
MINING
PASTORAL
SUGAR
Mackay
Longreach
Rockhampton (1864)
SUGAR
PASTORAL
Bundaberg
Maryborough (1868)
QUEENSLAND
Roma
MINING
Dalby
BRISBANE (1864)
PASTORAL
Toowoomba (1864)
LEGEND
Towns
Economic Activity
(Date) - Census year in which non-Aboriginal district population passed 10,000

Colonial Queensland: principal towns and major economic activities

political economy of the colonial period. The first section introduces the socio-economic context of colonial Queensland and outlines some of the important administrative features of policing organisation deriving from the imperial (especially Irish and English) models of policing. Later sections discuss the experience of the Native Police, the policing of social relations contingent on the pastoral, mining and sugar industries and finally the role of the police in the organisation of urban life.

The bonds of empire

European settlement in Queensland, which was little advanced in 1859, was almost geographically complete by 1900.[4] As late as the 1890s the police reports still indicate a level of resistance of aboriginal inhabitants of the northern rain forests to the despoilation of their lands by timber-getters and aspirant farmers. Prior to this, occupation had proceeded at the frequently giddy pace from the rich pastoral lands of the south-eastern Darling Downs, along the coast north for a thousand miles to Cairns and Cooktown, and out through the west and north-west in pursuit of grazing land for exportable cattle and sheep. Settlement often went in advance of government authority – hence the perennial call of small rural communities and townships for the establishment of new police stations and courts of petty sessions, the indispensable institutions of colonial government and social order. The pressures this created on policing may be measured by the figures prepared by the Commissioner of Police for his first annual report in 1865. European occupation of the colony had extended from 195,500 to 400,000 square miles in the four years, 1860–64, while the estimated settler population had grown from 30,000 to 75,000 in the same period. Expansion of police numbers failed to keep pace with this growth. Throughout the following decades there was a steady decline in the police–population ratio, though by 1900 it was still relatively high by Australian standards.[5]

What were the prevailing forms of settlement in Queensland and how did they affect the tasks of policing? While the dominant image of Australian settlement is of the prevalence of pastoralism and its attendant economic and social culture, the political economy of Queensland was more varied. But, as the form of settlement which provided a permanent social structure in rural areas, pastoralism was central to the colony's interests. In Australia the wool industry became the major source of export income from the 1870s. In turn it attracted a large proportion of British investment in the Australian colonies, and indeed stimulated the massive inflow of British capital into Australia in the 1870s and 1880s: during this period 'the Australian colonies actually absorbed, for a time, over half the net British overseas investment'.[6]

Queensland shared in this economic fortune, but was badly affected when the boom ended in the 1890s. The social consequences of the collapse of wool prices included a significant degree of labour conflict, requiring policing intervention.

Prior to that, however, pastoralism posed other problems for policing. Significant inroads into the structure and culture of the indigenous population were made by the spread of pastoralism. It was the most invasive form of occupation, because of the extensive land use it demanded and the destructive consequences of the introduction of exotic animals.[7] Throughout the period of colonisation of Australia to the 1930s, many of the bloodiest encounters between aboriginal and settler populations were occasioned by the conflict inherent in the spread of pastoralism. Pastoralism, however, did not make Queensland distinctive. It was the introduction of sugar cultivation through plantation production, using migrant indentured labour from the nearby Pacific islands of Melanesia, that distinguished Queensland colonial life, politically and socially. The plantation economy posed different problems of policing a racial divide to those of the aboriginal/settler frontier.

Finally, like most other Australian colonies Queensland was the site of significant mining development, in the south-east, centre and north of the colony between the 1860s and the 1890s. Policing of the goldfields, sites of immigrant rushes in these decades, posed special questions for the police, here as elsewhere. These ranged from the frontier problems of monitoring unstable and constantly mobile populations to the demands of government for revenue (licensing requirements produced some of the greatest tension on Australia's first goldfields in Victoria in the early 1850s) and the control of racial violence. Police responsibilities typically included duties as mining warden in such areas, making them the key state agencies on these fields and in the surrounding towns.

These three elements were the principal foundations of the political economy of Queensland in its early decades. They suggest a strong rural base and population, but the rural dominance can be exaggerated. The high export orientation of these economies and the extended area of settlement produced a considerable number of coastal ports and regional cities in addition to Brisbane, which served principally the pastoral south-east. Towns like Bundaberg and Mackay were dominated by the Melanesian labourer presence (constituting a third of their total population in the 1880s) in the surrounding sugar districts. Others, like the mining city of Charters Towers, Queensland's second largest centre in the late 1890s, were dominated by European (principally British and Irish) immigrant populations. Areas in the southern part of the colony, particularly in the rich Darling Downs, had significant populations of Irish and German settlers in the late nineteenth century.

[37]

If there was one single factor which governed imperial policing in settler societies like Australia, it was the high mobility and new character of social relations. The greater part of the process of settlement in colonies like Queensland was coincident with the organisation and refinement of modern, bureaucratic policing. Police, that is to say, may be seen as having played a crucial role in the *production* of the dominant forms of social order in such a colony. If we are to characterise policing practices in a society such as colonial Queensland we need to trace the effects of the interplay of two competing forces organising policing. On the one hand there were the demands of a centralised, bureaucratic organisation, subjecting police officers in often very distant and isolated centres to the disciplinary and staffing requirements of the whole organisation. On the other, there were the demands imposed by the variety of local conditions.

The forces enhancing police autonomy were considerable in the later nineteenth century. The police force in Queensland was given shape by the reorganisation brought about by the Police Act of 1863. Its principal effect was to bring the disparate police forces under the one head of the Police Commissioner. Only the Native Police remained a separate entity (but under the ultimate control of the Police Commissioner as commandant), until 1897. Centralisation brought with it the capacity to break up the links between police and local settlers. The first Commissioner, D. T. Seymour, early sought to remove long-resident officers, some of whom 'having continued for many years at the stations of which they were first appointed, had acquired property in, and formed connections with the people of the district'.[8] In the first decade vestiges of the fold system of magistrates' control of local police units were retained, with police magistrates being required to monitor police duties on a monthly basis.[9] The residual powers of magistrates were largely removed at the end of the 1860s, when their duties in relation to police discipline were abolished. From then on the authority of the Commissioner's office in Brisbane was *de jure* unfettered. The absorption of the Native Police in the 1890s meant the subjection thereafter of all police to a common set of rules, regulations and administrative processes.

The governance of the police themselves was secured through the adaptation of a variety of styles of imperial policing. The first rules of the force were adapted from those used in the Victorian force since 1854. Later manuals and codes drew on both the *Irish Constable's Manual* of Sir Andrew Reed and Howard Vincent's *Police Code and Manual of Criminal Law*, as well as on colonial codes, for example that for British Guiana, sent to the Queensland commissioner in 1899.[10]

The austere standards of nineteenth-century police administration encompassed two important principles in Queensland. First, relations between local communities and their police were kept as distant as possible through constant transfers of staff. Those police who stayed long enough in the force could expect to see service in areas throughout the colony over their career. Michael O'Sullivan, a chief inspector and acting commissioner at the end of his career, served at the south-western stations of Roma, Dubadilla, St George and Taroom in his first six years of appointment from 1883 before service at Rockhampton, Winton and Mt Morgan in the centre of the colony in the 1890s: only appointment to the Central Investigation Bureau in Brisbane at the turn of the century ended his migratory path. The pattern was typical.[11] This constant movement of staff was modelled on the administration of the Royal Irish Constabulary, rather than on the English local constabulary.

Second, discipline was maintained through a constant monitoring of police duties by senior officers and through recurrent, irregular inspections. The presumption in the gazetted rules of the force was that it was necessary to 'protect the public against the ignorance or improper behaviour of constables'.[12] A constable was required to report to his sergeant every occasion he used his whistle; while on duty, he was not to enter into conversation with any person, except on matters 'relative to his duty'. Even within the force the requirements of discipline forbade the giving of gifts to departing senior officers:

> for if the subordinate ranks of the service are permitted to express their approval of the conduct of their superiors, they might also assume it as a right to condemn it; and as the expression of either praise or censure would be alike opposed to all discipline and good order, they are both equally and strictly forbidden.[13]

The rule against gift-giving from within or outside the force could be and was invoked by the Police Commissioner on occasion.[14] In practice, of course, austerity must have given way to expediency and a measure of local sociability, evident in the autobiography of Michael O'Sullivan.[15] And the readiness with which police sought to use local influence to advance their promotion or resist transfer indicates the good relations which were enjoyed by the police with citizenry.[16] But the strictness of police office contributed its fair share to the high turnover in the colonial forces and the frequent disciplinary actions for drunkenness, dereliction of duty and departure from beat. These problems were of course not unique to Queensland.[17]

The bureaucratic nature of the organisation clearly offered a formidable challenge to the mediating influence of local and regional variations in policing practices. The extent to which it did so, however, must be tested through detailed analysis.

[39]

The Native Police

Settlement in any of the Australian colonies typically advanced beyond the *de facto* boundaries of government authority. This simple fact had critical consequences for the character of social relations on the frontier. For while there were forces of sympathy, paternalism or social discipline among some of the rulers and the urban settlers, they were rare on the frontier. Police stations and courthouses came after settlement had already made its claim on the lands and lives of the aborigines. The response to frontier disorder, prompted above all by the demands of settlers for protection from aboriginal resistance or retaliation, found shape in the institution of the Native Police.

Formed initially in the Port Phillip district and outer pastoral regions of New South Wales, the Native Police was organised into units of aboriginal troopers under the authority of white police officers. The recruiting of the troopers was varied: the preferred mode was to recruit aborigines from locations distant from the districts being policed. According to the Queensland surveyor-general in 1861 the native troopers in Western Australia, where he had earlier been, 'were selected from prisoners from other districts who had behaved themselves well, and whose period of sentence had nearly expired'.[18] In Queensland, however, many problems were regarded as stemming from the recruitment of native troopers from or near the districts where they were to act, a policy which was condemned in a number of official inquiries. Part of the problem with recruiting in Queensland was the enormous distances involved in securing troopers for the northern parts of settlement: hence recruitment by the white officers took the pragmatic turn of enticing local young aborigines into action against people of their own or adjacent areas.[19] One result of local recruitment was a high incidence of kidnapping of aboriginal women from the groups being dispersed, itself a provocation of further conflict. Later in the century, as troopers were replaced by black trackers, attached to the regular police force, the government supplied rations to the trackers' 'gins', who accompanied them on patrol.

The mode of operation of the police is starkly represented in the directions given to Native Troopers by the commandant, Frederick Walker, in 1851, prior to their departure on an expedition:

> What the Governor wants from you is to make charcoles quiet, he does not want them killed, and he *won't let* white fellows do so. If they won't be quiet, you must make them − that's all. But you will not shoot unless your Officer tells you. Mind if the charcoles begin to throw spears or nulla nullas *then* don't you wait but close up knock them down.[20]

Under a policy of 'dispersal' the police were responsible for intervening against any signs of aboriginal resistance which could not be managed by the settlers themselves. With the spread of settlement into the varied conditions of Queensland, especially in its northernmost parts, such a policy, it has been argued, began to founder.[21] Dispersal was unsuccessful in forest regions where aborigines had the advantage of greater knowledge of the difficult terrain; or else it was fundamentally at variance with a basic need of the settlers themselves, the need for labour. The forces for change in the policing of the aborigines were therefore multiple: from the voices of concern, metropolitan, urban, philanthropic; from the centripetal tendencies of government administration in Australia, of which the colonial police forces were an exemplary instance; and from the contradictions of settlement itself, for which the aborigines were one moment an impediment but next an available resource, if only they could be 'brought in'. By the 1880s these contradictory pressures had brought about significant changes in policing relations on the frontier.

In the first place a centralising tendency was evident in the decision from the 1870s to reduce the size of the Native Police by subsuming their functions within the ordinary duties of the Queensland police. As settlement stretched into remote areas in the north and west of the colony the Commissioner proposed moving the Native Police detachments out 'to the newly-settled country, and attaching in the more thickly populated districts, a native tracker to each ordinary police station'.[22] Wholesale replacement of the Native Police was not possible at that time because 'the services for which they are retained could not be performed by the ordinary police'.[23] 'The services', primarily those of dispersing troublesome camps, punishment raids and killing the most intractable aborigines, were not the only points at issue. Elementary matters like the provision of suitable police buildings, necessary for the discipline perhaps more than the comfort of the white police officers, also played their role in delaying the replacement of the Native Police. Over the next twenty years, however, the number of Native Troopers declined from about 200 in the mid-1870s to just over a hundred 'Native Trackers' by 1895. By 1897 the concentration of duties in the one force was accomplished. This movement was one which was directed from Brisbane.

But beside this centripetal administrative act we should note the development, at a local level, of the very practices of conciliation and pacification which became the cornerstone of aboriginal policy throughout much of Australia in the first half of this century.[24] In 1881 the Commissioner reported conciliation attempts in the northern districts, intended 'to make them understand that if they abstain from injuring the persons or property of settlers they will have no cause to complain of the treatment they will receive in return'.[25] Inducements were offered in terms of food above all, with promises of shelter in camps or pastoral stations or on the fringe of towns. In the following decade an important responsibility of the police in the north was the distribution of food to the often starving aborigines, their stocks of native food depleted by the inroads of pastoralism and mining.[26]

Such initiatives were far from benign in consequence for the aborigines: conciliation and pacification were essential conditions for the subordination of the aboriginal population in the coming century. The police played a central role in the construction of these conditions. Following the incorporation of the Native Police in the general force in 1897 and the passing of new legislation, police assumed an additional office of 'protector of aborigines', with extensive powers of removal and surveillance of the aboriginal population. The twofold role of the police was amply demonstrated in the history of the Native Police and its passing: on the one hand, an instrument of suppression of resistance to the spread of pastoral settlement, on the other the development of new techniques for the administration of the surviving population.

Policing the bush

Just as the transitions in the policing of aborigines mark out different phases in the consolidation of settlement, so the varieties of settler rural experience created constant changes in rural policing. Great demands were placed on policing resources by the intermittent eruptions of the gold rushes, particularly at Palmer River in the north in the 1870s and then around Charters Towers in the 1880s and 1890s. These produced large increases in population and high mobility, creating opportunities for gold theft and other crimes which were a focus of much popular attention in the period. A different kind of social crisis was produced by intense conflict in the pastoral industry in the 1890s, when striking shearers created the most substantial challenge to state and economic authority in any Australian colony in the nineteenth century. Outside these conditions of crisis policing, the roles of police were perhaps less obtrusive than in the cities and larger towns. This did not stop incidents of tension between officious or interventionist police and local citizenry. But the distance which might characterise policing behaviour in urban areas was less expected in the bush, and incidents of police favouritism in the administration of justice indicate the levels of tolerance which might be displayed: Michael O'Sullivan's partiality to a St George squatter is unashamedly recounted in his autobiography, while the high regard in which he was held in the mining district of Mt Morgan was rewarded at a civic function on his departure in 1898.[27]

The policing of the goldfields required both flexibility in organisation and a level of vigilance which was of a different order from that in some settled rural areas. Some fields, as on the Palmer, might have an effective life of only a few years.[28] In his 1871 report Seymour noted that it had been necessary to open three new stations, with two more anticipated, on the northern fields. Three years later, however, 'the unsettled state of the diggings rendering it injudicious to erect permanent buildings at any particular spot', the police on the Palmer were being housed in portable buildings and tents. By 1878 the population on these northern fields had considerably decreased and some manning reductions were made.[29]

Other rural areas had their own distinctive policing requirements. Of constant concern was the incidence of stock and horse stealing. The former could be on a substantial scale, organised on lines which took advantage of pastoral areas with little fencing and, until 1871, no branding requirement.[30] The policing and prosecution of these offences were fraught with difficulties of proof and hindered by local resistance to such controls. In 1873 the failure of the jury to convict in a cattle theft trial at Roma led to the government's withdrawing the Western District court from sitting in the town for two years. In the aftermath of the trial the judge reported that while waiting for his coach he had been 'surrounded by a mob of ruffians; some with black flags and a banner, and others disguised. All set up a roar at me and shouted "a groan for the judge; down with him"'. In the same district, as late as the early 1900s, police pursuit of alleged stock thieves, the Kenniff brothers, resulted in small-scale guerilla warfare between police and small farmers.[31]

Horse stealing bore some of the same marks of social resistance or simply of a conflict in values. John McQuilton's work on the social contexts of horse stealing in north-east Victoria provides strong evidence for cultural sanctioning of the process of 'borrowing' a horse for short-term use.[32] Understandably, perception of the legitimacy of 'borrowing' depended on the property-owning status of the observer. Official police comment indicates the ambiguity of the context, on the one hand blaming the 'criminal classes', on the other identifying the local rationale:

> From all that can be learnt, the majority of the horses carried away were not taken for sale, but ridden off by swagsmen seeking employment, and members of the criminal class, to facilitate their transit from one part of the colony to another, after serving which purpose the horses are turned adrift.[33]

Seymour's response to the high incidence of this offence, like his reaction to the complaints of settlers about the depredations of aborigines, was to identify the causes of the problem as much as to pursue individual offenders: hence his advocacy of Queensland's adoption of Victorian horse-stealing legislation to control the trade in stolen animals, and his endorsement of branding requirements to suppress cattle stealing. Changes in the pastoral industry, above all the fencing of properties, appear to have reduced the incidence of stock theft by the 1890s.

A much more substantial threat to social order was posed by the labour unrest of the early 1890s. Rapid advances in unionisation of the work force in the later 1880s were of major impact in Queensland, with its sizeable rural labour market. Union attempts to enforce a closed shop in the 1890 shearing season, to protect wages and advance conditions, were met by an unusually united campaign of defence by pastoralists, organised around the 'freedom of contract' slogan. Striking shearers organised camps outside sheep stations and western towns and attempted to restrict the entry of non-union 'scab' labour. In the first of the strikes police resources were inadequate to the protection demanded by squatters for their work forces of non-union labour: the government resorted to the swearing of special constables and the use of the armed militia. Three years later another major strike brought another emergency. Substantial areas of western Queensland were proclaimed 'disturbed districts' under the Peace Preservation Act, a strategy clearly adapted from the Irish Land War of the 1880s.[34]

The 1894 report of the Police Commissioner (William Parry-Okeden, who had been sworn in as a sub-inspector of police and district magistrate during the troubles), conveys the sense of threat which the labour troubles aroused. Constables who had initially been employed in watching woolsheds and homesteads and escorting non-unionist labourers and shearers were formed into patrols 'which were constantly on the move, and were able to keep the numerous travellers under supervision'. The burning of a major woolshed and the attempted burning of another, where forty shots were fired, were among the most serious events of the strike:

> There was throughout the proclaimed district an evident feeling of insecurity, and terror existed among all classes. There were many men who were anxious to work but were afraid, not knowing how far they would be protected by Government. As a consequence it would appear as if a very large number of the men were in sympathy with the perpetrators of outrages, but I feel sure that those who were implicated or concerned in outrages and disturbances, or who had knowledge of the perpetrators, were greatly in the minority. It was fear that caused numbers of quiet and respectable men to go out on strike and into camps.[35]

Police deployment increased in these districts from fifty-one in 1893 to 153 in 1894, with patrols still in place some months after the decline in tension.[36] In Queensland, as in Victoria and New South Wales, the open confrontation between labour and the police in the early 1890s soured relations between the two for many years. But the police response after this was to play a more discreet role in the management of most labour disputes.[37]

Rural policing, therefore, was characterised by sometimes intensive demands on the resources and methods of the colonial police force. The functions of rural policing, however, were not limited to the pastoral and mining districts of the colony. The peculiar status of Queensland as a part plantation society posed other questions of policing.

The sugar industry and Melanesian labour

The two principal centres of the sugar industry in Queensland were Mackay and Bundaberg. The Melanesian (or Kanaka) population in each centre, a constantly changing one from the 1860s to the early 1900s, comprised groups from different islands, often from traditional enemies.[38] In the servile relation of indenture they were largely the responsibility of their masters on the plantations; infractions of the law by such people were frequently handled by the masters. But by the later 1880s there were substantial numbers of time-expired Kanakas who were not subject to the same controls. Methods of dealing with these groups, whose drinking and opium-taking were seen at times as a threat to social order in the towns, were more directly the prerogative of the police. Policing the Kanakas therefore posed different challenges, depending on the economic/legal status of the individual Kanaka as well as the behaviour of the group.

Study of the policing records indicates the distinct experience of Kanakas in the criminal justice system. In Bundaberg in the 1880s and 1890s they made up the overwhelming proportion of assault charges, charges which were brought as a result of attacks on masters or on other islanders. As table 3.1 shows, Kanakas accounted for sixty-four of the eighty prosecutions for assault in the three years 1890–92, at a time when they made up about 38 per cent of the adult (over fifteen) male population in the area. Writing of the other region of large Kanaka settlement, Mackay, Clive Moore has suggested that the 'Queensland setting may have provoked an even greater degree of violence than that normal in the islands', where 'wars and killings were part of the way of life of nineteenth-century Melanesians'.[39] A high proportion of the violence was vented within the islander population. But deposition records also suggest that a proportion was directed at masters and overseers on plantations and farms.

The seriousness of the charge of assault produced a much higher rate

Table 3.1: Birthplace of offenders, Bundaberg, Queensland

Birth place	1884–86	1890–92	1900–02
(a) Charge			
	Assault		
Australia	1	3	1
Melanesia	17	64	14
Great Britain	6	6	1
Ireland	5	4	1
Other	2	3	4
Total	31	80	21
	Master and Servant		
Melanesia	36	6	21
Non-Melanesian	20	9	1
(b) Conviction as percentage of charges laid			
	Assault		
Non-Melanesian	57.1	81.3	85.7
Melanesian	88.2	76.2	64.3
	All charges		
Non-Melanesian	43.6	48.1	38.1
Melanesian	54.0	78.3	62.6
n =	636	594	954

Source: Watchhouse records, Bundaberg police station, QSA.

of imprisonment of Kanakas relative to other social groups in this area, although conviction rates were not consistently excessive compared with those for non-Melanesians. In contrast to the Irish, the next most imprisoned group in the early 1890s, the Kanakas were also likely to be in prison for periods exceeding one day, a quarter of them receiving sentences of over one month. Understanding the vulnerability of Kanakas to assault charges requires assessment of their position as indentured labourers under European masters. As indicated by the watchhouse sample the employment relationship produced a much higher use of Master and Servant actions against the islanders at a time when the use of this form of labour discipline was in decline.[40]

At lower levels of offence the Kanakas experienced policing in ways which were largely shared with the European population in Bundaberg. But their less frequent habitation of the town meant that they were considerably less prominent in the public order and other charges, at least in these sample years. Nevertheless, drunkenness made up a large proportion of police actions against them here, as in Mackay. Illegal provision of drink to Kanakas was common, and occasional incidents of violence or rowdiness on the part of drunken islanders were capable of inspiring passionate local European reaction, not always sympathetically viewed by the police. Following one such outbreak of press hysteria in 1887, police in Bundaberg were critical of local settlers. 'The press here,' reported Sergeant Kelly, 'when writing on matters touching on Kanaks are not reliable as the writers write for a purpose.' Police considered Europeans were as much to blame for sly-grogging as the much vilified Chinese traders (as prosecutions for illegal supply of drink indicate), while fears of racial violence were exaggerated. There had been few quarrels between whites and Kanakas in recent years, while 'those that took place originated in drunken white men interfering with Kanakas'.[41] While such a police response to charges of inaction was perhaps characteristically defensive, there appears some ground on the basis of charging patterns to suggest that police priorities in relation to Kanakas were dependent on the quite specific challenges posed by the presence of large numbers of young male islanders, little acculturated to the limits on physical violence expected in settler society. Hence the unusual position of Melanesians in the predominantly European economy influenced the criminal justice system in a way which was unique to the sugar belt.

Urban policing

At the founding of the Queensland police, in 1864, the proportion of police located in Brisbane and its suburbs was less than 17 per cent. Two decades later nearly a quarter of the colony's police were responsible for keeping order in the rapidly growing capital. Frontier conditions and a diversified economy had played a major role in determining the allocation of resources and the organisation of the police. But the progressive reduction of the native threat and the greater stability, economic and social, of the European population by the 1890s saw the emergence of new preoccupations in policing. These are evident from the late 1870s. They signify the extent to which Brisbane, the capital of the youngest of the Australian colonies, was the locus of a complex of social changes and policing responses common to the other colonial cities.

The apparatus of policing, transmitted from Ireland and London in the rules and organisational framework of the Queensland force, found its home most comfortably in the city. The characteristic police duties of patrolling the beat for prevention of crime and disorder were oriented towards the maintenance of order on the streets: hence the high volume of arrests for public drunkenness. But the role of the police extended beyond the arrest of drunks in the late nineteenth-century city, targeting a variety of behaviour and practice which police sought to bring under legal regulation or else, in a contrasting and hidden way, sought to franchise perhaps for their own personal gain or in sympathy with the cultural condoning of these practices. The regulation of prostitution, for example, was an area of ambiguity in state policy and in policing. While the policing of prostitution did not constitute a high proportion of police work in terms of arrests, the key place of the police in its regulation in Queensland suggests yet another dimension to the varieties of police responsibility in the colony.

Queensland was one of the two Australian colonies possessing Contagious Diseases legislation.[42] Passed in 1868, the Queensland Act allowed for medical inspection of prostitutes, monitored by the police. While fallen into disuse by 1910, the Act was an important instrument in the regulation of prostitution and of women's lives in Queensland. Although the Contagious Diseases Act applied throughout the state, police figures from the late 1890s seem to indicate that the policing of prostitution was largely a concern of the urban police. Prostitutes were arrested for a wide range of offences, and police decisions to arrest, as well as the choice of charge preferred, have to be understood in the context of the priorities affecting the regulation of sexuality. While the Contagious Diseases legislation provided the occasion for vigorous campaigns in many places against state-condoned vice, as a policing mechanism it was only one of a number of options: when it fell from use it was replaced by police use of the Traffic Act as a means of controlling street-walking.

A summary of the prosecution figures for prostitution in late colonial Brisbane suggests the dimensions of police involvement with the regulation of the practice. During the 1890s there was an increasing use of the Contagious Diseases Act, particularly when compared with the declining use of the disorderly prostitute charge after 1892. Peaks in the use of the latter charge (a Vagrancy Act offence which was more likely to result in the imprisonment of the woman concerned) may be indicative of more than increased police scrutiny: 1886, constituting one peak, was a year of high immigration and appears to have impacted severely on the social resources of the colony, while the early 1890s were years of very severe economic depression. In each case it is possible that greater numbers of women sought economic relief in the earnings which might come from prostitution, simultaneously placing themselves at greater risk of attention from the police, whether for reasons of protecting the existing trade or in response to local complaints. But the figures are indicative of less than a third of police arrests of prostitutes. For the period 1877–93 aggregate figures are available for arrests of prostitutes so described in the watch-house record. These indicate the intensive focus of police on the activities of prostitutes, relative to the low appearance rate of women in the criminal justice system generally. Designated prostitutes regularly made up one-third of females arrested in these years, in 1893 well over half. Further research on prostitution in Brisbane would be required to suggest the micro-decisions involved. But the extensive use of a range of public order charges in addition to the provisions of the Contagious Diseases Act confirms the historical picture developed elsewhere of the regulatory function of policing in this area of the social and sexual order. Unlike gambling, another object of policing which received much less consistent attention in this period, prostitution was a constant target of surveillance, the end of which was not 'crime' prevention but policing control. Condoned through legislation which had its imperial rationale in the desire of the British government to preserve the health of its visiting naval forces (in Queensland the colonial innovation was to extend this measure to the civil population), prostitution was regulated in ways which continued into the twentieth century, eventually becoming the basis of organised police corruption on a substantial scale.[43]

Conclusion

Policing in Queensland played a vital role in the construction of the colonial social order. As the foremost agent of the state, much more indeed than a mere repressive or crime-preventive arm, the Queensland police were indispensable to the management of social conflict in key areas of the economy at times of great tension or over the longer period in districts with particular population mixes demanding close attention. By the end of the colonial period the police had become one of the state's major bureaucracies.

The long period of occupation of aboriginal land had been marked by the main departure from the Irish and English models of policing, in the shape of the Native Police. Absorbed finally only in 1897, this military policing solution to the aboriginal resistance to alien settlement was the principal exception to the presumption that policing should be accountable to the land. When overt conflict between organised pastoral interests and organised labour broke out in the 1890s, the legitimacy of colonial policing faced its most serious challenge. But within the bounds of predominantly European settlement this was the exceptional occasion. The bulk of policing business was mundane, inflected as it might be in particular districts by the imperatives of economic and social practices and relations. Policing such a colony as Queensland meant a variety of strategies of social management, a flexibility which was made possible by the unified and centralised force established from 1864.

Notes

1 On the origins and organisation of Australian police see H. King, 'Some aspects of police administration in New South Wales, 1825–1851', *Journal of the Royal Australian Historical Society*, 42, 5 (1956), pp. 205–30; cf. M. Sturma, 'Policing the criminal frontier in mid-nineteenth century Australia, Britain and America', in M. Finnane (ed.), *Policing in Australia: Historical Perspectives* (Kensington, N.S.W., 1987); D. Philips, 'Law', in G. Davison *et al.* (eds.), *Australians 1888*, (Sydney, 1988); B. Swanton *et al.* (eds.), *Police Source Book* 2 (Canberra, 1985). The most important history of an Australian police force is R. Haldane, *The People's Force: a history of the Victoria Police* (Carlton, 1986).

2 *Progress Report from the Select Committee on the Management and Working of the Police Force*, Queensland Legislative Assembly, Papers, 1869, evidence, p. 105–6.

3 See *Commission of Inquiry into the Criminal Investigation Branch*, Queensland Legislative Assembly, Papers, 1899, vol. 4.

4 See G. Bolton, *A Thousand Miles Away* (Canberra, 1963); R. Fitzgerald, *From the Dreamtime to 1915* (St Lucia, 1982); W. R. Johnston, *The Call of the Land* (Brisbane, 1985); Beverley Kingston, *The Oxford History of Australia*, 3, *1860–1900* (Melbourne, 1988) especially ch. 1.

5 Commissioner of Police, *First Report*, 1865, p. 7 (hereafter *Annual report*, year); cf. S. K. Mukherjee *et al.*, *Crime and Punishment in the Colonies: a stastical profile* (Kensington, N.S.W., n.d.), pp. 148–9.

6 N. G. Butlin, *Investment in Australian Economic Development, 1861–1900* (Cambridge, 1966), p. 36.

7 N. Loos, *Invasion and Resistance: aboriginal–European relations on the north Queensland frontier, 1861–1897* (Canberra, 1982), p. 28.

8 *Annual report*, 1865, p. 1.

9 See, for example, Queensland State Archives [QSA], COL/A29, 62/1447. Return of duty performed by the Chief and Ordinary Constables of this District, Dalby, April 1862.

10 Cf. M. Finnane, 'Police rules and the organization of policing in Queensland, 1905–16', *Australian and New Zealand Journal of Criminology*, 22 (1989), pp. 95–108, and copies of manuals in Queensland Police Museum, Brisbane.

11 See QSA, staff file A/47938, and M. O'Sullivan, *Cameos of Crime* (2nd ed., Brisbane, 1947).

12 *Rules for the General Government and Discipline of Members of the Police Force of Queensland, 1869*, r. 224.

13 *Ibid.*, r. 7.

14 QSA, Police staff file, A/40203.

15 O'Sullivan, *Cameos of Crime*.

16 Cf. *Annual Report*, 1897, p. 3; 1875, p. 1.

17 The defaulters sheets on police staff files, QSA, show the frequency of disciplinary infractions and the relatively common experience of dismissal. Cf. Haldane, *People's Force*, pp. 49–50, 109, on Victoria; on New South Wales, R. Walker, 'The NSW Police Force, 1862–1900', *Journal of Australian Studies*, 15 (1984), p. 32; H. Boritch, 'Conflict, compromise and administrative convenience: the police organization in nineteenth-century Toronto', *Canadian Journal of Law and Society*, 3 (1988), p. 155, on disciplinary problems in the Toronto force (I owe this reference to Rob McQueen), and C. Steedman, *Policing the Victorian Community: the formation of English provincial police forces, 1856–80* (London, 1984), pp. 92–3.

18 *Report from the Select Committee on the Native Police Force*, Queensland Legislative Assembly, 1861, evidence of A. C. Gregory. See Marie Hansen Fels, *Good Men and*

True: the aboriginal police of the Port Phillip District, 1837–1853 (Melbourne, 1988), for an account which explores the perspectives of the aboriginal police recruits themselves in a rather different context from that prevailing later in Queensland, for which see, for example, R. Evans et al., Exclusion, Exploitation and Extermination: race relations in colonial Queensland (Sydney, 1975), pp. 55–66.

19 See the evidence to the 1861 Report (n. 18); similar complaints formed the object of criticism in the 1858 New South Wales select committee on the murders on the Dawson river (relating to the northern districts, i.e. Queensland); L. E. Skinner, Police of the Pastoral Frontier (St Lucia, 1975), pp. 323–4.

20 Cited in Skinner, Police of the Pastoral Frontier, p. 54.

21 See especially N. Loos, Invasion and Resistance (Canberra, 1982).

22 Annual report, 1874, p. 1.

23 Annual report, 1875, p. 2.

24 C. Rowley, The Destruction of Aboriginal Society (Ringwood, 1972).

25 Annual report, 1881, p. 1.

26 Cf. Loos, Invasion and Resistance, for a detailed history of this process.

27 O'Sullivan, Cameos of Crime, p. 50.

28 Bolton, A Thousand Miles Away.

29 Annual report, 1871, p. 2; 1874, p. 1; 1878, p. 1.

30 Annual report, 1871, p. 2.

31 For the 1873 case, Brisbane Courier, 4 February 1827, and Queensland Parliament Debates, 15 (1873), pp. 363–78; on the Kenniffs see R. Joyce, Samuel Walker Griffith (St Lucia, 1984), pp. 228–32.

32 J. McQuilton, The Kelly Outbreak (Carlton, 1979).

33 Annual report, 1872, p. 1.

34 A point not lost on Labour Party critics in the parliamentary debate on the legislation; Queensland Parliamentary Debates, 6 September 1894, vol. 71, pp. 473, 477.

35 Annual report, 1894, p. 1.

36 Ibid., p. 4. The strike receives detailed attention in S. Svenson, The Shearers' War (St Lucia, 1989).

37 Cf. R. Walker, 'Violence in industrial conflicts in New South Wales in the later nineteenth century', Historical Studies, 86 (1986), pp. 54–70.

38 See K. Saunders, Workers in Bondage (St Lucia, 1982); K. Saunders, 'Indentured labour in Queensland', in K. Saunders (ed.), Indentured Labour in the British Empire (London, 1984); C. Moore, Kanaka: a history of Melanesian Mackay (Port Moresby, 1984).

39 Moore, Kanaka, p. 269.

40 See Saunders, Workers in Bondage, chapter 6.

41 See papers in QSA, COL/A500, A87/3997, and COL/A601, 89/11130; on drunkenness see C. Moore, ' "Me blind drunk": alcohol and Melanesians in the Mackay district, Queensland, 1867–1907', paper for Medical History Section of ANZAAS, Townsville, 1987.

42 The history of colonial prostitution and its regulation in Queensland in detailed in R. Evans, 'Soiled doves: prostitution in colonial Queensland', in K. Daniels (ed.), So Much Hard Work (Melbourne, 1984); E. Barclay, 'Queensland's Contagious Diseases Act, 1868', Queensland Heritage, 2, 10 (1974), 27–34, and 3, 1 (1974), pp. 21–9; D. Sissons, 'Karayuki-san: Japanese prostitutes in Australia', Historical Studies, 68 (1977), pp. 323–41, and 69 (1977), pp. 474–88.

43 Cf. M. Finnane, 'The Fitzgerald Commission: law, politics and state corruption', Australian Journal of Public Administration, XLVII (1988), pp. 332–42.

CHAPTER FOUR

The policing of colonial New Zealand: from informal to formal control, 1840–1907

Richard S. Hill

By 1840, the year in which the islands of Aotearoa/New Zealand were annexed by the British, the imperial state had developed a complex range of mechanisms for effecting social and racial control. These controls ranged from the overtly coercive ('condign', to borrow from J.K. Galbraith) extreme of suppression by outright warfare to control of the minds and therefore the behaviour of the populace. The location of the various modes of policing along this continuum of control measures can be viewed from two perspectives. First, there is a *strategic* perspective; the overarching mode of policing which is utilised by the state throughout an extended period of time. Second, specific types of policing were employed in response to problems of order: these *tactical* modes generally had an organic relationship with the strategic approach but sometimes departed (perhaps drastically) from it. In the early years of the colony of New Zealand the policing strategy was that of *imposing* order upon a population, both Maori and white (*pakeha*), that was perceived by the state to be turbulent and untamed. As both races' modes of general behaviour became increasingly acceptable to the state, partly because of policing methods, mostly because of socio-economic developments, the strategy of instrumentalist policing, of *order-imposition*, gradually gave way to a replacement strategy located towards the other end of the continuum. This overarching approach focused upon *maintaining* the (relatively acceptable) degree of order which had been reached in *pakeha* and Maori societies. The goal of generally acceptable behaviour by the two races, *en masse*, had more or less been attained within fifty years of the annexation of the territory. The general policing strategy had changed accordingly, to that of *order-maintenance*.

Within this overall framework of altering strategies, a wide range of policing tactics were utilised to meet problems specific to time and place. These tactics were usually borrowed from English, Irish and imperial policing practices; the history of policing colonial New Zealand is one of the introduction of what were seen at the time as 'models' from overseas, and their adaptation to the peculiar indigenous circumstances of the colony.[1] The following account outlines in the most general of terms the various major strategic and tactical alterations in the policing mode in response to changes, in the perception of the state's decision-makers, in policing requirements.

Minimal policing, 1800–46

The state's function, in the final analysis, of imposing and maintaining a condition of societal 'order' which maximises the creation and protection of private profit can be readily perceived in the policing orientation of the state towards New Zealand. In 1800, several decades before formal annexation, New Zealand was an informal colony of the British colony of New South Wales, whose entrepreneurs were coming to appreciate the profit to be gained from exploiting the islands' natural resources.

The key impediment to this exploitation was the Maori, a warrior people disinclined to allow themselves to be exploited, but generally willing to trade with the *pakeha* to gain goods that would enhance their modes of existence. The Maori, well over 100,000 strong and communally organised, were perceived by the *pakeha* to be living (in the words of the Minister of Native Affairs in 1860, C.W. Richmond) in a situation of 'beastly communism'. Most tribespeople dwelt in the (warmer) North Island. The tribes (*iwi*) were subdivided socio-politically into *hapu* (sub-tribes) and *shanau* (extended families). At each level *runanga* (councils) discussed the regulation of tribal life, including customary law and its enforcement. In the final analysis, however, social control lay in the hands of the chiefly caste (*rangatira*) and its allies (such as the *tohunga*, the priest or 'expert').

Tribal warfare (not least between *hapu*) was endemic but had traditionally caused minimal social disruption. With the purchase in bulk by some tribes of European firearms, the 'musket wars' of the 1820s ensued. These, coupled with the ravages of other aspects of contact with the *pakeha* (especially liquor and disease), led to widespread devastation among certain tribes and *hapu*. White entrepreneurs visiting, and later residing in, New Zealand, maltreated the Maori, regarding brown-skinned people as primitives who could be exploited with impunity. Their ethnocentric view of Maori society was strengthened by their observation of social disintegration among *hapu* in close proximity to *pakeha* settlements.

It was the self-perceived role of the British and New South Wales states to regulate interracial contact on the new imperial frontier. The policing imperative was to ensure that the sealers, whalers, traders and so forth

[53]

c

who visited or settled in New Zealand did not provoke the Maori into retaliation which would threaten the profit-making activities of the Europeans. But since British global policing requirements were so great, the most meagre of resources were available to prevent interracial conflict and general turbulence in New Zealand. A handful of officials, such as naval captains, missionary justices of the peace and the British residency institution, operated a policing strategy of 'minimum intervention'.[2]

From time to time demonstrations of force were used despite that strategy. This was to ensure that the inhabitants of Aotearoa, mostly the indigenous people, knew that in the final analysis the British Empire could not be trifled with; the visiting, for example, of exemplary military punishment upon a tribe which had violated Eurocentric codes of behaviour to show that the British state had the *capacity* to wield overwhelming coercive might when necessary. The most dramatic instance of this occurred in 1834. After the barque *Harriet* had been wrecked on the Taranaki coast, and some of its crew had treated the local Maori with brutality, a confrontation had occurred. Some *pakeha*s were killed, the rest captured. The ship's owner, John Guard, a typical whaler of his time in believing that the only way to 'civilise' the Maori was to 'shoot them to be sure!' was released in order to procure a ransom.

Although the captives included his wife and children, he persuaded the New South Wales authorities to endorse and finance a punitive expedition. When the warship *Alligator* and a support ship arrived in Taranaki and a chief offered to mediate, he was tortured until all but one of the captives were returned. With Guard's son still detained, the expedition destroyed three villages, wounding and killing many 'innocent' (a word used by a House of Commons committee) Maori. When the final captive was handed over unharmed (all had been well treated) his escort was slaughtered. The official in charge of these acts of war issued a proclamation that future molestation of British subjects would similarly incur 'most severe punishment'. A dozen years later, well after annexation, the officer in charge of police in the region recorded that the affair was 'fresh in the memory of the natives'.

Despite such incidents, the British military position was not strong. In view of the coercive weakness of the British in New Zealand the main policing strategy was a system of 'indirect control', using indigenous authority within the tribes and sub-tribes. The chiefs selected for this role were, in return for benefits of various types, required to impose 'certain minimal standards of order' upon key areas. In acting in this capacity (sometimes specifically designated as policemen, more often not) they were laying the groundwork of greater *pakeha* involvement in New Zealand. This expropriation of indigenous authority and its adaptation to settler purposes would be a recurring theme in the history of colonial New Zealand. Maori chiefly agencies of indirect and preparatory control, then, were the key actors in the pre-annexation policing strategies of the British in New Zealand.[3]

By the end of the 1830s New Zealand was rapidly heading towards large-scale British settlement, much of it privately organised from London. At annexation in 1840 there were some 2,000 *pakeha*s in the country; by 1845 a further 9,000 settlers had joined them. To control this development required a rapid formal acquisition of the islands of Aotearoa. Loss by the Maori of their *substantive* sovereignty would clearly meet armed resistance, so the overall strategy of low-key control continued, particularly towards the Maori who, at least 100,000 strong, outnumbered the *pakeha* many times over. At first the state attempted little more than decreeing *nominal* sovereignty over much of the newly acquired territory. Then, on 14 January 1840, New Zealand became a formal possession of the empire. From that date British law came into force, and the first policemen arrived when the official party, headed by Lieutenant Governor William Hobson, reached the main settlement of Kororareka later that month. A number of important Maori chiefs signed the 'Treaty' of Waitangi on 6 February, thinking that, in the words of Chief Nopera Panakareao, the Maori retained the 'substance of the land' while the whites were getting only its 'shadow'. It was a holding operation that worked; the five 'dismounted Mounted Policemen' who arrived with Hobson were the only land-based overtly coercive forces in a territory of 103,000 square miles until a hundred troops landed that April. Nopera and others only gradually came to realise, as immigration increased, that the reality of the situation was that it was the *pakeha*s who had gained the substance of the land, and the Maori who were being left with the shadow.[4]

As the rudiments of formal administration were established, policing was confined mostly to the environs of the small number of scattered white settlements. From New South Wales (of which New Zealand was a dependency until 1841) the new colony adopted the police magistry system. In each settlement the police magistrate selected and controlled constables, who operated a London Metropolitan beat system adapted to the harsher realities of the antipodean colonies. It was a system generally acceptable to the early settlers, who prided themselves on inhabiting a 'free' colony, in as much as it did not embody the overtly militaristic characteristics of the Australian forces concerned with repressing convicts, bushrangers and aborigines. The detachment of New South Wales Mounted Police which had arrived with and (in enlarged form) continued to 'guard' Hobson offered a contrasting mode of policing: the heavily armed and overbearing mounted troopers were detested. Outside town

[55]

boundaries the countryside tended to be 'controlled', if at all, by the *pakeha*, through the mechanism of expropriating the services of 'friendly' chiefs.[5]

The armed police forces

The major modes of control were dramatically altered in the mid-1840s. The catalyst was the outbreak of Maori insurrection in 1845, first in the far north with the sacking of Kororareka in March and then in the southern part of the North Island. George Grey had, as Governor of South Australia, been successful in subduing aboriginal resistance. When late that year he arrived at the colonial capital of Auckland it was to fulfil the same function as Governor of New Zealand. He was given a sizeable imperial military force to crush the rebellions. Complementarily he introduced new institutions along the lines of his experiments across the Tasman Sea. Overarching a willingness to swear in 'native police' was the concept of rapidly pressing 'civilisation' upon the Maori, of firmly engineering their 'amalgamation' into the white society and economy. They would be both forced and cajoled into becoming a people of brown-skinned *pakeha*s.[6]

At the same time Grey sought to repress the unruly behaviour of the labouring and *lumpen pakeha*s who inhabited the settlements and frequented their innumerable grog shops. A single type of coercively oriented police force would accomplish this task, as well as his 'native policy'. Men assigned to duties such as fighting the insurrectionists, occupying their land and forcing them to adhere to the modes of behaviour (and, hopefully, the *mores*) acceptable to *pakeha* officialdom would also be patrolling beats in the *pakeha* towns, equipped with an overt display of weaponry. In 1846–47, therefore, the police magistracies were phased out and replaced by separate judicial and policing institutions. The new Resident Magistrates had the task of imposing British concepts of legality upon both races, those in the countryside being assisted in this by chiefly Maoris on state salaries or receiving fees or perquisites of various kinds.

Secondly, the institution of the Armed Police Force (APF), a militarised police responsible direct to the Governor, was established. The APF was, for convenience, split into three autonomous forces: one headquartered at Auckland, one at New Plymouth, and one (later called the New Munster APF) covering (from Wellington) the southern North Island and all the South Island. Discipline was strict; the men were young and imbued with the ethos of *imposing* and *controlling*: the Irish constabulary was perceived as the major model, although a modified London Metropolitan beat system continued in the towns. When APF rules were codified in 1852 what were understood to be the broad outlines of the two models were amalgamated. As with the rural units of the Irish constabulary, the police were highly mobile, often moved in small detachments, were demonstrably coercive in orientation, and conducted unremitting surveillance while on their patrols.

It had not been uncommon for imperial authorities to utilise the services of indigenous people for policing purposes. The practice reflected their possession of specialist knowledge about their own communities, as well as the appropriation of indigenous control institutions for indirect policing functions. But their mode of employment had been in an auxiliary or supplementary capacity. Grey, however, boldly proposed to make young chiefly Maori men an integral part of the mainstream policing of the colony. Soon, then, amidst considerable racist opposition from many whites, Maori constables were patrolling the streets and coercing *pakeha* and non-*pakeha* alike. The scheme was part of Grey's grand design to 'amalgamate' the two races, albeit (of course) on European terms. Maori police were supposed to learn appropriate ways of action and thought, take them back to their tribes, and coerce and cajole their people into wholeheartedly adopting the *mores* and procedures of the *pakeha*s. The state's activities would therefore, in a newspaper's (typical) words, 'transform the native grub into a civilised butterfly'.[7]

The Armed Police Force system ushered in a forty-year period characterised by a strategic policing mode located towards the condign end of the control continuum. In that period, various tactical modes of policing came and went in response to various imperatives specific to time and place. Most significantly, once a certain minimal degree of 'order and regularity' had been imposed upon the populace in the nucleated white settlements, it was possible for a devolving system of policing to gradually accompany a devolving system of governmental administration.

This development was formalised in 1853 when, under a new constitution, New Zealand ceased to be a Crown colony and acquired 'representative' institutions of government. Each of the six major settlement areas now became provinces which were, by delegation of the General Government, self-governing in many key areas, including that of policing. By and large the ruling elites in each province (ultimately there were ten administrations) took over the existing Armed Police Force detachments in their area of control and continued the same type of system. By then the sizes of the APF detachments had decreased and they had become less overtly coercive in their tactics, following what was perceived as the 'taming' of the rural Maori and the town *pakeha*. This development accelerated in the initial years of the provincial system, partly because of the very limited resources of some of the provincial governments and partly because of relative social quietude in many areas of the colony.

A number of tribes, for example, prospered in trading with the *pakeha* and were therefore disinclined to resist *pakeha* settlement. Small provinces in particular could not afford elaborate forces, while Otago's Scottish Free Church settlement attempted a communal 'moral policing' regime. Tiny sub-provincial forces were established, part-time police prevailed in tranquil settled areas, and policing tasks were often devolved upon rural justices of the peace.[8]

Yet over and above such tactical adjustments, specific to time and place, the general strategy of coercive policing remained intact. There were many reasons for this, most significant among them being increasing interracial tension in the North Island. Provincial governments encouraged white immigration, and the Maori were coming to realise that the *pakeha* wanted more than nominal sovereignty over Maori districts and that white settlement had an insatiable appetite for acquiring the land which had been owned communally by the indigenous people. By the end of the decade of the 1850s, when the white population for the first time surpassed that of the Maori (the latter having fallen below 60,000), most of the tactical moves away from coercive policing practices were in the process of reversal.

War and gold

Events of 1860–61 were to confirm in the eyes of the decision-makers the correctness of their strategic approach, and lead to an enormous tightening of the state's coercive grip upon sizeable sections of both races. This second phase of the strategy of repressive policing came about because of two phenomena. First, renewed warfare broke out in Taranaki in 1860, heralding a decade of Anglo-Maori wars in the North Island. The most significant new factor in the wars was that major tribes had coalesced behind a Maori king.[9] This phenomenon had arisen after the failure of tribal attempts to prevent large-scale alienation of land. Key Maori leaders had argued that the *pakeha* settlers had been so successful because a centralised state machinery controlled their strategies of conquest in a co-ordinated fashion; the Maori tribespeople should emulate this by pan-tribal unification of resistance to further *pakeha* encroachment upon their way of life. The resultant new movement, Kingitanga, was based essentially upon the important Waikato federation, and in 1858 Chief Te Wherowhero (once the leader of a pro-British police unit) was installed as King Potatau I at the royal capital of Ngaruawahia. Kingitanga aimed to place all Maori land under the *mana* of the new monarch, its ownership to be subject to decisions by the Kingite authority structure. Although this grand aim was never realised, even areas subject to Kingite sway, tribes and *hapu* of the powerful Tainui confederation (and others) generally joined.

The Kingite resistance movement established a rival sovereignty, complete with its own police and military forces, in the fertile Waikato lands. Once again Grey was called upon to be Governor. In a display of imperial coercive might, the Kingites were pushed into an interior territory of little attraction for the *pakeha*. A significant portion of the fighting was done by corps created with a militarised policing role in mind. The first was the Colonial Defence Force, whose units had been established on Irish constabulary lines; second was the Military Settler corps, who were paid for their services partly by grants of land confiscated from the Maori. In the aftermath of the wars these armed settlers constituted occupation police in frontier areas bordering on the King country.

As usual, however, the Maori were themselves to loom large in the operations to 'tranquillise' the North Island. Indeed, in reappointing Grey as Governor the Colonial Office had hoped that his expertise in the subjugation of indigenous peoples by policing modes might bypass the need for outright warfare. In the Cape Colony, for example, Grey had implemented a system of 'indirect rule' whereby indigenous institutions had been 'guided' by white officials; on arrival in 1861 he proceeded to adapt the principle to New Zealand conditions. Traditional chiefly control had been mediated through indigenous institutions called *runanga*, or assemblies. Under Grey's scheme the *runanga* of many collaborationist or neutral tribes and subtribes in the North Island were designated official agencies of state governance. Guided by *pakeha* officials, these institutions of indirect control could impose their own laws, so long as such customary laws were not too 'repugnant' in white eyes. Each 'official *runanga*' had a police force paid for by the state. Dozens of new forces were established in New Zealand under the system. Although Grey still invaded the Waikato, and although rebel 'no go' areas remained in New Zealand for some twenty more years, the 'official *runanga*' police had been an important means of making Maoris 'parties to their own submission'.[10]

The second reason for the renewed phase of condign policing happened a year after the outbreak of war. In 1861 New Zealand's first huge gold rush began in Otago, in the South Island. This placid rural settlement was suddenly inundated with thousands of rootless, usually young and often turbulent men. The province's population doubled to 30,000 inside six months. Extreme violence and disorder threatened, particularly when word reached the dying Australian goldfields that fortunes could now be made in New Zealand. The Otago provincial government, realising that an entirely *new* policing structure was required, looked across the Tasman Sea for a goldfield force it could use as a model. There, in Victoria, a successful goldfield policing system had evolved, after a shaky start which included the bloody suppression of the insurrection at the Eureka Stockade. The Victoria police force, considered to be one of the most professional in the world, was yet another force modelled essentially on what were seen as the key characteristics of the rural detachments of the Irish constabulary. It also incorporated strong London Metropolitan Police characteristics, especially in the towns.[11] It was a force specifically adapted to the conditions peculiar to antipodean goldfields and their environs. It existed to impose standards of behaviour, to discipline unruly masses of people. Otago imported not only the Victorian system but also many of its personnel; a sizeable proportion of these had, in turn, Irish or colonial policing experience. The new Otago Police were headed by a commissioned officer from Victoria, St John Branigan, an Irishman who had seen military service and been a member of the Cape Colony force.[12]

The system established by Branigan in 1861, amidst profound social turbulence, was to be the key model in New Zealand for a long time to come. The Otago force became a legendary policing operation and was soon being spoken of as on a par with that of Victoria or even Ireland. A firm paramilitary hierarchy and discipline were put in place, and a system of police districts and sub-districts set up throughout the province. Armed police worked urban beats; even more heavily armed police, often mounted, patrolled the countryside and the sprawling, raucous diggings, and operated lines of gold escort to Otago's capital, Dunedin.

The style of policing taken from Victoria spread to other goldfields in the South Island and influenced facets of policing in other provincial forces of both islands. Its overtly coercive proclivities, seen to derive from Irish methods, were what made it distinctive in the eyes of observers. The Canterbury force, it was noted in 1867:

> is formed on the model of the Irish Constabulary rather than of ordinary police. They are in fact a semi-military force, trained and disciplined in military style, and accustomed to regard themselves and to be treated by their superiors after the manner of regular soldiers.

This was 'quite foreign to English institutions'. Specialist departments of policing also followed overseas models: detective and water police branches were established, as were reward funds, systems of professional training at a central depot, the publication of a *Police Gazette*, the division of ranks into classes, and so forth. Along with this expansion of policing methods from Victoria came policemen from that colony who exercised control over the organisation of New Zealand policing. Most of the senior colonial policemen until the end of the century had been among those who had crossed the Tasman Sea from Victoria in the 1860s.[13]

By 1867 state officials assessed that the backbone of military resistance by the insurrectionist Maori in the North Island had been definitively broken. At its peak there had been 14,000 effective troops in the field, more than were immediately available for the defence of Britain, against Maori forces which never exceeded 20,900 at any one time. Most of the imperial regiments now withdrew, the Military Settler corps were disbanded, the 'official *runanga*' mechanism had been formally disbanded (although a number of their 'native constables' were retained as part-time specialist police by Native Department officials). The colony needed both a standing army and an occupation police for the conquered areas. An Armed Constabulary was set up to combine the two roles, following the report of the civil service commissioners a year before, which recommended 'an armed constabulary force, foot and mounted, similar to the Irish armed police'. Again, therefore, 'the Irish constabulary model' was consciously utilised, particularly the *modus operandi* of the countryside surveillance patrol in relatively hostile territory.[14]

Constabulary control

The Armed Constabulary, superimposed upon racially 'troubled' areas nominally controlled by provincial forces, was a General Government organisation. Its arrival ushered in the third phase of the strategy of condign policing. Unlike the provincial, *runanga*, part-time and other constables, its members were sworn to serve anywhere in the colony. The government, moreover, envisaged that eventually it would be more efficient if the provincial governments were to allow their policing tasks to be taken over by the highly mobile Armed Constables. The new force, then, would gradually evolve into a civil police as subjugation of the Maori countryside and the *pakeha* diggings proceeded.

Almost at once there was a hiccup in this development, and the constabulary's role rapidly moved along the tactical continuum to the position of extreme coercion. For there had been a resurgence of insurrection on both seaboards of the North Island, and the Armed Constabulary accordingly became little more than the colony's army. Hundreds of 'constables' fought in these last phases of the Anglo-Maori wars. But by late 1869 the forces of rebel leaders Titokowaru and Te Kooti had been forced into interior fastnesses, well away from major settlement areas. The government began to 'demilitarise' the Armed Constabulary and place it back on its destined evolutionary course. Again it was felt that the Irish system, but as modified by Victoria and remodified by Otago, was the appropriate model. Commissionar St John Branigan of Otago was brought to Wellington and made Commissioner of the Armed Constabulary.

There were Maori constables in the Armed Constabulary, particularly after specialist Maori corps ('the Flying Column', patrolling the borders of the Urewera) were incorporated into it; but it was predominantly a *pakeha* force of occupation. In the latter phases of the wars the 'friendly Maori' had fought as *kapapa*, or auxiliaries. Auckland and Wellington Provinces had provincial forces composed predominantly of Maori police well into the 1850s, but by the onset of the wars the growing polarisation of race had removed this phenomenon. With the Maori now, at law, perceived to be subdued, there was little need for indigenous policing personnel, although in 1882 the remaining twenty-eight part-time 'native constables' (remnants of the 'official *runanga*' system) were taken over from the Native Department by the policing authorities.[15]

It was the Armed Constabulary which now patrolled in the Maori districts, particularly those considered 'troublesome'. At the same time the Armed Constables prepared the way for expanded white settlement by pushing roads through the forests, draining swamps, building bridges and the like. In 1870 the Auckland provincial government allowed its policing organisation to become absorbed by the General Government force, the colony's central government hoping that this would give a positive lead to other provincial administrations. Despite some interest, however, no other province followed: control over the means of coercion was too important for provincial regimes to let it go. Auckland's vast sprawl, economic problems and high population of resistant Maoris had made it the exception. By the early 1870s the General Government had come to view devolved policing, and devolved political control, as anachronistic. This was the more so following Julius Vogel's comprehensive state-led immigration and public works schemes of the 1870s. The nucleated settlements were now linked by much better communications and transport facilities.[16]

In 1876 the provincial governments were abolished, and over a few months their police forces were absorbed into the Armed Constabulary. The resultant organisation, the New Zealand Constabulary Force, therefore combined policing and military functions, controlled from Wellington (the colonial capital since 1865).[17] But the force was soon split into two sections; the Police Branch, which included most of the previous provincial men, and the Reserve Branch (later called the Field Force), which was located at strategic garrisons in the countryside. As far as civil policing was concerned, the four main centres, the rural towns and the 'settled' localities were becoming more stable and tranquil. After the wars there was more land available to absorb potential farmers. With these developments, policing became less overtly coercive. For example, in 1878 foot police ceased to be issued with rifles. In 1880, with the onset of 'the long depression', the number of civil constables was drastically reduced and reached a low point of 441 colony-wide the following year.

The last of the great Maori resistance movements to develop, that centred at Parihaka, was forcibly suppressed by the constabulary in 1881. In any case, and significantly, it had not been a military threat to the *pakeha* but a movement of 'passive resistance' to land confiscation.[18] By the mid-1880s the last of the no-go areas, the King country, was being opened up for *pakeha* penetration as leaders on both sides of the border made their peace. Complementarily, as the racial frontier stabilised, the fears of *pakeha* New Zealanders about 'the enemy' began to focus upon perceived external 'threats'. For some time, especially since the Russo-Turkish war of 1877–78, there had been concern that great-power rivalry would lead to warfare in which New Zealand, with its long and undefended coastline, would be vulnerable to naval attack. Successive reports by naval experts recommended a standing army which was oriented towards a harbour defence system. One of those experts, Sir William Jervois, was Governor when in 1885 another 'war scare' panicked the colony. The time was ripe for change.

With the perceived threat to the colony now an external one rather than that of the Maori, the Field Force was retrenched, withdrawn from

New Zealand Constabulary Force Reserve Branch officers in the field during the invasion of Parihaka, 1881

Members of the New Zealand Constabulary Force at the harbour fortification of Fort Kelburne, Ngauranga, 1885

the interior and altered into a military machine aimed at repelling invasion. Most of its members had ceased all meaningful connection with the Police Branch, which continued to move strategically along the control continuum, away from the pole of order imposition and towards that of 'passive' policing and consensualism. In 1886 the constabulary was split by legislation into the New Zealand Police Force and the standing army or Permanent Militia (later called the Permanent Artillery). It was a very practical move, repealing as it did the various Acts of Parliament on policing organisation since 1846 and removing what had become an organisational anomaly. It was also a symbol of the change in state strategy from overtly coercive policing to one which, in the final analysis, rested on the concept of order maintenance.

Increasingly, most people most of the time (even amongst the Maori, at least in interpenetrated areas) obeyed most of the codes of behaviour laid down by the political executive and applied through its justice system. Hegemonic influences were successfully at work, accompanying sweeping socio-economic and racial change; the goals of instrumentalist policing could be gradually superseded as a policing ethos by those of a consensualist force disciplining individuals rather than masses. The constable was now an ancillary in enforcing generally accepted societal norms rather than a key actor.

Order-maintenance policing

Constables came to be symbols of the coercive potential of the state. They were embodiers of state-desired 'virtues', exemplars of state-desired behaviour, rather than simply coercive imposers. The arrival of the 'disciplinary society' was at hand, which most citizens had internalised 'correct' rhythms of behaviour and 'appropriate' patterns of belief. In general terms, society was increasingly self-regulating, a concomitant phenomenon of the growth of social bonding. Accordingly the police force's strategic mission required that it be essentially an unarmed policing body of relatively 'benign' disposition.

Within this overall strategy, of course, tactics could still be coercive: on a nightly basis all around the colony, for example, at pub closing time; when armed expeditions went into the mountain fastnesses of the Urewera, or to the Hokianga in 1898 to suppress the 'Dog Tax Rebellion' among local tribespeople; when strikers and their allies were resisted and strikebreakers protected during the great maritime strike of 1890 (and in the industrial strife of 1912–13). Moreover, the state maintained the mechanisms for the deployment of coercive power, should it be needed. Written into the 1886 legislation, therefore, was a provision that all recruits to the police force were to come from the Permanent Militia;

police training remained in essence and by design military training. New recruits to the police were also to undergo annual refresher courses in artillery training. The constables were to constitute a reserve military force, while conversely the gunners were brought on to policing duties when the police force needed strengthening – not only for crowd control, but also, from time to time, for beat policing. But the retention of a close military/police relationship proved to be over-cautious, in view of the rapid 'stabilisation' of New Zealand society by the end of the century (including the general quiescence of the Maori, whose numbers had dropped to a record low of 40,000). In the mid-1890s, when the population of the colony reached 750,000, the formal links between police and military no longer needed, atrophied. In 1896 control of the police force passed from the Defence Minister to the Minister of Justice.

It was logical that such developments should occur, and by the mid-1890s the ratio of police to population had sunk to a nadir of 1 : 1,530. But in shaking off the military and quasi-military orientation of the past, the police hierarchy, itself rooted in that very past, could come up with little in the way of new methodology for the control of a 'conditioned' Western society. Inefficiencies were exacerbated by constant interference in police matters by the heavily interventionist Liberal government. Public concern, orchestrated by temperance and prohibitionist leaders, enraged at police incapacity to check the colony's undoubtedly immoderate drinking habits, forced the government to take decisive measures in 1897–98.[19] First, a retired chief inspector from the Criminal Intelligence Department of Scotland Yard, John Bennett Tunbridge, was imported as Commissioner of Police; the government could rely on him to have knowledge of modern policing methods in what was regarded (despite the presence of the Maori) as a 'kindred' society. Second, the government succumbed to demands for a Royal Commission of Inquiry into the force. This, and a series of other such inquiries early in the next century, were to identify the problems and suggest solutions.

Guided by Tunbridge, the 1898 commission recommended a large number of reforms which the commissioner and his successor from 1903 (Walter Dinnie, another chief inspector from the London Metropolitan Police) progressively implemented: specialist police training for recruits, for example, a pension scheme and compulsory retirement age in order to remove blockages to promotion. It was assessed, moreover, that the government response to societal stabilisation of lowering police coverage had gone too far: the ratio of police to population would now gradually rise, although the New Zealand force remained the cheapest *per capita* in Australasia.[20]

By 1907, when New Zealand moved in constitutional status from colony to dominion, its population of 962,000 was policed by a force totalling 699 regulars, together with some three dozen auxiliaries such as part-time police, including 'native constables', and police matrons in the four cities. The process of reform under Dinnie was continuing: that year the *Police Gazette* was revitalised and produced more frequently, another command level was introduced to the cities, compulsory weekly instruction for junior constables implemented, and educational qualifications for entry were raised.

Around the turn of the century the former Police Commissioner George Whitmore expressed a truism among the *pakeha* in claiming that, after the Anglo-Maori wars, the Maori felt that 'the struggle against British supremacy was a useless one'; the two races were 'now practically one people'. This ethnocentric judgement ignored the continuance of the Maori way of life and the social control devices in rural communities, but did reflect satisfaction on the part of the state that 'the subjugation of the native' had been satisfactorily completed. 'It is easier to grow into the undisturbed sovereignty of New Zealand than to conquer it,' *The Times* had advised the colony in 1863; conquest had of course then ensued, but in the post-war pacification era the evolution of the Maori towards acceptance (at least, to all intents and purposes) of the dominance of the European had been so marked that the state felt no need for Maori constables in the regular police, although a handful of mixed-race men were enrolled. Where specialist indigenous knowledge was needed (usually in remote areas) a few Maori were still employed as part-time 'native constables'.

In 1907 both of the Parihaka resistance leaders, Te Whiti-o-Rongomai and Tohu Kakahi, died, taking with them, it was widely felt, 'the fast-dying idea of a Maori nationhood'. 'No longer can the hope of a reconstituted Maori race be maintained ... The rapid absorption of the native race is inevitable.' That year the state moved against one of the remaining areas of Maori customary practice deemed 'repugnant', that of fohungaism. It was seen to be evil because the *tohunga* 'generally take a hostile attitude to the laws which are in force', as the Native Minister (a mixed-race Maori), James Carroll, noted; under their guidance tribespeople tended not to join the work force, send their children to school or become *pakeha*-ised. There was a specific purpose behind the Act, too; an attempt to suppress the Tuhoe prophet Rua Kenana, whose millennial message preached self-determination for the Maori people. The last armed police expedition to move into an area of Maori 'rival sovereignty', in fact, would occur in 1916, when Commissioner John Cullen led an invading force to Rua's capital of Maungapohatu in the rugged Ureweras. It culminated in a bloody gun battle, with Maori loss of life (including Rua's son) and police injuries, before the leaders of the movement were arrested. It was the last organised Maori armed resistance to the state; long before it, to all intents and purposes, Maori people were as 'controlled' as the *pakeha*.[21]

The colony's white population had become subdued, the Maori subjugated; 'order and tranquillity', by and large, prevailed. There was still a paramilitary policing ethos present in the centres of the four cities, but even these on-street methods were far more benign than in the past. And out in the suburbs, in the small towns and in the countryside the policeman was evolving into the phenomenon perceived by the public as the archetypal 'English bobby'. In 1846 policemen had been required to transfer every three months to a new area: fraternisation with locals precluded effective techniques of suppression. Sixty years later it was not uncommon for policemen to be stationed at the same spot for decades, fully integrated into the local community. The strategy of overt coercion had been definitively replaced by the strategy of consensual policing.[22]

Notes

1 For all facets of New Zealand policing to 1867, including an elaboration of this model, refer to Richard S. Hill, *Policing the Colonial Frontier: the theory and practice of coercive social and racial control in New Zealand, 1767–1867* (Wellington, 1986). This constitutes the first volume (in two parts) of *The History of Policing in New Zealand*. Most of the material for that volume and the present chapter was gleaned from a study of contemporary newspapers and primary sources in New Zealand; the bulk of the latter is held at the National Archives of New Zealand, in Wellington.

2 For a selection of readings on officialdom in this period see Robert McNab (ed.), *Historical Records of New Zealand* (2 vols., Wellington, 1908, 1914); E. J. Tapp, *Early New Zealand: a dependency of New South Wales, 1788–1841* (Melbourne, 1958); Harrison M. Wright, *New Zealand, 1769–1840: early years of Western contact* (Cambridge, Mass., 1959); R. A. A. Sherrin and J. H. Wallace, *Early History of New Zealand* (Auckland, 1890); A. T. Yarwood, *Samuel Marsden* (Melbourne, 1977); Judith Binney, *The Legacy of Guilt: a life of Thomas Kendall* (Auckland, 1968); J. R. Barton (ed.), *Earliest New Zealand: the journals and correspondence of the Rev. John Butler* (Masterton, 1927); *Historical Records of Australia* (Series I, 1914 f). For archival sources see CO 209 series, Public Record Office, Kew, and British Resident's Papers (BR 1/1–2), New Zealand National Archives. Richmond's views on the Maori: *New Zealand Parliamentary Debates*, 1860, pp. 185–6.

3 An overview of the use of Maori police by the New Zealand state can be found in Richard S. Hill, 'Maori policing in nineteenth century New Zealand', *Archifacts: Bulletin of the Archives and Records Association of New Zealand*, 2 (1985). For the *Alligator* affair see William Barrett Marshall, *A Personal Narrative of two Visits to New Zealand* (London, 1837), and summary in Hill, *Policing the Colonial Frontier*, pp. 66–7.

4 For the standard interpretation of the 1830s and the context of annexation see Keith Sinclair, *A History of New Zealand* (London, 1959 and various updated editions). For newer perspectives, apart from the author's *Policing the Colonial Frontier*, chapters 1–2, see essays in W. H. Oliver (ed.), *The Oxford History of New Zealand* (Wellington, 1981); Ian Ward, *The Shadow of the Land: a study of British policy and racial conflict in New Zealand, 1832–1852* (Wellington, 1968); Peter Adams, *Fatal Necessity: British intervention in New Zealand, 1830–1847* (Auckland, 1977). For a brief overview of New Zealand history which incorporates the findings of recent historiography see the 'History' chapter by David Green in the *New Zealand Official Yearbook, 1987–88* (Wellington, 1987). The most recent study of the annexation is included in Claudia Orange, *The Treaty of Waitangi* (Wellington, 1987).

5 Hill, *Policing the Colonial Frontier*, chapters 2, 3, 5. For the major archival sources see Colonial Secretary's Papers (IA series), New Zealand National Archives.

6 Alan Ward, *A Show of Justice: racial 'amalgamation' in nineteenth century New Zealand* (Auckland, 1973); G. C. Henderson, *Sir George Grey* (London, 1907). For control of indigenous peoples in an Australian context see Robert Clyne, *Colonial Blue: a history of the South Australian Police Force, 1836–1916* (Adelaide, 1987).

7 Hill, *Policing the Colonial Frontier*, chapters 4–5; IA and NM (New Munster) series, New Zealand National Archives; *Hawke's Bay Herald*, 11 December 1858.

8 For a brief discussion of one such mode see Richard S. Hill, 'Part-time policing: an historical perspective', *New Zealand Law Journal*, December 1987. For the provincial forces of the 1850s refer to Hill, *Policing the Colonial Frontier*, chapter 6; and for (uneven) archival coverage of 'the Provincial Period' see the archives of each province at the New Zealand National Archives, and the Canterbury Province archives at the Canterbury Museum, Christchurch.

9 Keith Sinclair, *The Origins of the Maori Wars* (Wellington, 1957). For a revisionist version of the various Anglo-Maori wars see James Belich, *The New Zealand Wars and the Victorian Interpretation of Racial Conflict* (Auckland, 1986).

10 Hill, *Policing the Colonial Frontier*, chapter 10.

11 The only comprehensive history of Victoria's police force is Robert Haldane's *The People's Force: a history of the Victorian Police* (Melbourne, 1986). For Otago: Hill, *Policing the Colonial Frontier*, chapter 7.

12 For Branigan see the entry by the author in the *Dictionary of New Zealand Biography* (Wellington, 1990). Archives on Branigan's force may be consulted at the Hocken Library, University of Otago, Dunedin; see also the Otago Province *Police Gazettes*.

13 Hall, *Policing the Colonial Frontier*, chapters 8–9; *Lyttelton Times*, 24 June 1867; *The Press* (Christchurch), 4 July 1867.

14 For the Armed Constabulary and its complementary and successor forces see the second volume of *The History of Policing in New Zealand* by Richard S. Hill (forthcoming). The main archival source is the Police series at the New Zealand National Archives.

15 Richard S. Hill, 'Incorporating Maoris into the New Zealand police', *Journal of the Police History Society*, 4 (1989).

16 Raewyn Dalziel, *Julius Vogel: business politician* (Auckland, 1986).

17 See Richard S. Hill, 'The New Zealand Constabulary Force', *New Zealand Police Association Newsletter*, October 1986, for a brief summary. For the 1870s onwards see tables, reports, etc., in the annual *Appendices to the Journals of the House of Representatives*, especially section H; from 1877 *New Zealand Police Gazettes* hold useful information.

18 Refer to the 1981 edition of Dick Scott, *Ask that Mountain: the story of Parihaka* (Auckland, 1975).

19 For nineteenth-century social bonding processes see Miles Fairburn's 'Local community or atomized society? The social structure of nineteenth-century New Zealand', *New Zealand Journal of History*, October 1982, and his *The Ideal Society and its Enemies: the foundations of modern New Zealand society, 1850–1900* (Auckland, 1989). For the latest research and findings on the Liberals see David Hamer, *The New Zealand Liberals: the years of power, 1891–1912* (Auckland, 1988).

20 For the most accessible of the official inquiries see *Appendices to the Journals of the House of Representatives*, 1898, H-2, and 1909, H-16B; and National Archives, Wellington, file No. P1, 05/547 of 1905. For a brief summary of police training refer to S. I. Young and Richard S. Hill, 'Police training in New Zealand', in L. B. Mason and M. F. Gordon (eds.), *Trentham in Retrospect* (Porirua, 1982). For pensions see Richard S. Hill, 'The rise and fall of the first New Zealand police superannuation scheme', parts I and II, *International Police Association Journal* (New Zealand), September and December 1985.

21 George S. Whitmore, *The Last Maori War in New Zealand under the Self-reliant policy* (Loncon, 1902); A. J. Harrop, *England and the Maori Wars* (London, 1937); for the prophets' deaths, file P1/273, 07/2581 at the New Zealand Archives; for Rua, refer to Judith Binney, Gillan Chaplin and Wallace Craig, *Mihaia: the prophet Rua Kenana and*

his community at Maungapohatu (Wellington, 1979), and to Peter Webster, *Rua and the Maori Millenium* (Wellington, 1979).

22 Some idea of the evolution of New Zealand policing can be gained by a critical reading of regional police histories sponsored by the New Zealand police to commemorate the 1986 centenary of the modern police. Details are available from Chief Inspector Sherwood Young, Police History Liaison Officer, Royal New Zealand Police College. For the period since the first world war refer to Gra'eme Dunstall, 'The New Zealand police: aspects of its constitutional position, organisation and morale since 1920', *International Police Association Journal* (New Zealand), June 1986. For tentative conclusions on the modern situation see Neil Cameron and Warren Young (eds.), *Policing at the Crossroads* (Wellington, 1986).

CHAPTER FIVE

Patterns of policing in the post-emancipation British Caribbean, 1835–95

Howard Johnson

The transition from slavery to freedom in the British Caribbean raised, for the colonial economic and political elite, the question of exercising control over the free labour force. The challenge of emancipation for the former slaveholding class was to retain dominance over the ex-slaves without the extensive coercive powers which slavery had allowed. Policing, as the experience of slavery had established, was central to such control. As Elsa V. Goveia observed in her classic analysis of the West Indian slave laws of the eighteenth century: '... the experience of the British colonies makes it particularly clear that police regulations lay at the very heart of the slave system and that without them the system itself became impossible to maintain'.[1] In the years after slavery, policing activities remained of crucial importance to the attempts by the colonial elite to maintain the existing social and economic order. This chapter examines the principal methods which were employed to police the labouring classes in the British Caribbean in the post-emancipation period. Reference will be made to general trends in the colonies but a more detailed discussion will centre on the sugar colony of Trinidad and the non-plantation colony of the Bahamas.[2]

New policing legislation, 1830s–80s

In the post-emancipation British Caribbean the colonial state, which had a monopoly of law-making and coercive agencies, continued (on most islands) to be dominated by a small white elite with homogeneous interests. In Trinidad, which was a Crown colony, the unofficial membership of the Legislative Council initially reflected the sugar interest. Although representation on that body had been extended by the 1880s to include the mercantile sector and the large cocoa planters, their economic interests rarely conflicted with those of the sugar planters.[3] In the legislative colony of the Bahamas, the House of Assembly was controlled throughout the nineteenth century by an agro-commercial bourgeoisie which was further bound by family ties.[4] Laws and government policies often reflected the interests and concerns of these ruling groups, a fact that was evident to contemporary commentators. In 1888 Dr J. Chittenden, an English doctor resident in Trinidad, observed:

> With the exception of the Religious bodies the European has never regarded either the coolie or African labourer imported by him as destined for anything but a mere serf, the wonderful and rapid progress they had made has been in spite of him and due to their own unaided efforts and merit; after the emancipation which was in reality little more than a name as the relationship between the classes remained as bad or worse than before, the European having the control of the Government and of capital took care to make laws to suit himself and to the detriment of his coloured neighbour, these especially as effecting property exist still and are as one-sided as ever.[5]

In some sugar colonies the planting class attempted, through 'a variety of legal compulsions',[6] to recreate the social relations of production which had previously existed on the slave plantations. In these arrangements the police were undoubtedly envisaged as the instrument for maintaining the existing class structure. In Jamaica an annual police Bill enacted between 1835 and 1838 stipulated that persons who were found carrying agricultural produce without the written permission of the owner of the land where it was cultivated should be arrested. This legislation, ostensibly intended to prevent praedial larceny, could also be used to obstruct the peasant cultivator in marketing his crops.[7] Jamaican planters (or their representatives) clearly anticipated that this legislation would discourage former slaves from engaging in peasant cultivation which would deplete the labour supply available to the sugar estates. In Jamaica and Trinidad vagrancy legislation, with broad definitions of what constituted an offence, was also calculated to coerce the ex-slaves to work as agricultural labourers.[8] These attempts at 'class legislation', with a reliance on the police for enforcement, were eventually disallowed by the Colonial Office, which was, at this stage, alert in preventing the reintroduction of a new system of slavery.

Colonial Office officials had definite ideas about the general principles on which a police law should be framed and drafted, in consultation with a committee of the recently established Metropolitan Police, the legislation for which was to be used as a guideline in the West Indian colonies. In a circular despatch to the governors of the West Indian colonies in January 1839 Lord Glenelg, the Secretary of State for the Colonies, enclosed this model for legislative action and emphasised the need for establishing a professional police force. Glenelg suggested that among the principles shaping the framing of a police law should be

'The confiding the business of Police to Public Officers paid for that purpose, and not to Constables nominated by the owners of different Plantations, or other private persons'. This stipulation was prompted by the earlier attempts of the planters to establish what were essentially private constabularies. Glenelg also specified that the lower ranks of the police force should be placed under the command of officers who should possess 'the means of rendering their control efficient'. The model police legislation was concerned, as Glenelg noted, with the 'constitution and government' of a police force rather than with defining the crimes which such a body would prevent.[9] With the establishment of professional police forces in the early years after emancipation, the policing functions which slave owners had previously exercised, primarily in the rural areas, were thereby vested in the civil authorities. They also assumed the duties of those police forces which had been established in the major towns of colonies like British Guiana, Trinidad and the Bahamas 'for the safety and protection of the lives and property of the inhabitants'.[10] In Nassau, for example, a police force which depended on volunteer patrols and night guards had been introduced in the late eighteenth century by the recently arrived American loyalists.[11]

In slavery and in freedom the primary functions of the police force were to maintain public order and to prevent and detect crime. These tasks involved surveillance of the activities of those persons who formed the base of the colonial social structure. During the slavery era in Nassau both the night guards and the police were expected to deal with the problem of the social control of the urban slaves and the free poor.[12] This function was especially important in a context where many of the slaves worked independently on the self-hire system and thus did not come under the direct supervision of their owners.[13] Members of the night guard were required to patrol the streets and lanes of the town and its suburbs in order 'to prevent all mischiefs arising from fire, and all murders, burglaries, robberies, breaches of the king's peace, riots, and all other outrages and disorders, and all tumultuous assemblies, as well of white persons as of free people of colour or slaves ...'. They were also empowered to arrest and detain slaves who were found on the streets, without a letter or ticket from their employers or owners, after the goal bell had been rung.[14] The preoccupation with the suppression of disorder is also evident from the preamble to the Police Act of 1827, which referred specifically to the need 'to guard against dangers arising from ... disorderly meetings of negroes, and others, and to limit the number of houses for retailing spirituous liquors within the same ...'. The maintenance of public order was closely linked with the vigorous enforcement of the licensing laws. The police were also assigned to enforce municipal regulations relating to the prevention and fighting of

[73]

fires, and public health, such as the arrest of persons who threw dead carcasses into the Nassau harbour, except when the tide was running out, since it posed a health hazard. Policemen were, moreover, responsible for killing all stray dogs, goats and sheep and were expected to ensure that no rotting foodstuffs were offered for sale in the town.[15]

With full emancipation, the functions of the police force in the Bahamas remained essentially the same.[16] Judging from the general police regulations which were in force in March 1842, there was a determined effort to circumscribe the social (and potentially disorderly) activities of the urban labouring classes. The main objective was to remove recreational activities from the streets and public places of Nassau and its suburbs. These activities, it was implied, inevitably resulted in behaviour which was unacceptable to the 'respectable classes'. Legislation which was originally enacted in 1833 (and was still in force in 1842) made it illegal for persons to congregate in or near public places, except on business:

> ... That all assemblages of persons of either or both sexes, and of whatso-ever age, by day or night, on the Public Parade, or in or about the Market House, the Vendue House, or elsewhere, in or near the Streets or High-ways, aforesaid, for any lewd, vicious, idle or disorderly purpose or purposes, whatsoever, or otherwise than in the regular performance or in pursuance of some lawful duty, calling, employment or object; all loitering, carous-ing, or the like, in or about any Shop or Place where Liquors are sold by retail; all loud wrangling, scolding, quarrelling, shouting, singing, or whistling ... all violent, scurrilous, or highly abusive Terms of reproach, tending to a breach of the Peace ... all profane cursing or swearing, obscene or other indecent language ... all playing of Cricket or other like Game or Games, on the said Parades, or in or near the said Parades, or in or near the said Streets and Highways, and all Flying of Kites or other like pastimes in or near the same ... are hereby declared to be unlawful.[17]

As may be imagined, a major aspect of the policeman's duties in the post-emancipation years involved patrolling the streets and public places on the lookout for violations of public order by members of the urban lower classes.

In the Bahamas (as in the plantation colonies of the British Caribbean) the police force was used to enforce legislative restrictions on the economic activities of the labouring classes. In New Providence a law of 1837 made it illegal to hawk or retail certain kinds of goods without a licence. Hawkers who wished to sell dry goods had to obtain a licence, which was granted only after an expensive and complicated process. Those who sold food and small craft items produced by themselves were exempt.[18] This legislation was intended to protect the merchants from the economic competition of former slaves and free non-whites (usually women) who had hawked goods, on behalf of their owners or employers, during slavery.[19]

In the post-emancipation years the police forces in major sugar colonies like British Guiana and Trinidad became involved in the control and management of a labour force for the plantations. The performance of those duties was associated in part with the establishment by 1854 of a system of indentured Indian immigration, with long-term contracts. By that date the Colonial Office had ended its initial opposition to the introduction of a system which, in important aspects, recreated a slave labour force for the sugar estates.[20] The police forces were of central importance to the operation of this system, for the failure of the Indian immigrant to comply with the provisions of his contract was a criminal rather than a civil offence. Infractions of the laws which were enacted for the control of the indentured labour force could also result in criminal convictions for the Indian immigrants. As H. A. Alcazar, an unofficial member of the Trinidad Legislative Council, remarked in 1897 of the system of indentured Indian immigration: '... with regard to its effect on the employer, the system is not very different from slavery, with the gaol substituted for the whip'.[21]

The extension of the routine functions of the police force to include the control of the plantation labour force was formalised in Trinidad by Ordinance No. 7 of 1868. The ordinance created a private constabulary for the sugar estates – a situation which Lord Glenelg, in 1839, had been anxious to avoid. By the provisions of the ordinance, proprietors could apply to the inspector of police for estate personnel, usually a headman or a granger resident on the estate, to be appointed as estate constables with police powers. In effect, these estate constables were selected and paid by the proprietors and were also subject to dismissal by them.[22] This system of estate constables had already been operating for twelve years before the Colonial Office became aware of its existence. In a despatch of 10 December 1880 the Earl of Kimberley, Secretary of State for the Colonies, asked Governor Henry Irving to explain:

> the exact position of 'estate constables', as it appears somewhat anomalous to give the powers of public police constables to persons who are appointed to keep order on particular estates and are paid by owners of estates and may apparently be dismissed by them at their pleasure.[23]

In his reply the governor, Sir Sanford Freeling, pointed out that a system of estate constables had long existed in Trinidad and elsewhere in the West Indies. He also noted the opposition of the unofficial members of the Legislative Council to the discontinuation of the system and warned that such an action would result in sharply increased expenditure on the police force.[24] Colonial Office officials regarded these arguments as adequate grounds for approving the continued operation of the system.[25]

Ordinance No. 7 of 1868 also provided for the appointment of assistant constables whose duties can be interpreted as the control of a primarily Creole labour force. Under section 27 of the ordinance, wardens of rural districts were authorised to appoint, and dismiss, assistant constables who performed ordinary police duties or assisted the wardens in collecting taxes, serving notices and detecting squatters. It can be argued that the planting class anticipated that, by collecting taxes and detecting squatters, the assistant constables would force Creoles, who had withdrawn their labour from the estates, back to estate employment. These Creole rural and estate constables, 'with their local knowledge and acquaintance with the inhabitants of every out of the way Estate and Village', also provided the regular police with information they could not otherwise obtain.[26] The lower ranks of the police force were filled with Barbadians who did not speak nor understand the French-based creole which was spoken in the rural districts of the colony.[27]

In the Bahamas, by contrast, police intervention did not immediately become necessary for the control of a labour force. In the post-emancipation years there were few opportunities for regular wage employment outside New Providence, except in the salt and pineapple industries which were carried on in a few islands of the archipelago. In both those enterprises the proprietors developed credit and truck systems which were effective in mobilising and retaining a labour force.[28]

Police activities in both Trinidad and the Bahamas were concentrated in the major towns. In Trinidad, the population of Port of Spain increased by 47 per cent between 1839 and 1851, partly as a result of rural–urban migration and in-migration from other eastern Caribbean colonies.[29] The colonial government attempted to deal with the social problems connected with urbanisation by a stricter policing of the suburbs of Port of Spain. The reorganisation of the police force in 1868 involved both an increase in numbers and a greater surveillance of the urban population which, as a press comment in 1869 indicated, extended even to harmless social activities:

> Police: who has now the temerity to ask and who dare ask where are the Police? The question is as unnecessary now as before it was impertinent. The Guardians of day and night, and of times neither day nor night, have suddenly become ubiquitous. Let there be a burglary – the swift and ready arm of the Police is at once laid on the burglars. A robbery! and in a twinkling the culprits are in 'durance vile'. A cart unattended, and the pound receives a new burthen. Two gentlemen or ladies speaking for a moment on the side-walk, and the *gloved* hands of the Police are gently (!) laid on their shoulders. Men taking a glass of rum in a back store, the police are anxious to know the quantity and strength of their potations.[30]

Police numbers in the Bahamas were also increased in 1864 following the rapid growth in Nassau's population associated with blockade running during the American Civil War. Up to that point the colony had relied on a police force which was relatively small and was, moreover, a combination of paid and unpaid constables.[31] In his response to Lord Glenelg's recommendations of 1839, Governor Francis Cockburn had remarked:

> ... however essential & important an extensive & well defined system of Police may be in the more compact & populous of the West India Colonies, it does not appear to me to be of such Paramount necessity in the scattered & thinly settled islands of the Bahamas.[32]

In 1864 Governor Charles Bayley, with greater revenue available from blockade running, decided that a reorganised police force was essential for dealing with petty crime, which had increased with the influx of approximately 2,000 'strangers' into Nassau.[33] Acknowledging the seriousness of the situation, members of the House of Assembly requested Bayley to secure the appointment:

> of some properly-qualified officer or non-commissioned officer of the London Metropolitan, or other Police Force of the United Kingdom, conversant with the duties he would have to perform, so as to organize an active and vigilant Police in the Colony ...

This was a proposal which Bayley endorsed.[34] In the late nineteenth century proposals for the reorganisation of West Indian police forces would be increasingly accompanied by requests for British officers to fill the senior ranks.

Race, class and social disorder: the maintenance of paramilitary policing

Routine policing of both urban and rural areas was the main responsibility of the police forces throughout the British Caribbean, but the security of lives and private property and the stability of the economic environment depended ultimately on imperial troops which were locally based. As in the slavery era, a fear of the black majority persisted, and imperial garrisons continued to be seen as an important method of safeguarding the social and economic order. Roger Norman Buckley has demonstrated that the West India Regiment (composed of diverse ethnic, language and national groups) was successfully employed, from its inception in the late eighteenth century, to buttress the slave systems in the British Caribbean.[35] Divisive techniques were used in recruiting soldiers for the West Indian regiments to forestall the possibility of any collective action on their part or the development of sympathies with the black population in the colonies where they were based. Writing in 1861 of the Bahamas, Governor Charles Bayley explained how the West India Regiment, composed primarily of black soldiers, could be successfully deployed against people of their own race:

> The negro creoles, so far as I have observed, have strong local attachments. They each profess (& I believe feel) an ardent affection for the island which gave them birth; & invariably consider its attractions superior to those of the others. The Jamaica Creole despises Bahamas, the Antigua Creole Barbadoes [sic] & the Barbadian despises all other islands but his own. With prejudices or affections so vehement, it is evident that no Creole soldiers could safely be trusted to act by themselves against a tumultous or seditious movement of their own countrymen in their own island. But in any regiment moderately well disciplined and containing natives of all the islands & of Africa, the local sentiment of a past would be lost & swamped in the military subordination of the whole body.[36]

Governors in the more racially heterogeneous society of Trinidad were of the opinion that the presence of white troops was even more important for the maintenance of public order and economic stability than black troops. This view was expressed by Governor Robert Keate in 1859 when, because of the high mortality rate of white troops stationed in the colony, it was proposed that black troops should replace them entirely. In fact Keate linked the continued economic development of the colony by white capital directly with the presence of white troops, especially in a society which was composed of 'uncongenial and in-flammable materials':

> I should be very unwilling to assert that when called upon these [black] Troops would be found wanting in the discharge of their duty, nor do I for a moment suppose that such an impression prevails any-where, but to such an extent does the confidence reposed in them depend upon the fact of their being quartered side by side with, and enjoying the support and example of the white Troops, that I feel sure the withdrawal of the latter would destroy all feeling of safety among those who are devoting their energy and intelligence to the development of the prosperity of the island, and that a very serious check would thereby be given to its advancement. One has only to observe the uneasiness and anxiety which prevails, when the slightest rumour arises of disturbances in the country Districts to feel assured of the reality of the conviction entertained that in the present stage of the social progress of the Colony we are, as I have heard it, with some-what of an exaggeration expressed, 'living on the crust of a volcano'.[37]

Keate was aware of the necessary division of 'control work' between the police and the troops. He was, however, convinced that the police force effectively quelled local disturbances because of the presence of the troops:

This duty [suppressing disturbances] of course falls to the local Police to perform, but if the Police, such as it is, is in any degree adequate to perform it, and if there is any confidence in its power to do so among the quiet and industrious portions of society, and any wholesome apprehension of it among the disorderly, it is entirely because it is known and felt that in an emergency there are troops at hand to fall back on.[38]

Keate's opinions on the role of the imperial troops in internal policing were reiterated by subsequent governors of the colony. In 1866, after the Morant Bay 'rebellion' in Jamaica, Governor Manners-Sutton assured Edward Cardwell, the Secretary of State for the Colonies, that the presence of imperial troops effectively protected both the lives and the property of the white minority and acted as a deterrent to popular insurrection.[39] Keate's view was also repeated by Sir Sanford Freeling after the Carnival disturbances in 1881:

... I do not think it prudent, that under any circumstances, so long as European troops are stationed in the West Indies, this important Colony should be left without a detachment, the moral effect of those Troops being always much greater than that of Black soldiers, however useful and well disciplined the West India Regiments.[40]

By the last decade of the nineteenth century, policing functions which had earlier been divided between a civil police force and the imperial troops were exercised by a militarised police force in many of the Caribbean colonies. This development was primarily the result of the British government's decision to withdraw the scattered detachments of imperial troops from the Bahamas, British Honduras, Barbados, Trinidad and British Guiana, had concentrated them at two points, Port Royal in Jamaica and Port Castries in St Lucia, which were regarded as strategically important. In a circular despatch of 19 June 1885 the Earl of Derby informed governors of the colonies concerned about the imminence of the withdrawal of the troops and urged them to consider what strengthening of the police forces would be required as a result of the decision.[41]

After 1885 the major external impulse for the reorganisation (and militarisation) of the police forces in the British Caribbean came from the Colonial Office.[42] But there were internal developments which also prompted local governments to improve and strengthen the police. In Trinidad the police were strengthened in the 1880s in order to cope with what was perceived as the endemic lawlessness of Port of Spain and San Fernando.[43] In 1882 Captain A. W. Baker, the inspector-commandant of police, argued an increase to the police force of 100 men:

With the present strength in case of disturbances in the distant parts of the Colony, the towns of Port of Spain and San Fernando would be left unguarded and the inhabitants and their property left at the mercy of a number of Roughs who may at any moment take it into their heads to rise.[44]

Sir Sanford Freeling authorised the addition of only fifty men to the police force, but endorsed Baker's arguments about the need to strengthen the police:

> The suburbs of Port-of-Spain are insufficiently patrolled, and the necessity for reinforcing the existing Police Stations in the large Towns and villages which are springing up, as well as for creating new Stations becomes every day greater. A series of burglaries have but recently been reported so close to Head Quarters as the Savannah and the new houses on the Tranquillité Estate building lots for which the available patrols are entirely insufficient.[45]

At the beginning of the 1880s one of the main targets of the colonial authorities' efforts to suppress disorder was the annual Carnival. Carnival, which had been dominated by the white upper-class Creoles before emancipation, was gradually taken over in the years after slavery by the urban proletariat of Port of Spain.[46] Members of the 'respectable classes' were disgusted by the drunken disorder and the obscene singing, dancing and masquerading of the lower classes, which were features of the Carnival celebrations, but they were also alarmed by the possibility of revolt. This class and racial fear of the white elite is obvious from the comments of Governor Keate in May 1859:

> ... on the two days preceding Ash Wednesday, but for the presence of the troops, the Town of Port of Spain would be annually at the mercy of the lowest scum of its very mixed population who seem to think they have a vested right in a kind of Saturnalia of eight and forty hours duration which they call by the name of Carnival.[47]

In the 1880s Captain Baker attempted to suppress certain features of Carnival − an aspect of what David Vincent Trotman has described as 'the struggle for cultural hegemony' in nineteenth-century Trinidad.[48] When in 1881 policemen on Baker's orders attempted to extinguish the torches held by the Canboulay bands, thirty-eight policemen were wounded and twenty persons arrested and charged with affray in the fracas which ensued. Official fears about the direction in which the Carnival celebrations could develop were reflected in R. G. C. Hamilton's recommendation, in his report on the disturbances, that a man-of-war should be sent to Trinidad during the following Carnival.[49] Sir Sanford Freeling also appealed to the Colonial Office, without success, for the arrival of the squadron of the North American and West Indian station in the colony on its annual cruise to be timed to coincide with the Carnival festivities.[50]

The lingering fear of colonial administrators that disturbances might develop from the Carnival celebrations resulted in the Trinidad police force assuming a paramilitary character prior to the Colonial Office's announcement of the withdrawal of the imperial troops. In 1884 Sir Sanford Freeling increased the police force by fifty constables and four noncommissioned officers recruited from the Royal Irish Constabulary. He anticipated that the appointment of the officers would result in greater efficiency of the police force in drill and the knowledge of the use of firearms. Freeling's decision was prompted by the inefficiency of the police in those areas, as their performance in controlling the crowds at the Carnival celebrations in the towns of San Fernando and Princes Town had demonstrated. According to Freeling, 'At Princestown some of the Police dropped their Cartridges when endeavouring to load, while the rifles of others went off in the air before they could take proper aim.'[51] In a minute to the Inspector Commandant of Police in March that year, Freeling called his attention to:

> the extreme importance of all the men in the Force being instructed sufficiently in drill to enable them to act together in whatever numbers they may be, also in the use of the rifle sufficiently to be able to know how to load and use them without flurry up to 200 yards. Also to be able to use the bayonet without danger to themselves and with effect against others.[52]

Fear of the indentured Indian immigrants' potential for violent protest became another reason for strengthening the Trinidad police force in the 1880s. This violent protest was primarily a response to the efforts by estate managements, during the economic depression in the sugar industry in the 1880s and 1890s, to reduce production costs by increasing the amount of work allocated for each task.[53] Indentured immigrants frequently went on strike and sometimes physically assaulted estate personnel. In October 1882, for example, there were riots at Cedar Hill and Fairfield estates.[54] These disturbances on the sugar estates constituted 'collective bargaining by riot' on the part of the indentured immigrants.[55]

The 'disturbed state of the Coolies' was one factor which influenced the colonial authorities' decision to increase the police force by fifty constables in 1882. Captain Baker, like Hamilton before him, felt that a British naval presence would have a great 'moral effect'. Baker's proposal was undoubtedly inspired by a report from one of his detectives 'that the Coolies at their gatherings and meetings are discussing the strength of the Force at the disposal of the Government, also the feasibility of cutting off communication with Port of Spain'.[56] The continued labour militancy of the indentured immigrants on the sugar estate was met with force. In October 1884 a riot on El Socorro estate by indentured

[81]

immigrants over increased tasks ended with the arrest of immigrants, who had assaulted the overseer, by policemen bearing guns and fixed bayonets.[57] This use of armed police against the Indian immigrants was similar to the existing practice in British Guiana, where, after riots in 1869 by indentured Indian immigrants, the police force was armed and increased by 150 men.[58]

The series of strikes by the indentured immigrants created widespread fear of the alien Indian presence. Behind the self-assertiveness of the Indian immigrants the white elite saw the most sinister implications. This fear increased with an awareness of the growing number of Indian immigrants resident in the colony, as is evident from an editorial in the *Port of Spain Gazette* in October 1884, on the eve of the Hosein celebrations:

> Admitting that there are 30,000 adult males and 10,000 adult females East Indians among us, those 40,000 human beings have scarcely one feeling in common with the rest of the people among whom they live. They are among us but are not of us. They are united whilst we are divided.[59]

The leader writer (like other members of the colony's middle and upper classes) was convinced that the Indians' 'insubordination', as demonstrated by their labour militancy, should be met with force rather than with concessions.[60] The expected confrontation between the indentured immigrants and the forces of 'law and order' came the same month, during the Hosein celebrations, when armed police, supported by a group of soldiers, fired on a procession of Indians outside San Fernando, killing twelve of them and injuring 104.[61] The colonial authorities had attempted to regulate this Indian festival, like the Creole Carnival, because they feared it might provide the Indians (and the Creoles who increasingly participated in the festivities) with the opportunity for collective action. As an editorial in the *San Fernando Gazette* in December 1884 suggested, the colonial government 'feared that under the cover of the license on this occasion opportunity would be taken for a more generous and serious onslaught on their employers by the Coolies'.[62]

Members of the colony's middle and upper classes regarded this show of force by the colonial government as having a 'salutary effect' on the Indian immigrant community.[63] They also hoped that this demonstration of the willingness to use force would intimidate other sections of the 'lower orders', especially the urban 'dangerous classes'. After the Hosein riots the *Port of Spain Gazette* was moved to comment, 'Let us hope this terrible lesson may have a salutary effect not only on the Coolies, but on the heterogeneous collection of loafers, prostitutes, roughs, rogues and vagabonds which infest our two towns'.[64]

As our discussion has suggested, the Trinidad police force in their task of 'urban pacification'[65] as containment of rural class conflict functioned to maintain class inequalities. This was a role which the police force was especially equipped to perform. The positions of officers and noncommissioned officers were mainly held by Englishmen and Irishmen with military experience or previous service in the paramilitary Royal Irish Constabulary,[66] and the lower ranks were overwhelmingly dominated by black Barbadians, who were widely disliked by the Creole population, including members of the middle class. Few Trinidadians ever joined the police force.[67] The police hierarchy, as Captain Baker commented in 1885, also reflected the colony's class and racial structure, which they were expected to maintain:

> There are 435 men of all ranks in the police at Trinidad, including 30 additional this year. The staff consists of 2 inspectors, Englishmen, each having charge of one of the two divisions, northern and southern ... 1 sergeant major, from the Irish constabulary for each division; 5 sergeant superintendents, one a black man, the others old soldiers and Irish constabulary men; 21 sergeants, partly white and partly coloured; 26 corporals, of mixed races; 3 grades of constables, full strength 350, some of whom are also white, the others chiefly Barbadians, and only two or three natives of Trinidad in the whole force, who are usually worthless from stupidity.[68]

In the Bahamas the prospect of the withdrawal of the imperial troops aroused racial fears among the members of the white elite. In 1882, when the question was raised by the Earl of Kimberley, Governor Sir Charles Lees pointed out the importance of maintaining a garrison in the colony for, *inter alia*, ensuring the security of the white minority. He admitted that the colony's population was 'docile and law-abiding' but warned that it was 'almost entirely composed of a race easily excited, and when under the influence of passion, capable of but little self control'.[69] In 1885 Governor Henry Blake was more explicit about racial antagonisms:

> While I cannot speak too highly of the general conduct of the population, the fact remains that there is a strong feeling on the part of black & coloured peoples against the white population of Nassau. I have heard this from too many sources to leave any doubt on the subject.[70]

White perceptions of the dangers of withdrawing the troops were articulated in a memorial to Blake, in 1885, signed by all the members of the House of Assembly, asking for a reconsideration of the decision:

> Such a step as this we cannot but regard as one that will be absolutely fatal to the future progress of the Colony, its good government will be placed in jeopardy, and insecurity to life and property will under these circumstances universally prevail.[71]

An incident in 1886 further convinced the white minority of the likelihood of social disorder from a hostile black population, when a 'serious disturbance' broke out in Nassau after a white man, with powerful political connections, shot dead a black policeman.[72] The racial dimension was inevitably of profound importance to the white community. Lord Knutsford's proposal, in 1888, for replacing the troops by a strengthened police force did little to allay white fears. Both white Bahamians and the Governor, Sir Ambrose Shea, believed that locally recruited policemen, with ties to the community, would take sides with the black population in the event of disturbances in which race was a factor. It was Knutsford who suggested (on the recommendation of Major George S. Clarke, secretary of the Colonial Defence Committee) that the members of the police force, like the West India Regiment, might be recruited from other West Indian colonies 'to prevent any feeling of local sympathy between [the] Police and the inhabitants of the Bahamas'.[73]

'Strangers' and 'other-islanders'

By 1888 the colonial government in both Trinidad and the Bahamas identified the 'lower orders' as constituting the main threat to social and economic stability. This perception was reflected in the plans for reorganising the police force and for strengthening local defence. In Trinidad this point was emphasised when in 1889 the West India Committee, alarmed by 'an insubordinate feeling among the lower classes', requested that the police force should be strengthened by the addition of fifty white men 'to be specially selected and of exceptional physique'. The West India Committee believed that such an addition would have 'considerable moral effect'.[74] Governor Sir William Robinson refuted the request on the grounds that such a force 'would be regarded as a standing menace not only to the negro population, but to the different nationalities and races from which the labourers are recruited'. The police force was, however, augmented by twelve sergeants recruited from the Royal Irish Constabulary and fifty constables.[75] With an eye on the Indian immigrant community, Robinson also proposed that men be recruited from the Indian constabulary, with experience 'in the criminal habits of Coolies'. He claimed that:

> ... crimes are not infrequently committed which are to be traced to the machinations of Coolies and the detection of which baffles the acumen of the ordinary native policeman. Coolies plot and commit crimes according to methods peculiar to themselves.[76]

This scheme was eventually abandoned after it was discovered that the colony would be unable to recruit Sikhs, as in the case of Hong Kong and the Straits Settlements.[77]

By 1890 the Trinidad police force resembled the Royal Irish Constabulary, with 'its armament and residence in barracks'.[78] This resemblance was further reinforced by the fact that men recruited from that organisation dominated the ranks of the noncommissioned officers. In a news item on 'The Armed Constabulary' in June 1890, the *Port of Spain Gazette* commented on the way in which the reorganised police force was expected to operate:

> The new military programme is beginning to take shape. A new body of 50 armed Police or Constabulary is to be added to the Police Force, and to be permanently stationed at the St. James Barracks ... It appears that there is to be in future a regular exchange of men between the Barracks and the Police Station, which will ensure the efficient training of the whole force as an armed body, whilst providing an ever ready body for any military emergency.[79]

The withdrawal of the imperial troops also encouraged the further development of the volunteer forces and led to their reorganisation along military lines. By 1890 two corps of Mounted Rifles and an artillery corps had been added to the original Rifle Volunteers. These volunteers were partly equipped with a grant of four sixty-four-pounder guns, 500 Martini-Henry rifles and 200 carbines from the British government and were officered and instructed by a permanent professional staff of seven with extensive military experience. European employees of British sugar colonies formed a large proportion of the volunteer force, especially in the country districts, but colonial administrators showed an early willingness to extend membership of the corps to other racial groups.[80] In 1888 Henry Fowler, the officer administering the government, had argued that it was safe to entrust all classes of the colonial population with arms, for there were 'sufficient race jealousies to prevent any common combination against the governing authority'.[81] Although the police and volunteer forces were responsible for different aspects of local defence, it is clear that the colonial administration contemplated the use of the volunteers (and their 'coercive technology') in the event of local disturbances.[82] In 1888, for example, Fowler observed that machine guns would be effective in preventing 'hostile boats' from landing in the colony and would also be 'very useful to the Police in case of any internal disorder for protecting the Police Barracks in the Town of Port of Spain'.[83]

In the Bahamas the police force was reorganised along more military lines in 1891. Legislation that year created a constabulary force which

[85]

D

was distinct from the existing police force. The colonial administration intended that the constabulary, recruited entirely from abroad, would eventually replace the locally recruited police force. The conditions of service were made deliberately unattractive to Bahamians. The Constabulary Act stipulated that the members of the constabulary should reside in barracks – a rule which extended even to constables and sub-officers who were married with permission – and specified that no more than 10 per cent of its members should be permitted to marry. Both regulations were calculated to prevent constables from forming local attachments.

The constabulary (specially trained and disciplined) were expected to replace the imperial garrison as an organisation of last resort for the suppression of internal disturbances, and the main duty of the police force would be to police the local population. This division of duties was made clear in a comment by the colony's attorney-general in a report on the Constabulary Act in July 1891:

> For some time at least there must be the two forces, one doing civil duty entirely, the other isolated and kept in Barracks, performing when necessary and advisable civil duty as a Police, but especially trained and disciplined, and kept in hand for any emergency.[84]

The men eventually recruited for the constabulary were Barbadians – the West Indian counterparts of the 'martial races' of India – who similarly served in the police forces of the colonies in the eastern Caribbean and in mainland British Honduras.[85] The Barbadian constables proved unpopular with the black Bahamian population, who were hostile to the strangers and complained about their aggressive and 'unnecessarily rough' treatment of prisoners. Members of the existing police force also resented the fact that they would eventually be replaced by the foreign 'interlopers'. In 1893 disturbances in the black suburb of Grant's Town (involving Barbadian constables and members of the local population) resulted in some changes in the organisation of the police force. The local police force was allowed to survive and was assigned primarily to police the suburbs where black Bahamians resided. The main duty of the Barbadians of the renamed Bahamas Police Force was to protect the property of the white minority in the city of Nassau and suppress any 'organized disturbance' in the suburbs.[86]

The practice of recruiting policemen from one area to keep colonists of another in check was used elsewhere in the Caribbean. By 1889, for example, a law was already in force in the Windward islands which allowed the police to be interchangeable throughout the islands of that group.[87] The idea of an interchangeable police force was also, reportedly, behind a scheme to consolidate the constabulary forces of the West

Indian colonies which was discussed by the governors of Jamaica, Barbados and British Guiana in November 1896. According to a report in the Jamaica *Gleaner*:

> The main argument advanced in favour of such a proposition is that as the Constabulary Force is at present constituted no interchange is possible; in the event of a riot in Barbados, say, or in the other islands it is hopeless to believe that the constable born in the country, knowing the people, having his brothers, sisters, wife, children and other relations in the place, would be likely to fire with any assurance at any rate into a crowd of rioters if called upon to do so. A constable born in Demerara would not have these qualms of conscience in St. Lucia, for instance.[88]

Nothing seems to have resulted from the proposal; but the notion that efficient policing was best carried out by a force of 'strangers' and 'other islanders' had become thoroughly ingrained.

Conclusions

In the immediate post-emancipation years the Colonial Office attempted to establish a civil police force (modelled on the Metropolitan Police) in the Caribbean which would be 'wholly free from local influence of any class of person'.[89] After 1838, however, the character of the police force was determined not by the model on which it was originally based but by the local context; the maintenance of the existing social and economic order remained a major concern of the colonial elite whose predominant position emancipation had left intact. In the Caribbean, policing was not, however, the responsibility of a civil police force only but also of the imperial troops stationed in the colonies. The troops were not involved in routine policing but were regarded as indispensable guarantors of the economic and social order, in a context where the middle and upper classes lived in constant fear of open class warfare and racial violence. The announcement of the withdrawal of the troops by the British government resulted in the militarisation of the police force in both Trinidad and the Bahamas. In those colonies, however, the impulse towards the arming and strengthening of the police also came from the identification of the 'lower orders' as the main threat to internal stability. Questions of class and of race had a powerful influence over the exclution of nineteenth-century policing in the British Caribbean.

Notes

1 Elsa V. Goveia, *The West Indian Slave Laws of the 18th Century* (St Lawrence, Barbados, 1970), p. 20.

2 The only historical studies of policing in the British Caribbean relate to Trinidad and the Bahamas. See David Vincent Trotman, *Crime in Trinidad: conflict and control in a plantation society, 1838–1900* (Knoxville, 1986), and Howard Johnson, 'Social control and the colonial state: the reorganisation of the police force in the Bahamas, 1888–1893', *Slavery and Abolition*, 7 (1986), pp. 46–58.

3 H. B. D. Johnson, 'Crown Colony Government in Trinidad, 1870–1897' D. Phil. thesis, University of Oxford (1970), pp. 150–62.

4 Howard Johnson, ' "A modified form of slavery": the credit and truck system in the Bahamas in the nineteenth and early twentieth centuries', *Comparative Studies in Society and History*, 28 (1986), p. 730.

5 Letter by Dr J. Chittenden, 25 June 1886 enclosed with evidence before the Trade and Taxes Commission, 11 July 1888, p. 7; *Trade and Taxes Commission Report, Evidence and Appendices* (Port of Spain, 1889).

6 The phrase is from Robert B. Seidman, *The State, Law and Development* (London, 1978), p. 30.

7 Philip D. Curtin, *Two Jamaicas: the role of ideas in a tropical colony, 1830–1865* (paperback edition, New York, 1970), p. 130.

8 *Ibid.*; Trotman, *Crime in Trinidad*, pp. 54–55. Cf. Martha Knisely Huggins, *From Slavery to Vagrancy in Brazil: crime and social control in the Third World* (New Brunswick, 1985).

9 Reprinted in *Votes of Bahama Assembly, 1839 to 1840*, pp. 118–21. See also William A. Green, *British Slave Emancipation: the sugar colonies and the Great Experiment* (Oxford, 1976), p. 164.

10 B. W. Higman, *Slave Populations of the British Caribbean, 1807–1834* (Baltimore, 1984), p. 229. The phrase is from 'An Act for establishing a Nightly Guard or Watch in the Town of Nassau, for the safety and protection of the Town and suburbs thereof', 3 Geo. IV c. 1 (1823).

11 D. Gail Saunders, *Slavery in the Bahamas, 1648–1838* (Nassau, 1985), p. 41.

12 For an excellent discussion of the role of the police force in a slave society see Thomas H. Holloway, 'The Brazilian "judicial police" in Florianopolis, Santa Catarina, 1841–1871', *Journal of Social History*, 20 (1987), pp. 733–56.

13 Howard Johnson, 'The liberated Africans in the Bahamas, 1811–1860', in Howard Johnson (ed.), *After the Crossing: immigrants and minorities in Caribbean Creole society* (London, 1988), p. 20.

14 An Act for establishing a Nightly Guard', 3 Geo. IV, c. 1 (1823).

15 'An Act for regulating the Police of the Town of Nassau, and the Suburbs thereof, and for other purposes therein mentioned', 8 Geo. IV, c. 2 (1827).

16 In the Bahamas the Act of 1840 for 'regulating the Police' specified the duties of constables as 'preserving the Peace, and preventing Robberies and other felonies, and apprehending Offenders against the Peace'; 'An Act entitled An Act for regulating the Police of the Bahama Islands', 3 Vic., c. 38 (1840).

17 *Laws of the Bahamas, in Force on the 14th March, 1842* (Nassau, 1843), p. 178.

18 *Ibid.*, pp. 183–4.

19 Johnson, 'The liberated Africans in the Bahamas', p. 29.

20 See Hugh Tinker, *A New System of Slavery: the export of Indian labour overseas, 1830–1920* (London, 1974). See also Alan H. Adamson, *Sugar without Slaves: the political economy of British Guiana, 1838–1904* (New Haven, 1972).

21 Memorandum by H. A. Alcazar on Indian immigration, 28 February 1897. *Parl. Papers*, 1898, HL (C. 8657), q. 716.

22 Sir Sanford Freeling to the Earl of Kimberley, 8 November 1881, No. 308, PRO, CO 295/291.

23 Kimberley to Irving, 10 December 1880 (draft), CO 295/288.

24 Freeling to Kimberley, 8 November 1881, No. 308, CO 295/291.
25 See minutes on Freeling to Kimberley, 8 November 1881, No. 308, CÓ 295/291.
26 Report of the Attorney General, 1 November 1880, enclosed in W. A. G. Young to Kimberley, 30 October 1880, No. 277, CO 295/288.
27 Freeling to Kimberley, 8 November 1881, No. 308, CO 295/291. For a discussion of this point see Howard Johnson, 'Barbadian immigrants in Trinidad, 1870–1897', *Caribbean Studies*, 13 (1973), pp. 16–18.
28 See Howard Johnson, ' "A modified form of slavery" ', p. 734; 'The share system in the Bahamas in the nineteenth and early twentieth centuries', *Slavery and Abolition*, 5 (1984), pp. 141–53.
29 Trotman, *Crime in Trinidad*, p. 43; Johnson, 'Barbadian immigrants in Trinidad', pp. 5–9.
30 *Port of Spain Gazette*, 17 February 1869. In 1848 the police force of Trinidad, which had a population of 65,411, numbered ninety-one. By 1871 there were 130 policemen stationed in Port of Spain, which had a population of 23,561. Trotman, *Crime in Trinidad*, p. 282.
31 Bee, for example, 'An Act to consolidate and amend the Laws relating to the stipendiary Police Force of the Colony', 23 Vic., c. 4 (1860), and 'An Act to consolidate and amend the Laws relating to the unpaid Constabulary Force of the Colony', 23 Vic., c. 5 (1860). In 1838, after full emancipation, six constables and twenty nightwatchmen were based in Nassau. By 1864 the strength of the police force stationed in Nassau and its suburbs was forty-eight. Between those dates the population of the island of New Providence had increased from 9,505 to approximately 13,320 – a figure which includes the transient 'strangers' who came to Nassau during the American Civil War. Blue Books for the Bahamas, 1838, 1861–64.
32 Francis Cockburn to Lord Glenelg, 30 March 1839, No. 18, CO 23/105.
33 Bayley to the Duke of Newcastle, 7 March 1864, No. 26, CO 23/174.
34 Speech opening the Bahama Legislature, 24 February 1864; 'Humble Address of the House of Assembly', 29 February 1864 and Bayley's reply to the House of Assembly's address, 29 February 1864, all enclosed in Bayley to Newcastle, 7 March 1864, No. 26, CO 23/174.
35 Roger Norman Buckley, *Slaves in Red Coats: the British West India regiments, 1795–1815* (New Haven, 1879), p. 117.
36 Bayley to Newcastle, 11 February 1861, No. 19, CO 23/165.
37 Keate to E. Bulwer Lytton, 10 May 1859, No. 85, CO 295/204.
38 *Ibid.*
39 Quoted in Trotman, *Crime in Trinidad*, p. 234.
40 Freeling to Major General Gamble, 24 October 1881, enclosure No. 2 in Freeling in Kimberley, 25 October 1881, Conf., CO 295/291.
41 Earl of Derby to West Indian governors, 19 June 1885, Conf., reprinted in Cab. 11/2. See also Cedric L. Joseph, 'The strategic importance of the British West Indies, 1882–1932', *Journal of Caribbean History*, 7 (1973), pp. 25–6.
42 See 'Report of Inspection in the West Indies by the Inspector-General of Artillery', 11 May 1889, pp. 2–3, Cab. 11/2. In Tobago the police force had been organised as a semi-military body as early as 1876; see Bridget Brereton, 'Post-emancipation protest in the Caribbean: the "Belmanna riots" in Tobago, 1876', *Caribbean Quarterly*, 30 (1984), pp. 121–2.
43 See Trotman, *Crime in Trinidad*.
44 Baker to the Colonial Secretary, 25 October 1882, enclosure No. 1 in Freeling to Kimberley, 7 November 1882, No. 260, CO 295/295.
45 Freeling to Kimberley, 7 November 1882, No. 260, CO 295/295.
46 See Andrew Pearse, 'Carnival in nineteenth century Trinidad', *Caribbean Quarterly*, 4 (1956), p. 184; Errol Hill, *The Trinidad Carnival: mandate for a national theatre* (Austin, 1972), pp. 16–21; Bridget Brereton, 'The Trinidad carnival, 1870–1900', *Savacou*, Nos. 11 and 12 (1975), p. 46.
47 Keate to E. Bulwer Lytton, 10 May 1859, No. 85, CO 295/204.
48 Trotman, *Crime in Trinidad*, chapter 8.

49 'Mr. Hamilton's report on the causes and circumstances of the disturbances in connexion with the carnival in Trinidad', 13 June 1881, West Indian No. 40, CO 884/4.
50 Freeling to Kimberley, 7 November 1881, Conf., CO 295/291.
51 Freeling to the Earl of Derby, 25 March 1884, No. 65, CO 295/301.
52 Minute by Freeling to the Inspector Commandant, 6 March 1884, Conf., enclosure No. 1 in Freeling to Derby, 25 March 1884, No. 65, CO 295/301.
53 Howard Johnson, 'Immigration and the sugar industry in Trinidad during the last quarter of the nineteenth century', *Journal of Caribbean History*, 3 (1971), p. 64. Cf. Walter Rodney, *A History of the Guyanese Working People, 1881–1905* (Baltimore, 1981), p. 153.
54 *San Fernando Gazette*, 7 and 14 October 1882.
55 The phrase is Eric Hobsbawm's, quoted by Brian R. Brown, 'Industrial capitalism, conflict and working-class contention in Lancashire, 1842', in Louise A. and Charles Tilly (eds.), *Class Conflict and Collective Action* (London, 1981), p. 132.
56 Baker to the Colonial Secretary, 25 October 1882; and minute by Baker to the Colonial Secretary, 27 October 1822, enclosures No. 1 and 2 in Freeling to Kimberley, 7 November 1882, No. 260, CO 295/295.
57 *Port of Spain Gazette*, 11 October 1884.
58 Adamson, *Sugar without Slaves*, pp. 154–5, 263.
59 Editorial, 'The coolie immigrants', *Port of Spain Gazette*, 18 October 1884. The comments in the editorial suggest that memories of the Indian Mutiny still influenced Creole perceptions of the Indian immigrants. See Donald Wood, *Trinidad in Transition: the years after slavery* (London, 1968), pp. 154–5.
60 *Port of Spain Gazette*, 18 October 1884.
61 See Wood, *Trinidad in Transition*, pp. 151–3, and Kusha Haraksingh, 'Indian leadership in the indenture period', *Caribbean Issues*, 2 (1976), pp. 33–6.
62 Editorial, 'Retrospect – 1884', *San Fernando Gazette*, 24 December 1884.
63 See, for example, the evidence given by the colonial civil servants to Sir H. W. Norman in his investigation of the Hosein riots in 1885; *Report on the Coolie Disturbances in Trinidad at the Mohurrum Festival* (C. 4366).
64 *Port of Spain Gazette*, 8 November 1884.
65 The phrase is from Phil Cohen, 'Policing the working-class city', in Mike Fitzgerald, Gregor McLennan and Jennie Pawson (compilers), *Crime and Society: Readings in History and Theory* (London, 1981), p. 116.
66 For a discussion of this point see Trotman, *Crime in Trinidad*, pp. 92–4.
67 Johnson, 'Barbadian immigrants in Trinidad', pp. 19–21.
68 Statement by Captain A. W. Baker, Inspector Commandant of Police, 5 January 1885, in Report on the coolie disturbances. Cf. Carolyn Steadman, *Policing the Victorian Community: the formation of English provincial police forces, 1856–80* (London, 1984), p. 2.
69 Lees to Kimberley, 29 December 1882, No. 155, CO 23/222.
70 Blake to Stanley, 8 August 1885, Conf., CO 23/226.
71 Enclosure (undated) in Blake to Stanley, 19 September 1885, Conf., CO 23/226.
72 Blake to Stanhope, 11 December 1886, No. 119, CO 23/228. Charles T. Sands Jr. was the son of a member of the House of Assembly and the nephew of the colony's attorney-general.
73 Shea to Knutsford, 22 November 1888, Conf.; and Knutsford to Shea, 19 January 1889 (draft), Conf., CO 23/230.
74 Nevile Lubbock, chairman of the West Indian Committee, to Knutsford, 29 October 1889, CO 295/326.
75 Robinson to Knutsford, 21 July 1890, No. 217, CO 295/329.
76 Robinson to Knutsford, 13 April 1889, No. 146, CO 295/322.
77 Robinson to Knutsford, 24 May 1890, No. 137, CO 295/328.
78 The phrase is from Clive Emsley, *Policing and its Context, 1759–1870* (London, 1983), p. 60.
79 *Port of Spain Gazette*, 4 June 1890.
80 See 'Retrospect of the past year', *Port of Spain Gazette*, 10 January 1890; H. G. Deedes

to Under-secretary of State, Colonial Office, 25 January 1890, CO 295/331; Robinson to Knutsford, 7 May 1890, Conf., CO 295/328. See especially enclosure No. 2, memorandum on Trinidad volunteer force permanent staff; and letter by 'Robin Hood', 17 November 1890, in *Port of Spain Gazette*, 21 November 1890.

81 Fowler to Knutsford, 25 October 1888, Conf., CO 295/319.

82 The phrase is from David Arnold, 'Crime and crime control in Madras, 1858–1947', in Anand A. Yang (ed.), *Crime and Criminality in British India* (Tucson, 1985), p. 80.

83 Fowler to Knutsford, 25 October 1888, Conf., CO 295/319.

84 See Johnson, 'Social control and the colonial state', p. 52.

85 Evidence of Dr Gooding, a doctor in St Philip, Barbados. *Parl. Papers*, 1898, HL (C. 8657), 569, q. 521; 'Report of inspection in the West Indies by the inspector-general of artillery', p. 1. For a discussion of the Barbadians as the West Indian counterparts of the 'martial races' of India see Johnson, 'Social control and the colonial state', p. 53. For the African parallel, see A. H. M. Kirk-Greene, ' "*Damnosa hereditas*": ethnic ranking and the martial races imperative in Africa', *Ethnic and Racial Studies*, 3 (1980), pp. 392–414.

86 This paragraph is based on Johnson, 'Social control and the colonial state', pp. 54–5.

87 See 'Report of inspection in the West Indies by the inspector-general of artillery', p. 5.

88 Reprinted in *Port of Spain Gazette*, 3 December 1896.

89 'Memorandum relative to police for West Indies' by Richard Mayne, 3 January 1839, No. V, CO 884/1.

CHAPTER SIX

Imposing the British way: the Canadian Mounted Police and the Klondike gold rush

William R. Morrison

In the late 1890s, at the height of imperialist sentiment in Canada, an event occurred in a remote part of the dominion which illuminated a number of official Canadian attitudes current in the period. This was the Yukon, or Klondike, gold rush, which took place between the summers of 1897 and 1899. The establishment of law and order during the gold rush shows the strength in Victorian Canada of the 'British connection' – that powerful combination of emotional attachment to Britain and her institutions on the one hand, and fear of American expansion and revulsion against American institutions on the other. In its extreme form the British connection led to enthusiasm for Joseph Chamberlain's Imperial Federation League and flirtation with the idea of eugenics.[1] In its milder version, as displayed during the Klondike gold rush, it furnished a kind of Canadian nationalism, based largely on invidious comparisons with American social institutions. The gold rush also provides a clear illustration of Canada's policy towards her northern regions, these internal 'colonies', as one historian has called them.[2] This famous episode is the best example in Canadian history of the extension of Canadian sovereignty for nationalistic and economic purposes over a people of different national origin, to a certain extent against their will – in short, an episode of imperialism.

What is now the Yukon Territory was acquired by Canada from Great Britain as part of the great transfer which conveyed the prairies and the continental region of the Northwest Territories to the young dominion in 1870.[3] Though the oldest part of Canada in terms of human habitation (man came first to North America through Alaska and the Yukon at least as early as 12000 B.C. and perhaps much earlier), no European set foot on it until Sir John Franklin explored its northern coast in 1825. Its interior was not penetrated by Europeans until the 1830s and 1840s, when agents of the Hudson's Bay Company established posts there. For another forty years it remained the preserve of 5,000–8,000 Indians and a handful of fur traders. In the early 1870s a few miners began to trickle into the region over the Chilkoot Pass. Most of these men were veterans of the California gold rush of 1849 or the gold strikes which occurred in British Columbia in the 1850s and 1860s. They operated on the reasonable principle that if there was gold in the southern and central Rockies there was likely to be gold in the northern end of the mountain chain as well. Throughout the 1880s and early 1890s they found promising amounts of gold, but no bonanza.

Despite the presence of the miners, the Canadian government for several years took virtually no action to establish its authority in the region. In 1887 a survey party had marked the Yukon–Alaska boundary in the vicinity of the main mining camps, but other than that there was no official presence in the Yukon before 1894. In that year Ottawa sent a two-man police detachment to the Yukon, prodded by the complaints of W. C. Bompas, Anglican Bishop of Selkirk, that his Indian charges were being 'debauched' by the miners, who gave them home-brew and abused their women; social conditions in the region, he claimed, were little short of scandalous.[4] The main plank of the Canadian government's northern policy was parsimony, but its fear of public embarrassment was also strong. There was also a strong suggestion from traders operating in the area that a gold strike might provide handsome royalties to the government. By 1895 the region's prospects were sufficiently bright for the federal government to create a provisional District of Yukon, bounded on the west by the international boundary at the 141st meridian, on the east by the height of land separating the Mackenzie and Yukon river drainage basins, on the south by the northern boundary of British Columbia (the 60th parallel), and on the north by the Arctic Ocean. The same year a detachment of twenty North-West Mounted Police was sent to the region. When in August 1896 substantial quantities of gold were discovered at Bonanza Creek, a dozen miles from the present community of Dawson, the white population of what is now the Yukon Territory was about 1,000. Almost all were miners, the rest traders or merchants.[5]

The Mounted Police[6] were in every way the logical body to send to the Yukon to establish Canadian sovereignty and represent the federal government there. The force was erected in 1873 by the administration of Sir John A. Macdonald to establish Canadian authority on the newly acquired prairies. The NWMP were to be:

> trained to act as cavalry, but also instructed in the Rifle exercises. They should also be instructed, as certain of the Line are, in the use of artillery, this body should not be expressly Military but should be styled *Police*, and have ... military bearing.[7]

The model for the Mounted Police, as well as for similar organisations in other parts of the empire, was the Royal Irish Constabulary.[8] That force was responsible for law and order, but it was organised in a semi-military fashion, and was responsible to central rather than local authority. Its members, unlike those of the regular British police forces, carried arms, and were subject to discipline and regulations more military in character than those of the police. Nor was it the only imperial model. Macdonald felt that there was a parallel between the problem faced by the NWMP in policing the prairies and that faced by the British in India:

> There the British had met the difficulty of maintaining law and order in a multi-racial society by recruiting members from each of the major religious and racial groups into both the Indian army and the local police forces. Macdonald ... [ordered] that the mounted police force 'should be a mixed one of pure white and British and French half-breeds.'[9]

Though this was not done – all the members of the force were white,[10] and it was only quite recently that the RCMP began to recruit Canadian Indians (and mostly as special constables on reserves) – it was not entirely anglophone, since there were always French-Canadians among its commissioned and noncommissioned ranks.

The Mounted Police have often been described by popular writers as a 'semi-military' force,[11] and the military aspect of their activities was particularly evident in their early years when, for instance, the commissioned ranks bore the military titles of colonel, major and so forth – instead of the civilian police nomenclature, commissioner, superintendent, which has been used for most of this century. The field artillery with which the police were originally provided, and the Maxim gun which they put in position on the Chilkoot Pass, were certainly not part of the armament of the regular police. Of more importance, however, was the political nature of the force. The NWMP were not only charged with the task of bringing law and order to Canada's northern 'colonies' but were also the agent of Canada's policy in regard to those huge undeveloped parts of the dominion. The vital distinction between the Mounted Police and other police forces lay in this political task. It was the fulfilment of this role which made the work of the police in the north so extraordinarily diverse. In the Yukon, for instance, they not only enforced the federal, territorial and municipal laws but also carried the mail and acted, among other things, as mining recorders, coroners, health officers, customs officers, land agents, returning officers at elections, prison guards and police magistrates. In doing so they demonstrated the fact of Canadian sovereignty over the region and made it clear that the Yukon was to be completely subordinate to the will of the central government.

[94]

The justification for referring to Canada's northern territories as colonies derives from the fact that in the Yukon, for example, there was no semblance of representative self-government in the Territory while the gold rush lasted. It was not until 1899, at the end of the rush, that elections were held for two members of the Territorial Council,[12] and a member of Parliament was elected from the Territory, and not until 1908 that the council was made wholly elective. Before that date, all members of the council were appointed from Ottawa, the purpose being to keep political power out of the hands of local residents, a majority of whom were foreigners, considered to be of dubious loyalty. And in a larger sense the destiny of the Yukon, particularly in economic matters, was for decades completely under the control of Ottawa, a condition which to a considerable extent still persists.[13]

The 'British' nature of the Canadian colonial regime in the Yukon was manifest in a variety of ways. The main motivation of the government in this respect was that of John A. Macdonald and the statesmen of his era: an affection for British traditions of government combined with fear and dislike of American institutions. Many of the officers of the force were graduates of the Royal Military College in Kingston, and had served in the militia, some seeing action in the Fenian raids of the 1860s and the two Riel rebellions. Most of them belonged to the Anglo-Saxon middle and upper middle classes of eastern Canada, or were French-Canadians who shared the same values. In the noncommissioned ranks of the force there was a strong British presence: 48 per cent of the recruits taken into the NWMP between 1895 and 1897 had been born in Britain.[14] Many of them had already emigrated to Canada, but the police also sought recruits in Britain, where it was expected that young men would be imbued with the ideals of empire, and would be unaware that the pay of a police constable, fifty cents a day plus a northern allowance of fifty cents, would not buy much in the Yukon, where the average labourer's wage was five times as much.

Most members of the police – and this was particularly true of the commissioned ranks – despised and feared the values of the American frontier, the individualism and the grass-roots democracy extolled by the historian Frederick Jackson Turner.[15] The idea that the Yukon ought to be governed by its residents was anathema to them. They wanted the Territory, as they had earlier wanted the Canadian prairies, to become:

> orderly and hierarchical; not a lawless frontier democracy but a place where powerful institutions and a responsible and paternalistic upper class would ensure true liberty and justice ... the Upper Canadian Tory tradition in its purest form.[16]

[95]

And this tradition, paternalistic and authoritarian, was almost entirely derived from British models.

The history of the Yukon during the gold rush period provides many examples of the clash between the American and the British frontier traditions. One of the best, and one which clearly shows the role played by the police in imposing the British way over an American population, is the attempt by the police to suppress the miners' meetings. These formed the basic governmental institution of the western American mining camps, where in lieu of formal authority the miners had constructed their own. The meetings were held at the request of any resident of the community, and dispensed civil as well as criminal justice in accordance with popular standards of fairness. Since Ottawa had not provided the Yukon with any kind of government, the miners simply imported the American system into the region, where it seemed to work well; an early observer reported that the decisions of the meetings were 'fairly just, inexpensive, quick in results, and promptly executed'.[17]

Just they may have been, but in both theory and practice they clashed directly with the British-Canadian system of centralised, paternalistic control, and as soon as the police were able to do so they suppressed them. In 1894 Ottawa had sent two members of the NWMP to the Yukon to reconnoitre the region, and the next year a detachment of twenty arrived at the main mining district of Fortymile, a substantial number for the task of policing the 500 people who wintered there, but not too many to demonstrate that Canada was now determined to see her writ run in the Yukon. The suppression of the miners' meetings was an instructive illustration of this determination. It was done by a simple show of force. Two owners of a mining claim had leased it to a third man, who had employed men to work it for him, had defaulted on their wages and then left the country. A miners' meeting was called which sold the claim to a fourth man and gave the proceeds to the workers. Because this procedure was not in accordance with Canadian law, the original owners of the claim appealed to the police. The officer-in-charge of the force, Inspector Charles Constantine, sent twelve men armed with rifles to the claim, gave it to the owners, and warned the miners that such a thing must not happen again. It did not. That was the end of the miners' meeting as a judicial institution, and the last time there was any organised opposition to the police.[18] The contrast with the disorder and violence of the American mining frontier was striking.[19]

The nature of the British influence in the Klondike gold rush may be seen both in the policy of the government and in the actions of the men sent to enforce it. At the height of the rush the police were commanded by Superintendent S. B. Steele, one of the more ardent imperialists of the day. Sam Steele, whom a popular biography calls the 'Lion of the

Frontier',[20] had a career that was so completely in the imperial mould as to seem worthy of fiction. His father and two uncles were British naval officers; one of them was a surgeon aboard HMS *Victory* at Trafalgar, and the boy grew up in an atmosphere of reverence for British tradition.[21] Men like Steele – and there were many of them in the English-speaking Canada of the nineteenth century – were true Tories. They believed in order more than in personal liberty; the 'peace, order, and good government'[22] enshrined in the Canadian constitution was their watchword. Britain, or Britain as they imagined it to be, was the model of order and respect for authority. The United States was the model of what a society ought not to be.

Thus Steele's first imperative in the Yukon, and that of his superiors, was the maintenance and preservation of public order, an order imposed and defined entirely from outside the community. What was not wanted was the lawlessness of the American frontier, an example of which lay across the path to the Yukon at Skagway, Alaska. Skagway was the port where gold seekers landed before crossing the Chilkoot and White Passes. Throughout most of the gold-rush period it was dominated by a thug named Soapy Smith, who ran the town with his gang, robbing, beating and murdering at will. Steele's autobiography makes much of the contrast between the disorder of Skagway and the peaceful nature of Dawson; the town of Skagway, he wrote, 'was little better than a hell upon earth'.[23] His scene of the Canadian–American border on the passes provides an even more vivid contrast. He reported that the pace of lawlessness increased as the travellers approached the border, then stopped abruptly:

> murder, robbery, and petty theft were of common occurrence, the 'shell game' could be seen at every turn of the trail, operations being pushed with the utmost vigour, so as not to loose [*sic*] the golden opportunity which they would be unable to find or take advantage of on the other side of the line in British territory.[24]

Perhaps the most notable feature of the police imperium was its paternalism. Not only was there no representative democracy in the Yukon as long as the gold rush lasted, but on several occasions which the police deemed to be emergencies they simply invented law to forestall public disorder. The best-known example occurred in the spring of 1898, when thousands of men were camped on the shores of Lake Bennett and Lake Lindeman, preparing to drift downriver to Dawson in jerry-built boats. When the ice went out on the upper Yukon river and the flotilla began to move through Miles Canyon a number of boats were swamped and ten men were drowned. Sam Steele then ordered a system of registration for the boats, and regulations for navigating the canyon:

[97]

women must walk around it, pilots were to be hired, and so forth. He justified these actions in a public speech which he later quoted in his autobiography:

> There are many of your countrymen [i.e. Americans] who have said that the Mounted Police make the laws as they go along, and I am going to do so now for your own good, therefore the directions that I shall give shall be carried out strictly, and they are these ...[25]

The penalty for non-compliance was a fine of $100. No one seems actually to have been charged with an offence under the rule. It would have been interesting to see what would have happened had Steele levied a fine under this non-law; probably he would simply have ordered the offender out of the country. Another example of extra-legal action occurred in November the same year, when a shortage of food in the Dawson region led to rumours of impending starvation. Though these proved to be exaggerated, the police were concerned that they might result in public disorder. Steele therefore announced that no one would be permitted to enter the Yukon without satisfying the police that he had sufficient cash or provisions to see him over the winter season, and notices to this effect were posted in the principal cities of the Pacific north-west. The regulation, like the rules for passing through Miles Canyon, was entirely the work of the police, and was not justified by any official statute or regulation. As law it was completely *ad hoc*, as the Department of Justice eventually decreed after the rush was over and the necessity of such measures had disappeared. They were also a good example of the paternalism which was central to the British way of governing frontier societies. In an American mining community such measures would never have been successful, nor would they even have been attempted; given the libertarian ethos of the frontier, they would have been vigorously resisted, and the American government lacked an efficient body like the Mounted Police with which to enforce them.

The Klondike during the gold rush gained a reputation in the rest of the world of being a violent, rowdy frontier society. The image of Dawson during the rush which made the greatest public impression was that fostered by Robert Service in poems such as 'The Shooting of Dan McGrew'.[26] Service knew what his public wanted – a 'colourful' mythology, derived from the American mining frontier, with gamblers, painted ladies, and disputes settled by the law of the six-gun. Thus 'Dan McGrew', whose climactic stanza runs:

> Then I ducked my head, and the lights went out, and two guns blazed
> in the dark;
> And a woman screamed, and the lights went up, and two men lay stiff
> and stark;

Pitched on his head, and pumped full of lead, was Dangerous Dan
McGrew,
While the man from the creeks lay clutched to the breast of the lady
that's known as Lou.

What is wrong with this picture, of course, is that, although there were
plenty of men who ended up 'pitched on their head' in Dawson saloons,
it was not from being 'pumped full of lead'. There was a law forbidding
the carrying of handguns which the police enforced strictly. There were
very few murders in the Yukon Territory during the gold rush, and
apparently none took place in a saloon.[27] But presumably a poem in
which the man from the creeks punched Dan McGrew on the nose, was
arrested by an unarmed constable and sentenced to ten days on the police
woodpile was not likely to sell.

The police enforced order in other ways as well. Saloons were permitted to operate twenty-four hours a day, except on Sundays. At midnight
Saturday they all closed, and remained closed until midnight Sunday,
when they all reopened. Sunday was thus quieter in Dawson than in
many cities in the south. On the other hand, the police permitted
prostitutes to operate, so long as they caused no public disorder. They
felt that prostitution tended to preserve rather than threaten public
order in a society made up largely of single young men. Thus, despite
complaints from moral purity organisations in southern Canada, prostitution was tolerated until several years after the rush ended. The same
was true of gambling, which was felt to be acceptable so long as no one
was permitted to carry a handgun.

The Mounted Police equated public order with British law and justice,
and disorder with the American system. Their mandate in the Yukon
was to suppress lawlessness and disorder, and, since they felt that contempt for law was an American trait, they were alarmed by the fact that
a large part of the Territory's population seemed to be made up of riff-
raff from the United States. Charles Constantine, who led the first police
expedition to the Yukon, observed that 'a considerable number of the
people coming in from the [Puget] Sound cities appear to be the sweepings
of the slums and the result of a general jail delivery'.[28] What happened
to Yankees who bragged and blustered in front of the police, displaying
an indiscreet contempt for British justice, is shown in a story, perhaps
apocryphal, told by Pierre Berton:

> One American gambler, so the story goes, who came up before Steele was
> contemptuous when the policeman fined him fifty dollars. 'Fifty dollars –
> is that all? I've got that in my vest pocket', he said. Whereupon the super-
> intendent added: '... and sixty days on the woodpile. Have you got that in
> your vest pocket?'[29]

[99]

Another extra-legal technique used by the police to control the Yukon's turbulent population was to arrest people they considered undesirable, then drop the charges if they agreed to leave the country. Sometimes they simply ordered them to leave; the process was known as getting a 'blue ticket'. An example which illustrates the political attitude of the police, as well as the state of free speech in Dawson during the gold rush, is given by Steele:

> Some of the people objected to Royalty in general, did not like monarchs, and would speak slightingly of ours. One of those was an actor in the theatres in Dawson, and when his conduct was reported by the sergeant he was given an opportunity to say he would sin no more or take his ticket for the outside. This had the desired effect.[30]

Most of the police officers who served in the Yukon during the gold rush seem to have regarded the Territory not essentially as a distant part of Canada; rather, they viewed it as an outpost of the far-flung British Empire. They spoke not of Canadian law and justice but of British law and justice, not of Canadian but of British pluck and hardiness,[31] qualities they deemed essential for survival in the north. When Steele wrote his annual report from Dawson late in 1898, he compared the Yukon not to the rest of Canada but to the empire as a whole, proudly asserting that 'in proportion to the population, crime is not very prevalent, and in fact the crime sheets of the Yukon Territory would compare favourably with those of any part of the British Empire'.[32]

It may be asked why Steele and his men were obeyed as readily as they were, why the Dawson actor did not simply tell Steele that it was a free country and that he would speak as he pleased about Queen Victoria. There are two answers. The first is that the police were not operating entirely on their own. They were representatives of a vast empire which commanded respect even from its enemies. Men like Sam Steele – and there were others like him in the force – were like characters in a G. A. Henty novel (even Steele's name was perfect for the genre): men who cowed refractory natives or insolent Americans with a word, men who commanded obedience without seeming to try. There was something intangible about these men, perhaps force of character is the best descriptive phrase, which was real, and acknowledged by their contemporaries. And behind them stood the moral force of the entire empire. The second reason these men were obeyed was more tangible than character and moral force, for the Yukon was not really a free country, nor were the police simply a small band of brave men surrounded by potential adversaries. At the height of the rush there were 350 members of the force in the Territory, supported by the Yukon Field Force, a 200 man detachment of the Canadian army. A force of 550 men controlling a community of 30,000 was a ratio of police to civilians ten times that of a modern Canadian town.[33] At about the same time the entire North West Territories, with a population of 160,000, mostly farmers and people in small towns, including a number of Indian reserves, all spread out over what is now Alberta and Saskatchewan, were policed by only 462 members of the NWMP, and that number included the training depot at Regina.[34]

Moreover the police not only enforced (and sometimes invented) the law, they also administered it. Steele acted as a police magistrate; members of the force thus arrested, tried and sentenced offenders, and also acted as prison guards. No one of any importance complained publicly about this conflict of interest. Had the offending actor not ceased his slanders, the police could have arrested him, probably on a charge of vagrancy, convicted him, and given him the choice of leaving the country or spending several days sawing stove wood for the police barracks. An appeal to a higher court in Edmonton or Victoria was impracticable; thus there was nothing to do but submit. Nor were the population of the Yukon particularly hostile to the police. The NWMP enforced a social order which was welcome to many citizens and settled mining and other disputes in what was perceived to be a fair manner. The civil servants who served in the Territory during this period were generally thought to be inefficient or corrupt, and the police provided a welcome contrast. In the tradition of the best of Britain's imperial servants, they were firm but fair in their dealings with the public.

In the gold-rush Yukon the police interpreted the British imperial mandate, and did so in a particularly Canadian way. The mandate involved a paternalistic imposition of fair and impartial justice, aimed at securing a peaceful and orderly society, and was successful in doing so. What was particularly Canadian about the way the mandate was interpreted in the Yukon was the extent to which it manifested itself in anti-Americanism. Though there was plenty of that in Britain at the time, where the supposed brash crudity and greedy aggressiveness of Uncle Sam provided material for generations of *Punch* cartoonists, it was particularly marked in the Yukon, where America was perceived as the antithesis of what society ought to be. But this has long been part of the Canadian character, not only because of the relative conservatism of Canadians, but because of the prolonged search for the elusive 'Canadian identity'. Unlike the citizens of other countries – the English, for example, who had a fairly good idea of their national character (and who taunted the Americans out of a fear of declining power) – Canadians were perennially uncertain about theirs, and were haunted by the thought that they were more like the Americans than they wished to admit. The Canadian identity was thus partly based on the British connection and partly on a rejection of the United States. In the Yukon, with its largely American population, it was a powerful combination.

In this respect the 'British way' was as much a negative as a positive force in the Yukon. To forestall the possibility of a democratic take-over of political power by Americans, representative government even at the municipal level was not granted to the Yukon until the rush was over, and the Territory's political development was thus delayed, and to a degree stillborn. When a totally elected Territorial Council was granted in 1908, it was marked by a degree of partisanship and narrow self-interest unusual even by the standards of the day. Since the federal government continued to appoint the Territorial Commissioner, who had the power of the veto and the purse, the Yukon's colonial status continued for decades. The Territory's political development bore scars from this delay which are evident still.[35] In the Yukon, as to a degree elsewhere in Canada, adherence to the 'British way' as a means of defence against Americans and Americanism has helped muddle questions of national interest and has delayed the emergence of a genuinely national identity.

Notes

1 On the imperialist impulse in Canada see Carl Berger, *The Sense of Power: studies in the idea of Canadian imperialism, 1867–1914* (Toronto, 1970); Robert Page, *The Boer War and Canadian Imperialism* (Ottawa, 1987); Robert Page, 'The Canadian response to the imperial idea during the Boer War years', *Journal of Canadian Studies*, 5, 1 (1970).

2 K. S. Coates, *Canada's Colonies: a history of the Yukon and Northwest Territories* (Toronto, 1985).

3 For a history of the region see K. S. Coates and W. R. Morrison, *Land of the Midnight Sun: a history of the Yukon* (Edmonton, 1988).

4 William Carpenter Bompas was fanatically devoted to his Native charges and had a low tolerance of those he suspected of debouching them. Other observers, the Mounted Police, for example, tended to discount his alarms on the subject. See W. R. Morrison, *Showing the Flag: the Mounted Police and Canadian sovereignty in the north, 1894–1925* (Vancouver, 1985). The gold rush had little real effect on the majority of the Yukon Indians. Most of the terrible decimation through introduced diseases occurred during the fur trade period. The Indians did work for wages periodically, cutting wood for steamboats, or working part-time in mining, but the majority of the region's Native population remained as hunter-gatherers for several decades after the gold rush. See Kenneth Coates, 'Best left as Indians: the federal government and the Indians of the Yukon, 1894–1950', *Canadian Journal of Native Studies*, 4, 2 (1984).

5 On mining in the Yukon before the gold rush see A. A. Wright, *Prelude to Bonanza* (Sidney, B.C., 1976).

6 Until 1904 the North-West Mounted Police, from 1904 to 1920 the Royal North-West Mounted Police, since 1920 the Royal Canadian Mounted Police.

7 National Archives of Canada, Macdonald Papers, vol. 516, Macdonald to D. R. Cameron, 21 December 1869, quoted in S. W. Horrall, 'Sir John A. Macdonald and the mounted police force for the Northwest Territories', *Canadian Historical Review*, LIII, 2 (1972), p. 181.

8 See Horrall, 'Sir John A. Macdonald'.

9 NAC, Macdonald Papers, vol. 516, Macdonald to William McDougall, 12 December 1869, quoted in Horrall, 'Sir John A. Macdonald', p. 181.

10 Over the past two decades the RCMP has made an effort to make the force more representative of the Canadian racial mix through the recruitment of 'visible minorities': blacks, Asians, Native Indians and women.
11 By writers such as R. C. Fetherstonhaugh, *The Royal Canadian Mounted Police* (New York, 1940), p. 3.
12 It was not until 1977 that the Executive Council of the Territorial Council was restructured to give it a majority of elected over appointed members.
13 On this subject see Coates and Morrison, *Land of the Midnight Sun*, chapter 9.
14 R. C. Macleod, 'The North-West Mounted Police, 1873–1905: Law Enforcement and Social Order in the Canadian North-west', Ph.D. thesis, Duke University (1971), p. 152.
15 Others, of course, embraced American values. Many men stationed on the southern prairies in the early days of the force deserted to the United States.
16 R. C. Macleod, 'Canadianizing the west: the North-West Mounted Police as agents of the national policy, 1873–1905', in R. D. Francis and H. Palmer (eds.), *The Prairie West: historical readings* (Edmonton, 1985).
17 William Ogilvie, *Early Days on the Yukon* (London, 1913), pp. 245–6.
18 The episode was described by a member of the police detachment which participated in it. See M. H. E. Hayne, *Pioneers of the Klondyke* (London, 1897), p. 124.
19 There is a substantial literature on law and order on the American mining frontier. Useful sources are R. D. McGrath, *Gunfighters, Highwaymen and Vigilantes: violence on the frontier* (Berkeley, 1984), D. A. Johnson, 'Vigilance and the law: the moral authority of popular justice in the far west', *American Quarterly*, 33, 5 (1981). A comparative study is Desmond Morton, 'Cavalry or police: keeping the peace on two adjacent frontiers, 1870–1900', *Journal of Canadian Studies*, 12, 2 (1977).
20 Robert Stewart, *Sam Steele: Lion of the Frontier* (Toronto, 1979).
21 The father had retired to Canada on half-pay and had become a local magnate in Upper Canada: a magistrate, a member of the Assembly, a colonel of the county militia, donor of land for the local Anglican Church, and a promoter of roads and canals. He was seventy in 1851 when Sam was born (his second wife was fifty years his junior; he survived her by five years), but he had more children, and lived to be eighty-four. Sam Steele's service to Queen and country began in 1865 when at the age of fourteen he lied about his age and joined a militia regiment being raised to fight the Fenians. In 1870 he volunteered to serve in the expedition commanded by Colonel Garnet Wolseley sent to put down a Métis rebellion in the new province of Manitoba. He then joined the artillery school in the fledgling Canadian army, and in 1873, at the age of twenty-two, was appointed sergeant-major in the newly formed North West Mounted Police. He served in the force until 1899, then commanded a detachment of police which volunteered to fight in the South African war. He was then appointed to the South African Constabulary, served with the Canadian army in the first world war, reached the rank of major-general and was knighted. When he died in 1919 he had achieved the perfect career of imperial service, or as close as a Canadian ever came to doing so.
22 The maintenance of peace, order and good government is one of the prerogatives of the federal government under the British North America Act, now called the Constitution Act (1867).
23 S. B. Steele, in NWMP annual *Report*, 1898, p. 4.
24 *Ibid.*
25 S. B. Steele, *Forty Years in Canada* (London, 1915), p. 311.
26 From *Songs of a Sourdough* (1907).
27 There were only three cases of robbery–murder during 1897–99, not many for a turbulent frontier of 25,000 or 30,000 people. The most notorious was an incident in which three miners were murdered by Indian youths; they were convicted and hanged. There were also a number of killings which could be called 'crimes of passion'.
28 NWMP *Report*, 1897, p. 309.
29 Pierre Berton, *Klondike Fever* (New York, 1958), p. 308.
30 Steele, *Forty Years*, p. 327.
31 Strictly speaking, they should have referred to English rather than British law, but the word 'British' was invariably used in this context, perhaps because so many of those

in authority in the dominion were Scottish. Among the Canadian-born the word 'English' eventually came to have connotations of elitism and what was called 'Downing Street domination'.

32 Quoted in Stewart, *Sam Steele*, p. 216.

33 Brandon, Manitoba, where my university is located, has a population of just under 40,000, and a police force of fifty-two.

34 NWMP *Report*, 1902.

35 Coates and Morrison, *Land of the Midnight Sun*, explore this theme in chapters 6 and 7. In 1977 the federal government ordered the Territorial Commissioner to accept whatever legislation was placed before him; he thus assumed the role, though not the title, of the Lieutenants-Governor of the provinces. The leader of the majority party in the Yukon council is now called the 'government leader', and is a provincial premier in all but name. However, since the revenue of the Yukon comes overwhelmingly from federal grants rather than from local revenue, Ottawa's power over the Territory is still very strong.

PART II

Colonial policing in Africa and India, 1860–1940

CHAPTER SEVEN

Guarding the extending frontier: policing the Gold Coast, 1865–1913

David Killingray

This chapter discusses the development of a formal system of policing in the Gold Coast over a period of nearly sixty years, the concluding date of 1913 marking the consolidation of British control over the territory that now approximates to modern Ghana. The chapter looks at the origins of the police and the way in which a dual system of policing developed, mainly an armed frontier force to secure the extending territory of the Gold Coast, but also a smaller unarmed civil police force to extend social control over the coastal towns and villages.[1] An uneasy contention existed between these two forms of policing. The origin of the police as an armed constabulary, the system of direction and control, and the continuing political instability of the Gold Coast, ensured that policing relied primarily on a paramilitary force. This in turn influenced, and was reinforced by, the kinds of European officers appointed to command the force and particularly by the recruitment of a rank and file that was for the most part alien and thus mercenary in nature. Official rhetoric often proclaimed evolution to a system of civil policing by consent; popular hostility to the police and political realities dictated that policing remained predominantly a paramilitary activity throughout the whole of the colonial period.

Origins of the police

The locally raised militia and detachments of the West India Regiment (WIR) stationed on the Gold Coast were regarded by both London and local administrators as unfitted for general police purposes. In 1845 the Secretary of State favoured the raising of a small 'Police establishment of some thirty, or even fifty if absolutely necessary, under the super-intendence of two or three intelligent sergeants, to be drilled and disciplined much in the same manner as the London Police'.[2] Ten years later the reform-minded Governor, Sir Benjamin Pine, argued that the regular maintenance of law and order required an armed police force, 'under strict military discipline', and subject to local control.[3] It would also be considerably cheaper than the WIR. No action was taken, but by the mid-1860s the need had become more urgent. Conran, the Acting Governor, argued that 'Fifty Policemen here [Cape Coast], thirty at Accra, and twenty at Anamaboe properly organized armed equipped and under a Gentleman Inspector and Magistrate would I feel confident be of more use than three times that number of soldiers'. His military experience carried weight in the Colonial Office, and a new police force was duly organised in 1865, each blue-serge-uniformed constable supplied with a set of handcuffs 'to be worn on the right side like the Irish Constabulary'.[4]

This new police force proved barely adequate for maintaining law and order in the Gold Coast and had to be briefly strengthened by a detachment from Sierra Leone. It was largely confined to the towns, and was occupied primarily with policing petty offences and public nuisances. With the prospect of a British withdrawal from the Coast, following the recommendation of the parliamentary committee of 1865, several officials urged that a local paramilitary force be created 'to meet if possible any special emergency without application to the military'. Acting Administrator Simpson proposed a 'Governor's Guard' to police the courthouse and guard Government House and the prisons; the force would be 'drilled as soldiers', but would never wear arms except on 'special duty', and would be the nucleus of a colonial force in the event of British military aid being withdrawn.[5] The Asante incursion of 1869 and the threat of war spurred on the creation of such a force.

The model was provided by the Lagos Armed Police, formed in 1863 by Captain John Hawley Glover. Recruits were drawn from local Yorubas and also runaway Hausa slaves. Known as 'Glover's Forty Thieves', the force guarded the Lagos hinterland and the trade routes to the British colony. The Hausas were already being identified as a martial race, but the term 'Hausa' was applied loosely to all Muslims who came from the northern Niger region, irrespective of their ethnic identity. It was a term soon to be transferred to men from the northern Gold Coast, who, in turn, were to be recognised as archetypal military material. In 1870 and 1871 Governor Kennedy of the Gold Coast suggested that a Hausa force might be raised from the Hausa settlements on the coast, and also from Lagos. By 1872 the force had been created at a cost less than one-third that of the WIR: 'Not only are the Hausas cheaper, but for service in Africa, and especially for service a few miles inland, they are also more efficient,' wrote Governor Hennessy.[6] The Gold Coast Armed Police, or the Hausa Police as they were sometimes called, became the paramilitary arm of the colonial government. The existing Fante civil police,

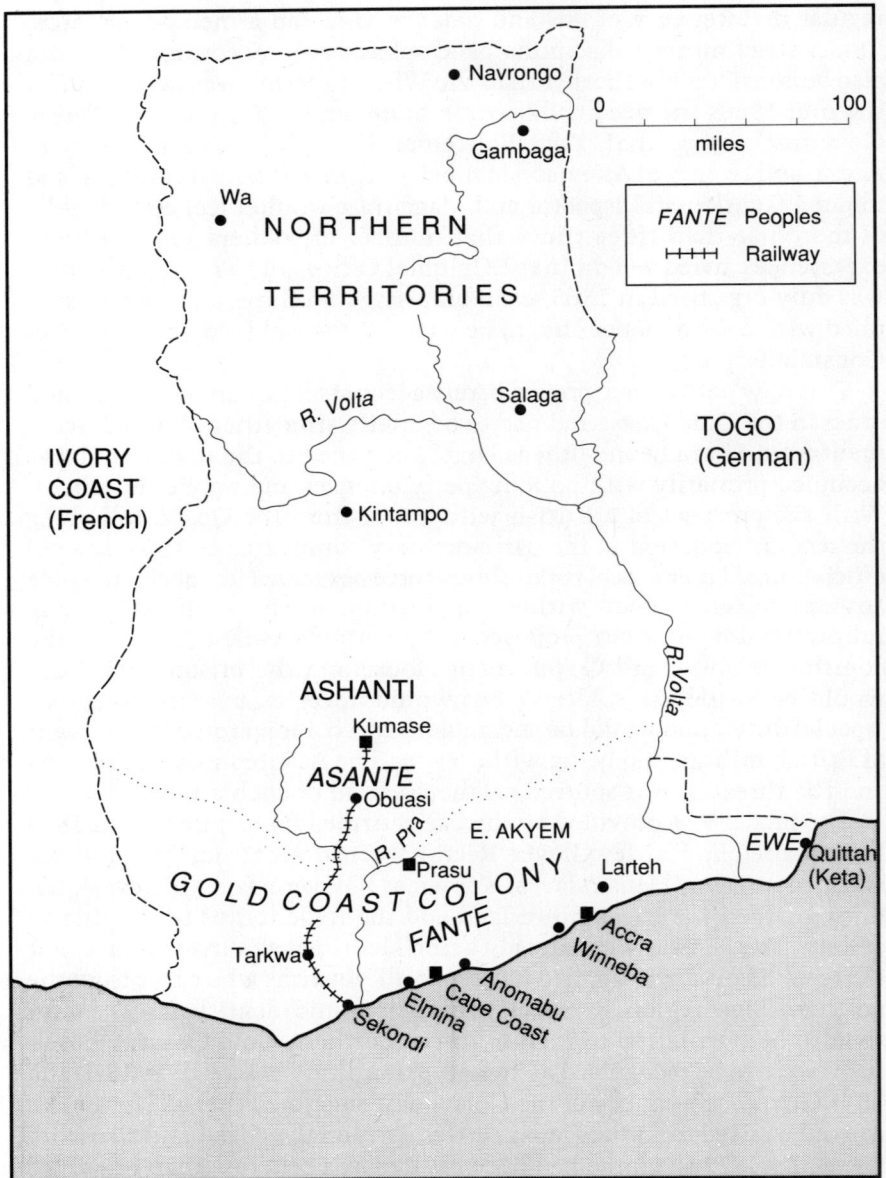

The Gold Coast, 1912

Hausa detachment of the Gold Coast Constabulary at Adwatan, 1887. *Further details in the list of illustrations*

never a very highly regarded body of men, together with the Hausa force, constituted a single force under the command of an inspector-general.

The proclamation of the colony in 1874 enlarged the role of the police, both armed and civil. There was no longer any ambiguity as to British responsibilities and the exercise of law. Territorial acquisition and extension, even under a system of indirect rule, demanded a larger, more effective armed police force. Under a reorganisation scheme of 1875 the joint civil–military police were to be increased to 1,000 men, each enlisted for a period of five years. The civil police, recruited mainly from coastal peoples, numbered 250. A small number spoke, and some wrote, English. They patrolled 'beats' in the towns armed with regular police whistles, batons and bullseye lanterns, and in emergencies could be issued with arms. The Hausa force became increasingly an infantry body, with light artillery. Each of the 500 men carried a breech-loading rifle and sword bayonet.[7] The Hausas served in the frontier districts, formed patrols and punitive expeditions to assert British sovereignty and authority, and guarded the key route north to Kumase at Prasu. They provided the coercive force which enabled British authority to be established throughout the Gold Coast in the last three decades of the nineteenth century.

The civil and military aspects of the Gold Coast Constabulary were ill suited to a common system of command. Constabulary officers, for the most part officers seconded from the British army, disliked the civil functions of police work. From the outset it proved difficult to reconcile control of joint civil and military forces, especially when the civil police were deemed by senior officials 'thoroughly worthless'.[8] When Lieutenant Colonel E. B. McInnis was appointed Inspector General in 1886 he brought his considerable Indian military experience to bear on the force; his aim was to model the Hausa Constabulary on an Indian infantry irregular regiment. As a result of his reforms the Hausa companies became a solely military force, and the civil police were placed under the control of civilian District Officers. A complete separation of the two branches of police now became essential, demanded by both colonial administrators and constabulary officers. Governor Griffith's views, endorsed by the Legislative Council in 1888, favoured a distinct force under specially appointed officers drawn, if possible, from the Metropolitan Police. The formal creation of separate forces came in 1894.

The newly appointed inspector-in-chief of the civil police, Captain Kitson, had little good to say of his new charge. With 336 men the force was well over a hundred short of establishment, and of those he thought more than 200 should be discharged as unsuitable. Kitson described the force as 'deplorable and demoralized'. It was, he said, 'the laughing stock of the Colony', while the Governor reported that it was 'choked with goal birds'. Recruits were of poor quality, undersized and unfit for service. Since 1887 large numbers of policemen had been discharged either as bad characters or as medically unfit; many had deserted, and neglect by officers and harsh control by sergeants had even led to a brief mutiny of police at Winneba in June 1888.[9] It was to take a long time before the civil police force reached the standard that officials thought even modestly satisfactory for regular policing of the towns.

Structure, direction and control

The War Office in London disliked the imperial commitment to police the West African territories when the burden of cost and occasionally men fell on the regular army. Britain's legal and judicial position on the Gold Coast, before annexation in 1874, was ambiguous.[10] Legal possession was limited to a few coastal forts. George Maclean, the Judicial Assessor from 1830 to 1843, extended British influence by a mixture of force, personal contact and local consent, with the aim of keeping trade routes open and recovering commercial debts. Curbing slaving, kidnapping and human sacrifice provided further moral imperatives for intervention in local African societies. This informal 'power and jurisdiction', acknowledged by the Fante 'Bond' of 1844, established a judicial system which blended English and customary law.[11] Maclean's system had placed local policing under local control, and this remained the general ambition of most colonial administrators in the Gold Coast thereafter. The Armed Police of 1873, and their military successors, the Gold Coast Constabulary and Gold Coast Regiment, and also the civil police, came under the direct control and authority of the Governor of the colony. When the constabulary was separated into civil and military forces in 1894 the governor acted as commander-in-chief of the military and directed the local organisation and conduct of the civil police. The senior officer of the constabulary continued to be an inspector-general, while a commissioner headed the civil police.

Most military and civil police officers were Europeans, mainly seconded or former army officers, many with experience in India or other parts of the empire. As the constabulary became a more professional military force so the pressure for a more efficient type of officer grew; inspectors-general were not prepared to accept the rakes and half-pay officers discarded by British and Indian regiments. Native officers also formed a regular part of the establishment, appointed up through the ranks from men who had a proven record of loyalty and ability to command. Inspectors and sub-inspectors came into the civil police by several routes. The majority were ex-army officers. By the early 1890s men with police experience in other colonies had received appointments to the force, and this included gazetted officers from Caribbean islands.

At the same time the first officers from British police forces joined the Gold Coast police, for example William Brown, a constable in the Renfrewshire Constabulary, appointed a sub-inspector in 1891. These officers brought to the Gold Coast force not only new ideas of police work but also a much needed sense of professionalism.

The day-to-day direction of the constabulary, and the civil police, was by District Commissioners. As British authority was extended constabulary officers increasingly filled this role and also acted as magistrates, thus combining the role of policeman, prosecutor and judge in local criminal and civil cases. The early criminal statistics for the Gold Coast are both brief and inadequate. They indicate the magisterial activities of constabulary officers more than the incidence of criminal activity in the colony.[12] For example, a report of 1882 shows that many officers were occupied mainly with offences under the Towns Police and Public Health Ordinance, dealing with cases involving the recovery of small sums of money, petty larceny and cases of assault. One District Commissioner reported that civil actions for debt or assault tended to predominate.[13] This 'system of combining civil with military employment ... is a mistake', reported Governor Ussher in 1880. Constabulary officers not only lacked legal training, so that their administrative and judical actions were often neither firm nor fair, but their dual role resulted in neglect of proper direction of the constabulary. As a result it was decided in mid-1888 to replace them as DCs by legal officers.[14]

Both the civil police and the armed constabulary drew on external models. But there was no single model; the Gold Coast police developed in a pragmatic way. They were fashioned from the experiences of the personnel employed and in response to local circumstances. Indian and Egyptian paramilitary policing provided examples of practice; the Royal Irish Constabulary offered a structural model and, after 1907, regular training facilities for all officers; the methods of organisation in English county forces, the London beat system, and some of the accoutrements of the Metropolitan Police, were transferred to the coastal towns; and officers from other West African colonies and the Caribbean islands also brought distinctive patterns and dimensions to civil police work. Constabulary ordinances drew on examples from a variety of colonies. Whatever the source of ideas and practices, they were adapted and shaped to the particular conditions of policing the Gold Coast. The system, in both origin and development, was essentially hybrid.

The extent of policing

The annexation of 1874 did not 'close' the frontier; it merely gave it judicial definition, albeit one that the British were unable to endorse for a considerable time. The British presence was thinly spread in an effort to secure some measure of internal control and also to guard the frontier, especially with Asante. Both within and beyond the colony were territories regarded by the administration as 'unsettled' or 'savage'. Limited manpower and poor communications restricted the effectiveness of the Hausa Constabulary, and many areas and actions went unpoliced. The constabulary was also regularly required to deal with urban riots and the faction or 'company' fights which every so often erupted, especially during the annual Yam Festival.[15]

A major aim of the British administration was territorial and fiscal control over the whole of the littoral. The incorporation within the colony of the eastern district of Keta and the lower Volta region would, in the words of Governor Ussher, 'protect British territory from violation and stop smuggling'[16] of tobacco, rum and trade goods and increase the colony's revenue. German annexation of neighbouring Togo in 1884 hastened this policy. New customs posts were created, and the Hausa force stationed in the area built blockhouses and redoubts; in a series of campaigns over a period of more than ten years they suppressed the independence and the trade of the south-eastern Ewe peoples.[17]

Redoubt at Keta (Quittah), 1886. *Further details in the list of illustrations*

British jurisdiction was proclaimed over the Volta district in 1880. For the rest of that decade the Hausa Constabulary was crucial in enforcing British rule and ensuring control over the lower reaches of the Volta river.

With the 'pacification' of the Volta region responsibility for anti-smuggling operations passed, in 1888, from the constabulary to the new Volta River Preventive Service. Formed from ex-constabulary men, uniformed, drilled and disciplined, the service combated the smuggling of trade goods and also prevented firearms and powder coming across the eastern frontier. Similar forces, under the Customs Department, were established on the western, south-eastern and north-eastern frontiers in the early twentieth century. Initially equipped with only side arms, the 281 strong Volta Service was issued with carbines in 1908 as a result of armed resistance to its activities.[18]

Policing the interior of the colony depended to a large extent on the support of chiefs. The authority of some had been eroded by British rule, and Lieutenant Governor Freeling was eager to strengthen their rule by creating local militias in each district. Chiefly authority was also vital to the maintenance and construction of roads, which, Freeling said, were essential 'both for strategical and trade purposes' and could not be built 'without assistance from our constabulary'.[19] Five years later, in 1882, Governor Rowe argued strongly that:

> Kings and Chiefs ... though their methods for the suppression and detection of crime are different from those approved by European opinion, still they have for many years been considered as the expression of the native mind in favour of social order and the rights of property.

There were, he reported, towns and villages all over the protectorate:

> without a policeman to represent the Government, ... [where] the assistance of the native chiefs is especially valuable in attempts to detect crime. In this matter the Police force is quite helpless, many of the men are strangers ... [without] knowledge of any political movement, and I would wish to do all in my power to encourage the Kings, Chiefs and Headmen to work with the Government.[20]

That was easier said than done. African opposition to British interference with customary rule and law, and the weakness of British legal institutions, led to the Native Jurisdiction Ordinance, passed in 1878 but enforced in 1883, which transferred authority from the chiefs to the Crown. It ushered in a form of indirect rule where chiefs had the power to make by-laws, police their own communities and conduct tribunals, but subject to the governor's *fiat*. In this way the administration in Accra attempted to regulate the native states of the interior and to bring them gradually under English law and practice.

[114]

British authority within the protectorate was tenuous and, as Freeling admitted in his report on the expedition to eastern Akyem in 1877:

> the late events ... prove the great difficulty there is in ascertaining with any degree of certainty what is really taking place even within the Protectorate; it likewise proves, (if more proof were wanted), that a considerable Force of Constabulary must be maintained and kept in the highest state of efficiency ready to march at short notice.[21]

A Hausa column on the march demonstrated the visible power of the colonial government to the people of the towns through which it passed. Douglas, reporting on his march to Larteh to arrest a chief for murder in late 1886, wrote:

> I feel sure that seeing so large a body of drilled and disciplined soldiers well provided with Snider rifles and ammunition impressed them greatly ... as expeditions such as those under my command are heard of, known and talked about over a wide extent of country – they have an effect far beyond their immediate field of action ...[22]

Between 1896 and 1900 the British used the constabulary to extend their control over Asante and the Northern Territories. The Asante rose in revolt in 1900, besieging the governor in the fort at Kumase, and additional military force was required to establish a rudimentary administration over such a large area. Once the rising was suppressed, and much to the surprise of many officials, Asante proved to be a relatively peaceful acquisition. The fort and strong garrison at Kumase cowed the heartland of the once powerful state, and similar smaller structures and detachments held key towns; the newly constructed strategic railway to Kumase gave military reinforcements rapid access to central Asante; and the new cash crop of cocoa offered a commercial and export diversion for Asante farmers. Although the rebellious potential of Asante continued to concern London more than Accra, and military men more than civil administrators, by 1907 the local authorities felt secure enough to reduce the military presence, principally in order to reduce defence expenditure. The 'day when soldiers and Maxims can be done away with and the country ruled with police'[23] was some way off, but a start had been made with civil administration in place of the military, and quasi-civil policing in the rapidly expanding towns of Kumase and Obuasi. By 1910 there were 102 men of the civil Escort Police in Asante compared with only seventy-five in 1909.[24]

The Northern Territories remained under quasi-military administration until 1920. Revenue was pitiably small and the cost of military occupation high. The imperial grant-in-aid was reducing and due to end in 1907, and military administration in the region, in the view of Governor Rodger, had 'proved a failure'; punitive expeditions raided recalcitrant people but then retired, rarely attempting a settlement.[25] In mid-1906 the Chief Commissioner proposed a civil administration and the replacement of the Gold Coast Regiment by a semi-military 'Gold Coast Frontier Police'. The outcome was the disbandment of the 2nd battalion GCR and its recreation as the Northern Territories Constabulary. 'Pacification' was now to be by a policy of gradualism, by an armed presence rather than by punitive expeditions. The final major military action, by the NTC against Frafra resistance in the Tong Hills, occurred in March 1911. Shortly after Sir Hugh Clifford arrived in the Gold Coast as the new Governor in 1913 he confidently informed London that 'throughout the length and breadth of the Gold Coast Colony and its Dependencies, there is no section of the population which it is desirable to disarm, or which can be described as under suspicion'.[26] His assessment was largely correct. The Gold Coast was 'pacified' and policing had become mainly a civilian-directed activity, although most branches of the police remained organised and equipped for military-policing roles.

Recruiting for the constabulary and the police

Although relatively small forces, the constabulary and the Fante civil police had the constant problem of recruiting the right kind of men in sufficient numbers. Throughout the late nineteenth century both forces were below establishment, with numbers regularly reduced by desertion and dismissal for indiscipline. Reliance on the supposed martial qualities of Hausas meant that the paramilitary constabulary was a mercenary force, recruited initially from the Niger region and finally from the northern periphery of the Gold Coast and also from neighbouring French territories. In using reliable aliens and strangers as policemen and soldiers the Gold Coast authorities followed policies already well established in Ireland and throughout the colonial empire.

Among the earliest recruits were runaway slaves; the armed constabulary in particular continued to enlist such men until the first decade of the twentieth century. In 1858 Benjamin Pine said that the Gold Coast Corps was unfitted to police the country as it was:

> composed of the off-scourings of the country; men who have plundered their masters or committed other atrocities ... slaves, generally bad characters ... sent back to them [their masters] with red coats on their backs, to enforce the orders of Government; which they, of course, do with all the insolence natural to their sudden change of fortune.[27]

Glover recruited runaway slaves for his Hausa force in Lagos, a practice he continued in Accra in 1873, buying slaves at £5 a head, until told to

cease by a disapproving Colonial Office worried at the likely consequences of the practice becoming public knowledge in Britain.[28] When
the Hausa Armed Police became the Gold Coast Constabulary in 1879
the majority of the 800 rank and file were former slaves.

Carnarvon, the Secretary of State, in May 1877 argued that the constabulary was vital for the defence and policing of the Gold Coast: 'the
efficiency and strength of this force is in my opinion the most important
consideration on the Gold Coast – everything else, however important,
is really secondary, and I grudge expense here less than in any other
detachment'.[29] For the next two decades, and as revenue permitted,
regular recruiting expeditions sought Hausas from several directions:
Lagos, its hinterland and the middle Niger valley were the obvious and
first favoured areas; less success was had in recruiting from the Hausa
zongos (settlements) on the Gold Coast; finally economy, politics and
results confined recruiting to the northern interior of the Gold Coast,
the region that was to become the Northern Territories. In official eyes
the ideal recruit was non-literate and preferably a Muslim. This ethnic
and geographical pattern of recruiting to the constabulary in the nineteenth century established the shape of future recruiting for the military
in the Gold Coast throughout the rest of the colonial period.

The first attempt to augment the Hausa force was in mid-1877. An
expedition to Lagos sought a hundred recruits but gained only thirty-six.
A further expedition in 1879, to Nupe, on the northern shore of the
Niger, with plans to secure 260 Hausas, brought back seventy-eight.[30]
Attempts were then made to recruit in the northern hinterland of the
Gold Coast, in the region of Salaga, which was expected to be a cheaper
source. Three recruiting expeditions, mounted in 1880, 1881–82 and
1887, proved less successful than expected. Few of the recruits were
genuine volunteers, most being escaped or manumitted slaves, many
of whom deserted on the long trek south. And there was widespread
suspicion in Salaga, and elsewhere in the north, that the recruiters were
slave raiding parties.[31] The poor results of these recruitment campaigns
left the Hausa force well below establishment, and so in 1889 the authorities made a further attempt to enlist men on the Niger.[32] But here even
economic inducements failed to secure many recruits and a further
expedition to Lagos, Ijeba-Ode and Ibadan in mid-1896 was only slightly
more successful.[33] Thereafter all efforts to secure recruits for the constabulary were confined to the Gold Coast.

In autumn 1896 the British were intent on keeping the French out of
the hinterland of the Gold Coast. The military occupation of Asante and
the Northern Territories, and the confrontation with the French throughout West Africa, made increased recruitment imperative. The British
were prepared to recruit from almost any source, including freebooters

[117]

from Zabirima raiding bands and soldiers (*sofa*) left over from Samori's depredations in the far north. As a result the constabulary, and its successors the GCR and NTC, included a number of ex-bandits in the ranks, some of whom continued their activities in uniform.[34] Few Fantes or coastal men entered the armed constabulary, except as clerks, and Asantes were regarded as unreliable and specifically excluded from any of the armed or paramilitary forces maintained by the colonial state until the manpower crisis of the first world war.

Recruits to the civil police came from a variety of sources, though principally from the coastal Fante, and included men from Sierra Leone, southern Nigeria and Liberia. Few officials thought highly of the Fante as policemen, armed or otherwise:

> I am unprepared to recommend the recruitment of any armed force from the Fanti Natives; as although noisy and turbulent they are not of a military temperament, and not in any manner to be trusted in an emergency involving the immediate interests of their own countrymen,

wrote Ussher in 1871. Time did not substantially change this negative opinion; according to Governor Griffith, the civil police were drawn from a variety of tribes and 'were suspicious of each other [so] that each man of one tribe acts as a watch upon a man of another tribe'.[35] Official neglect encouraged corruption, and the consistently high level of dismissals from the force indicate that it failed to secure the right kinds of recruits. Policing a community or the streets of a town required different skills and standards from those needed for the armed constabulary. As mercenaries the Hausa force had to be subject to strict military discipline and constant 'close supervision' by European officers. The possession of arms, Hausa as a *lingua franca*, a common origin as aliens, concentration in barracks, and Islam, all combined to give the Hausa Constabulary a strong sense of cohesion and *esprit de corps*. The Fante civil police possessed neither institutional virtue.

Yet, in theory, much more was expected of the Fante civil police. The language of command was English, although Twi was essential, especially in the six months that it took to train a third-class policeman; in 1898 the Governor deplored the absence of any European police officer who spoke the language.[36] Policemen literate in English and Twi were vital if the force was to develop the capacity to detect and repress crime, although this was unlikely while the police school for recruits ('not an ambitious school', according to the Governor in 1903) provided recruits with only 130 hours of training in English, reading, writing *and* police duties. And policemen, unlike soldiers, were expected to understand, interpret and administer the law, and to exercise personal judgement about people and situations. Kitson, the Commissioner, argued in 1904:

as a rule a good Policeman makes a bad soldier, and a good soldier is not necessarily a good Policeman. A Policeman has to act and act quickly on his own responsibility, a good soldier is a machine who only acts on instructions from a superior officer.[37]

These are qualities that very few civil policemen possessed, as was evident from their poor conduct of normal police duties, and highlighted in court proceedings, where they had to give evidence; here policemen were on their own and, in the words of one official, liable to be 'bamboozled by the native lawyers'.

The official expectation was that very gradually – and a time scale was rarely suggested – the civil police would evolve into an efficient force able to maintain law and order with a minimum of force while serving the interests of the community. The model in mind was that of an English county force: blue-coated black 'bobbies' on the beat equipped only with batons, members of a force possessing a strong sense of pride and purpose.[38] But this was an unlikely eventuality while the civil police were composed mainly of non-literates, remained small in numbers (244 in 1877, 342 in early 1888 and only 357 general police in 1913) and had to rely upon the support of the armed Hausas for regular patrol duties, for example during the spate of night burglaries in Accra in 1879–80. Loose official control, relatively low levels of pay, and public hostility towards the civil police, resulted in high rates of dismissal for indiscipline, large numbers of desertions and the refusal of time-served policemen to re-enlist.[39] Such a constant turnover in policemen made for an unstable, demoralised and unreliable force.

Civil police work was extremely unpopular and admitted as such by the colonial authorities. All too often a uniform seemed a licence to loot and extort, and as a result both the Hausa Constabulary and the Fante police were despised and hated by those they affected to police. Pre-eminently they were hated as unaccountable representatives of an alien colonial power imposing a range of new laws and measures of social control which lacked any semblance of popular consent. Hausa constables might be indifferent to public hostility; civil policemen, living within the community, were much more exposed to popular animus and also to family and communal pressures to pervert the law. The business of day-to-day policing, serving summonses, dealing with public nuisances (for example, people defecating on the beaches), petty theft, common assault, and the like, intruded into people's lives. Policemen had few friends, and their work was seen as 'dishonourable'. Chiefs, traders and common people all had reason to dislike them. In Accra in 1886 a large part of the population stoned the civil police: 'every man's hand is against a policeman who is looked upon as a traitor to his race', wrote the Colonial Secretary in 1895, and 'the Gold Coast native would rather do anything than to become a Policeman', stated the annual police department report for 1906. Similar reports by officials, and by those who experienced or observed the police in action, are numerous and frequent throughout the whole colonial period in the Gold Coast.[40]

So why did men join the civil police? It was clearly difficult to attract the right kind of men, and the authorities often took whoever they could get. For unskilled men the pay, at 1s a day, offered one of the few opportunities for wage labour; additional payment in kind, and a uniform, undoubtedly provided further incentives. Details of deserters, posted in the official *Gazette*, indicate that recruits to the civil police were mainly peasant farmers and often well under the stipulated height of 5ft 6in. The high and steady levels of desertion also show that men were not prepared to surrender their freedom of mobility and labour for contracts of up to five years. When other wage labour became available with the rapid expansion of the cocoa and mining industries at the beginning of the twentieth century, recruiting for the police became more difficult and desertions increased. A more professional and modern force suited to the changing needs of the expanding economy of the Gold Coast was unlikely as long as most policemen continued to come from the 'illiterate peasant class'.[41]

The changing structure of policing

The work of policing the Gold Coast hardly changed in form or function until well into the 1920s and 1930s. Although the number of police was increased by the creation of specialist branches − Escort, Mines and Railway Police − the overall number engaged in civil or general policing duties stayed roughly the same. The general police (as they came to be called) numbered 352 in 1919, a figure lower than for either 1910 or 1913. There may have been more policeman after the first world war (1,050 in 1919, against 901 in 1913) but with the increase in population, and also in recorded crime, the Gold Coast was probably less well policed than a decade earlier. In 1919 many areas were not policed at all, even in the coastal provinces, a picture that was little different from, say, 1905. And with the extension of the policy of indirect rule through the 1920s and 1930s, and this not exclusively in rural areas, the function of policing was passed to traditional authorities. The overall effect was a change in the organisation of the police but with little effect on the extent or nature of actual policing.

Large areas of the Gold Coast could still be defined as 'frontier' well into the twentieth century. Unlike the frontiers of settlement in Canada, Australia and parts of South Africa, where generally policing was with the consent of the community, the Gold Coast and the other colonies in West Africa had frontiers of administration with a mobile paramilitary police presence. Military discipline and armaments, especially artillery, and machine guns, introduced in 1888, were seen as essential to repress and intimidate a truculent and unreliable population. Even the civil police, created as an unarmed force, were rearmed by Governor Hodgson in 1897 following the withdrawal of the constabulary for service in Asante and the Northern Territories and serious riots in Saltpond and Accra. The police, Hodgson argued, must 'be able if necessary to charge with fixed bayonets'.[42] Only gradually in the twentieth century did the general police relinquish carrying firearms; the Escort and other branches continued as armed bodies.

The creation of a genuine civil police force composed of men with the office of constable in the English sense, able to determine points of law laid down in the Criminal Code of 1892 and juggle with ideas about the admissibility or otherwise of evidence, was far distant in the Gold Coast. Civil policing in the West African colonies implied direct control by the civil authorities, a force under police officers rather than military men, possibly carrying arms but not functioning as an armed body. Notionally, and to some extent in practice, civil police replaced the military once an area had become 'settled'. This was a slow process and also one that could be reversed. In 1907 the GCR battalion stationed in the Northern Territories was disbanded and reformed into the paramilitary NTC, but it was not until 1929 that a transition to civil policing occurred. The extension of territory and the rapid economic and social changes at the turn of the century left the colonial authorities uncertain as to the kind of policing required for the Gold Coast. Civil-style policing continued in the coastal towns, with the new cocoa trade adding responsibility for weights and measures and the licensing of motor vehicles. Some attempts was made to detect crime, and small detective branches, staffed by literate policemen, were established at Accra, Sekondi and Cape Coast by 1904.[43] Elsewhere there was a reversal to a frontier style of policing with the creation of separate Railway, Mines (in 1901) and Escort Police (in 1902) mainly composed of ex-soldiers.

These new branches – 'khaki police' as they were called – represented a great change in the structure of policing. As the value of gold and cocoa exports increased, so also did government revenue from taxation and the state-owned railway. This new and expanding capitalist infrastructure of mining, cash crops and transport, much of it in the form of movable property, needed regulating and protecting. A rapidly growing, and ethnically varied, migrant labour force in the gold-mining towns of Tarkwa and Obuasi (some 17,000 in 1902) led to a rise in crime. Mine closures and reductions in wages in the years 1900–06 resulted in increased labour militancy and official fears of serious civil disorder.

To help combat this, separate Mines and Railway police were established in 1901. The Mines Police, hired out to the mining companies, had been created 'specially and solely for the purpose of preserving law and order in different mining centres'. Local detachments of military volunteers, armed with rifles and machine guns, were also established from European employees on the railway and mines. During the years 1902–06 the mining companies frequently used the Mines Police to break strikes and to regulate labour disputes.[44]

The Escort Police had an initial strength of fifty men, all ex-soldiers from the Northern Territories. The force was created to guard specie, particularly for the mines and banks, to escort officials, accompany carrier caravans of the newly formed Government Transport Service, supervise convict labour and provide an additional armed force for the business of civil administration. As the military were withdrawn from policing Asante their place was taken by the Escort Police. By 1914, under Sir Hugh Clifford's plans for the reorganisation and expansion of the police, the Escort Police had become the largest branch of the police with 463 men.[45] Wherever the Escort Police operated it was hated as an alien force, but especially in Asante, where policemen from the Northern Territories were regarded as *odonko* – the slave class. The creation, and the often predatory activities, of the 'khaki police' branches marked a step back from real civil policing.

Policing in the Gold Coast by 1913 was largely a paramilitary activity. Although the civil police had been created as a separate body in 1894, and a detective branch had been added after 1897, the force was relatively small, its role confined largely to the coastal towns. The civil police had been rearmed and the recently established Escort Police, although under civil control, were in effect another paramilitary force. So also was the Northern Territories Constabulary. And in permanent reserve stood the Gold Coast Regiment, although it was but rarely used to aid the civil power after 1913. Paramilitary policing had for sixty years been, and continued to be, the crude but effective means of political control and social regulation throughout the Gold Coast. Paramilitary methods and practices, once established, were difficult to relinquish. To a certain extent the extending frontiers of the Gold Coast, and the tenuous nature of colonial authority, required that military policing in one form or another should continue to predominate.

By 1913 most branches of the police were alien occupying forces (little short of being 'Hausarised', according to the governor) regarded with hatred, fear or suspicion by all sections of the population. Despite increased government expenditure on the police the colony had advanced little towards effective civil policing.[46] Ironically, remilitarisation of the police occurred at a time when the Gold Coast was becoming more peaceful and there were fewer threats to the colonial presence. Official rhetoric in favour of unarmed policing remained at variance with the realities of Gold Coast politics and economics. Policing throughout the colonial period was imposed on the people and never enjoyed their consent. Without such consent it was inevitable that the police remained armed, or with ready and rapid resort to arms, and that any evolution to genuine civil policing and the professionalism that would accompany it would be slow. Colonial policing in the Gold Coast had little to do with serving the community and everything to do with upholding the authority of the colonial state.

Notes

1 The police in the Gold Coast have been neglected by historians. W. H. Gillespie, *The Gold Coast Police, 1844–1938* (Accra, 1955), is a semi-official history; see also S. K. Ankama, 'The Police and the Maintenance of Law and Order in Ghana', Ph.D. thesis, University of London (1967). On the Gold Coast Constabulary and its successor, the Gold Coast Regiment, see David Killingray, 'The Colonial Army in the Gold Coast: official policy and local response, 1890–1947', Ph.D. thesis, University of London (1982).

2 Stanley to Lilley, 7 October 1845, Public Record Office, Kew [PRO], WO 1/497.

3 Sir Benjamin Pine to Labouchere, 31 August 1857, PRO, CO 96/41/9322; and 10 February 1858, CO 96/43/3698.

4 R. Pine to Cardwell, 4 February 1865, CO 96/67/2305; E. Conran to Cardwell, 25 October 1865, CO 96/68/12038. The Digest of Rules for the Police Force are printed in S. K. Ankama, *Police History – some aspects in England and Ghana* (Ilford, 1983), pp. 44–8.

5 W. H. Simpson to Sir A. E. Kennedy, 8 July 1869, CO 96/81/85.

6 A. E. Kennedy to Kimberley, 25 July 1870, CO 96/85/8925; Kennedy to Kimberley, 17 February 1871, CO 96/87/2478; Hennessy to Kimberley, 31 May 1872, and enclosure by Col. Foster, dd. Elmina, 27 May 1872, CO 96/93/6426.

7 G. C. Strahan to Lord Carnarvon, 22 June 1875, enclosing 'Scheme for Reorganization of Constabulary Forces drawn up by Capt. Alfred Molony', CO 96/115/8274.

8 S. Freeling to Lord Carnarvon, 31 January 1878, CO 96/123/21.

9 W. B. Griffith to Lord Ripon, 3 December 1892, CO 96/227/151; F. M. Hodgson to Lord Ripon, 9 February 1894, CO 96/243/4355; W. B. Griffith to Lord Ripon, 15 February 1895, CO 96/255/4611; W. B. Griffith to Lord Knutsford, 'Police Mutiny at Winneba – Fanti Police', 30 November 1888, CO 96/195/25321.

10 British jurisdiction over the Gold Coast was defined by an order-in-council and the proclamation of 1874 to embrace the coastal forts and settlements (the colony) and the states within the British sphere of influence (the protectorate). For a brief introduction see Adu Boahen, *Ghana: evolution and change in the nineteenth and twentieth centuries* (London, 1975); and further David Kimble, *A Political History of Ghana, 1850–1928* (Oxford, 1963).

11 The final article of the Declaration of the Fante Chiefs – the 'Bond' – stated the purpose of 'moulding the customs of the country to the general principles of British law'. In the judicial system that developed, according to James Stephen, 'an English officer, in an adjacent, barbarous country (of which the Queen is not the sovereign) presides in courts held by the natives, and administers to them a kind of law made up of native customs and English forms and maxims'. Colonial Office [CO] minute by Sir James Stephen, 28 January 1846, CO 96/7/245. See further Carnarvon to Strachan, 20 August 1874, where Carnarvon refers to the 'peculiar jurisdiction' exercised by Britain over the Gold Coast; printed in G. E. Metcalfe, *Great Britain and Ghana: documents of Ghana history, 1807–1957* (London, 1964, pp. 369–712).

12 Regular and slightly more reliable criminal statistics date from 1895, but for the period under discussion they are more an indication of the development of police activity than an index of crime.

13 C. A. Molony to Lord Kimberley, 'Legal Work performed by DC', 24 July 1882, CO 96/141/15046.

14 S. Freeling to Lord Carnarvon, 13 April 1877, CO 96/121/94; H. T. Ussher to Hicks Beech, 25 March 1880, CO 96/130/6514; W. B. Griffith to Lord Knutsford, 31 July 1888, CO 96/192/17474.

15 For the often bloody faction fights see H. T. Ussher to Hicks Beech, 'Riot at Cape Coast', 8 November 1877, CO 96/128/19683; Sir S. Rowe, to Lord Kimberley, 'Riot at Mumford', 2 February 1882, CO 96/137/3803; W. B. Griffith to Lord Granville, 'Criminal Statistics 1885', 19 June 1886, CO 96/174/13001.

16 H. T. Ussher to Hicks Beech, 19 November 1879, and Colonial Office minuted by Hicks Beech, 10 December 1857, CO 96/128/19603.

17 Francis Agbodeka, *African Politics and British Policy in the Gold Coast, 1868–1900: a study in the forms and force of protest* (London, 1971), chapter 3.

18 W. B. Griffith to Lord Knutsford, 'Smuggling', 9 April 1888, CO 96/191/112. Very little has been written on the Preventive Service; see R. K. Gibbons, 'The Preventive Service in the Gold Coast', *Elder's Review of West African Affairs*, VIII, 32 (1930); also the annual *Reports of the Gold Coast Customs Department*.

19 S. Freeling to Lord Carnarvon, 'Our position on the Coast and Relations with Kings and Chiefs of the Protectorate', 13 March 1877, CO 96/120/4245.

20 Sir S. Rowe to Lord Kimberley, 6 March 1882, CO 96/138/6110.

21 S. Freeling to Lord Carnarvon, 13 September 1877, to which Carnarvon minuted: '... as regards the increase of the force I have long thought that it wd be very desirable. It is the key to our successful govt. of the West Coast and the point on which more than any other our attention sd be fixed', CO 96/122/12610.

22 Douglas to Colonial Secretary, 14 January 1887, enclosed with Griffith to Stanhope, 28 January 1887, CO 96/179/4152.

23 F. E. Fell, DC, Western Ashanti, letter to his mother, 12 July 1905, Rhodes House Library, Oxford, Mss. Brit. Emp. S311.

24 Colonial Reports – Annual: *Ashanti 1910*, p. 10.

25 Sir J. P. Rodger to Lyttelton, 26 June 1904, CO 96/418/25605.

26 Clifford to Harcourt, Conf., 25 August 1913, CO 96/534/32098.

27 Sir B. Pine to Labouchere, 10 February 1858, CO 96/43/3698; also Sir H. Holland, memo to W. Gladstone, 13 November 1873, CO 96/103/13327. Raymond Dumett and Marion Johnson, 'Britain and the suppression of slavery in the Gold Coast Colony, Ashanti and the Northern Territories', in Suzanne Miers and Richard Roberts (eds.), *The End of Slavery in Africa* (Madison, 1988), p. 93.

28 *Parl. Papers, Further Correspondence respecting the Ashantee Invasion*, No. 4 (1874), No. 20, Wolsley to Kimberley, 13 November 1873, enclosed with Glover to Wolseley, 6 November 1873. Glover to Sartorius, 28 October 1873, Royal Commonwealth Society Library, London, Glover Papers and Letter Book.

29 Colonial Office minute by Carnarvon, 26 May 1877 on S. Freeling to Lord Carnarvon, 13 March 1877, CO 96/120/4245.

30 S. Freeling to Lord Carnarvon, 30 June 1877, CO 96/121/9362; C. C. Lees to Hicks Beech, 5 February 1879, CO 96/126/3905; H. T. Ussher to Hicks Beech, 1 August 1879, CO 96/127/14114; H. T. Ussher to Hicks Beech, 29 November 1879, CO 96/128/4.

31 H. T. Ussher to Hicks Beech, 3 February 1880, CO 96/130/3347; H. T. Ussher to Lord Kimberley, 31 May 1880, CO 96/131/10055; W. B. Griffith to Holland, 11 April 1887, CO 96/180/9902.

32 W. B. Griffith to Lord Knutsford, 9 July 1889, CO 96/203/14735.

33 W. E. Maxwell to Sir J. Chamberlain, 21 March 1896, CO 96/271/14783; W. E. Maxwell to Sir J. Chamberlain, 18 January 1897, CO 96/288/3429.

34 W. E. Maxwell to Sir J. Chamberlain, 8 April 1897, CO 96/291/9469. Rodger to Lyttelton, Conf., 31 March 1905, enclosed with report of Inspector General on 2 Batt. GCR, CO 445/19/13706.

35 W. B. Griffith to Lord Ripon, 3 December 1892, CO 96/227/151.

36 F. M. Hodgson to Sir J. Chamberlain, 26 September 1898, CO 96/321/23803.

37 A. W. Kitson to Colonial Secretary, 22 March 1904, enclosed in Sir J. P. Rodger to Lyttleton, 6 April 1904, CO 96/417/14783.

38 See the Colonial Office minutes of January 1893 on the 'Separation and Reorganization of the Civil Police', CO 96/227/151.

39 E.g. F. M. Hodgson to Sir J. Chamberlain, 20 May 1898, reported that of 355 police seventy to seventy-five left each year, CO 96/315/13224. The Police Department Report, 1901, gave strength at 534 (establishment 611); of 291 men recruited in 1901 a quarter (seventy-two) were dismissed and eighty deserted. The Chief Commissioner reported: 'The recruits come in absolutely without any idea of civilization or discipline. ... After their day's duty is performed they return to their quarters in the town, and except when on parade or other duty they lapse back into their original savagery, and forget what little they have learned.' There was a 'shocking years record' for 1903; from a strength of 589 there were fifty-nine desertions, 113 resignations and 118 dismissals. Sir J. P. Rodger to Lyttelton, 6 April 1904, CO 96/417/14783.

40 E.g. Acting Inspector General to Colonial Secretary, 14 December 1882, CO 96/174/12993 of 1885; Griffith to Stanhope, September 1886, CO 96/179/2914; H. Bryan to Lyttelton, 7 October 1905, CO 96/432/38227. Complaints about the brutal and predatory behaviour of the Hausa Constabulary and the GCR were legion.

41 Colonial Reports – Annual: *Police Report 1910*, p. 12.

42 F. M. Hodgson to Sir J. Chamberlain, 20 May 1898, CO 96/315/13224.

43 Colonial Reports – Annual: *Police Report 1904*, p. 11.

44 Jeff Crisp, *The Story of an African Working Class: Ghanaian miners' struggles, 1870–1980* (London, 1984), pp. 25, 30–2.

45 Sir H. Clifford to Secretary of State, 19 June 1913, CO 96/532/23057. The figures for the police under the reorganisation schemes of 1913 and 1919 were:

	1910	1913	1914	1919
General	477	482	357	352
Escort	147	238	463	578
Railway	49	64	81	95
Mines	60	60	60	
Marine				9
Total	733	844	961	1,050

46 In 1908–13 expenditure on the police increased 63 per cent, from £29,937 to £42,245; under the expansion plan of 1913 it rose to nearly £50,000. Sir H. Clifford to Secretary of State, 13 June 1913, and Colonial Office minutes, CO 96/532/23057.

CHAPTER EIGHT

The ordering of rural India: the policing of nineteenth-century Bengal and Bihar

Peter Robb

For nineteenth-century India, it is difficult to distinguish, among the policies and instruments for maintaining order, a separate category concerned with the use of civil force. In the twentieth century, however, policing and the police may be regarded as belonging more or less to a single discrete sector of government. Several processes had to be completed before this could be so. There was an expansion of the functions and goals of the state, built upon a formalising of the concepts, power and procedures which identified public concern as against private interests. This included a shift of emphasis from the need mainly to defend the person and property of the rulers towards the attempt to manage conduct in society as a whole; it implied an ideal that rights should exist independently of might. In particular, crimes were defined as offences against a common weal. Police forces were created as public, professional bodies, to be substituted for private force; they were pictured as servants rather than masters. Thus policing was clearly distinguished from other executive tasks of government, including law-making and the administration of justice. The police developed institutionally, and they developed a sense of their own knowledge and expertise. Some important questions in regard to the police in India therefore concern the timing, extent and causes of their 'professionalisation'.

A second set of issues relates to the purposes of the police and their role in society. Institutional development and expertise do not prevent the police from representing in practice special interests in addition to their own. Just as the law is claimed to be an objective and impartial force but is a moral or political instrument, so too supposedly objective policing may be intended to discipline the work force, to encourage civil behaviour and personal rectitude, or to protect the interests of elites against masses. Clearly the Indian force was shaped both by its imported design and by the nature of the government it served – for example, by elements of indirect rule.[1] But how far did it serve imperial purposes,

[126]

and thus become identified with foreign oppression, while also being inhibited by the fear of confronting a society united against it? The main aim of this chapter is to define the role of the police in north-eastern India, and thus to account for the pace and manner of its development.

In the Lower Provinces of Bengal (most of present-day Bangladesh, West Bengal, Bihar and Orissa) the situation of the police and especially their local agency was somewhat different from that in other parts of India. The British supposed that a policing system based upon watchmen had existed in every village and market under the control of local revenue collectors or landlords (the *zamindars*); payment was through allowances to the *zamindars* and fees or land grants to the watchmen. These arrangements were abolished in 1793 and replaced by a *daroga* system, in which policing was mainly handed to direct employees of the government. Initially it was intended that the *darogas* should be paid through local contributions, but a separate police tax proved too difficult to collect and was dropped in 1797. Village watchmen continued to be employed privately, and a duty was placed upon *zamindars* and other village officials to report to the authorities on crimes and other matters, though many of the old allowances and revenue-free land grants were disallowed over the ensuing years; it was repeatedly argued that no policing could ignore the local dimension, and indeed *zamindari* police were permitted again after 1805.

Each *daroga* was responsible for an area averaging about twenty miles square (a *thana* or police circle) and an establishment of between twenty and fifty men; he himself served under the general control of the local magistrate, who was responsible for revenue and other administration and the majority of trials as well as for the management of the police. There were about 500 *darogas* in the Lower Provinces: 463 of them in Bengal and Bihar proper in 1853, by which time various reforms and modifications had been introduced, including the appointment of a Superintendent of Police in 1808 and the promulgation of a general police regulation in 1817. A consolidated manual of all circular orders relating to the police was prepared in 1854. At the same time (in 1853) the office of Bengal Superintendent of Police was abolished, and the supervising and reporting duties entrusted to Commissioners of Circuit, except for the work carried out by the Commissioner for the Suppression of Dacoity (robbery by armed gangs), established in 1852, and his few hundred paid informers.

The condition of the largest and most closely administered force in the region, in Calcutta, gives some insight into the problems which were faced well into the second half of the nineteenth century. In the 1860s few had hopes of promotion (there were 156 Indian officers to 2,715 constables) and low pay led to rapid turnover of personnel, with about half the force either resigning or being discharged each year. In addition, at any one time (it was reported in 1860) one-third of the men were unfit, a figure repeated at later periods also. The pattern of employment persisted even though there were few local men in the service – in the 1860s about two-thirds were up-country Hindus, and the Muslim remainder came largely from one district, Faridpur; again, in 1883 in the town police, 57 per cent of the officers and 93 per cent of the men were designated as 'upcountry' in origin, that is they were non-Bengali (particularly Bihari), while fifteen out of forty-five new recruits came from Faridpur. Over time problems remained with recruitment. In 1884 the local government reported that it was difficult to recruit Bengalis: few applied, and many of those were rejected on medical grounds. Sturdy men able to perform manual labour were discouraged by the low pay; on the other hand illiterate recruits were apparently preferred, because more 'dependable', up to and including the rank of head constable. To an extent this reflected stereotyping by the British, who tended to regard the Bengalis as physically inferior to and, because intellectually inclined, less reliable than some other Indian 'races', a factor which also influenced their expectations of the level of policing needed in Bengal.

The facts of police recruitment and retention created problems for training – much was left to (literally) 'native' wit – and for management. In 1861 the superintendent reported that police conduct was 'on the whole' satisfactory in Calcutta, and yet that year, out of a complement of 106 Europeans and 2,993 Indians, one European and twenty-two Indians had been convicted of crimes (0·7 per cent), fifteen Europeans and 104 Indians were dismissed (3·8 per cent), while 3,394 fines were imposed for neglect of duty (including forty-one upon Europeans). Similar figures for 1883 over the whole province suggest that this problem too persisted, though, perhaps significantly, at this time very much higher proportions of the police were convicted by the courts (3·3 per cent) and a much smaller proportion dismissed without judicial intervention (0·3 per cent).

In practice the policing was both socially intrusive and relatively light; that is, the definitions of crime were affected by the attitudes of the day, measures being taken, for example, against Sunday processions or undesirable 'superstitions', but the number of recorded crimes and of convictions was low. Assuming a population of 60 million in the 1820s (probably an underestimate), the annual incidence of executions actually carried out was about one per million, in comparison with one in 200,000 in England and Wales; the discrepancy was far greater in capital *sentences* (one in 10,500 in England and Wales), such sentences being carried out relatively infrequently in Britain but almost invariably in Bengal. Transportation and imprisonment, by the same calculations, affected one in 1,327 in England and Wales and one in 2,225 in the Lower Provinces, remaining in the latter case below 30,000 per annum in number. However, a steady increase was shown in such statistics. Over the nine years from 1843 to 1851, for example, the number of reported homicides in the Lower Provinces increased from 459 to 562 per annum, the total number of convictions from well under 40,000 to well over 50,000, while the acquittal rate declined from as much as 87 per cent of convictions to 60 or 65 per cent or less. These trends started from levels significantly above those of the corresponding nine-year period ending in 1826, in regard both to reported crime (including homicide) and to convictions. By the 1880s the number of offences had reached beyond 100,000, and the regular police force in the Lower Provinces totalled over 22,000 men, approximately one for every 3,000 people.

The functions of the British police establishment in the first half of the nineteenth century were designed more to maintain order and to impress the population than to investigate crime. The police inspector, as George Campbell remarked in 1852, affected a 'judicial [rather] than a thief-catching character'; typically obese, clad in fine linen, carried about in a palanquin, he reacted to serious crime by writing a report and then proceeding to the scene and holding court. Thus the British proclaimed the theory of the state's responsibility for many transgressions against person and property, but their practice in Bengal was rather to give a show when necessary as a marker of the importance and supremacy of the state; its interests, of course, especially in regard to revenue payment, were pursued rigorously. The borderline between these concerns was thin, however; the real difference was one of method, and hence the special effort against dacoity from the 1850s marked in some respects the beginning of the modern policing of crime; when the department was abolished in 1863 its officers formed the nucleus of a detective service the regular police, emerging as the Special Branch of the CID in 1887, a body which, however, became fully recognised and able to develop only after 1905. Another step in the direction of 'modern' policing was marked by the establishment of a separate Police Department, under an Inspector General, as recommended by a commission set up in 1860; further organisational reforms for Bengal were suggested by another committee of inquiry under John Beames, in 1891, which was promptly followed by a committee for implementation under Henry Cotton. These investigations revealed that, in comparison with the rest of India, where serious complaints were also heard against the police, Bengal employed many fewer men. Moreover, as a rule, the qualifications of the policemen were as low as their pay and prospects. The maintenance of an effective village agency had also remained elusive, despite a Chaukidari Act of 1856 and other measures in a long-drawn-out attempt to bring the local watchmen under official control.[2]

If we place this developing police force in a broader context of imperial purposes in India, it will be seen that it long remained a largely symbolic representation of power and order, playing its part alongside other such instruments rather than being a force for the detection and reduction of crime. Its evolution reflected these purposes. Hence we begin from a more general appreciation of the problem of 'ordering' a predominantly rural India, to identify the place occupied by the police in the policies of the state, and the extent to which policing was not merely a matter for the police. These questions in turn revolve around British goals and perspectives. State controls to protect the public were in concept and practice almost inextricable from coercion to preserve colonial rule. Collecting the land revenue, by force if necessary, or facilitating peaceful communications, or preventing the operations of marauding groups, and so on; each was arguably both a public good and a colonial necessity. And this link derived partly from the view taken by the British of Indian society and the objectives of their rule. Similar factors contributed, moreover, to delay and imperfection in the development of the Indian police.

Strategies of control

In north-eastern India the British adopted three different, even successive strategies of control during the nineteenth century. First they proposed a minimal government, using the force of armed power and legal regulation but working through Indian intermediaries. Secondly they attempted to intervene, chiefly through bureaucracy and by facilitating markets, to create a more prosperous and 'civilised' India, which would thus be welded to the colonial connection by self-interest and 'modern' institutions. Thirdly, they returned ostensibly to policies of social protection, depending particularly on the loyalty of rural elites and the cohesion of 'traditional' communities. At the same time several more continuous processes can be observed, which may be summed up as the widening of state functions, the generalising of law and institutions, and the separation of government into specialist, 'expert' departments. The British co-opted and remodelled indigenous authorities such as Hindu and Islamic law or local elites: they then extended the public domain while dividing the state machinery. But policing, defined as the imposition of order by coercion on behalf of the state, occurred in diverse public and private forms.

Innovations flowed, in particular, from the expectations of undivided sovereignty and of unitary or universalist law which the British government entertained and aroused. The impact of these tendencies was to be found in the strong pressure exerted by the state in favour of settled populations, and its fear, translated from Europe but reinforced in India, of migrants and vagrants. Over India as a whole, the law of property and measures encouraging the subservience of agricultural producers were thus reinforced by warfare against displaced or predatory forces (notably Gurkhas, Rohillas, Pindaris, Wahhabis and Pathans) and by semi-military campaigns against the 'hereditary criminals' subsumed under the term *thagi*. In eastern India too there were continual battles with marginal groups, the most famous of the nineteenth century being with the Santals.[3] Thus the state sought to define crime and moral behaviour. In the long run the ordering of rural society was as much a process of definition through administration, censuses and ethnographic study as of coercion through subordination to state power.

The character and methods of civil control in India remained complex throughout the nineteenth century. They involved much more than the police, while the police were involved with more than the maintenance of law and order. The business of controlling India began with Indian collaborators. Because the British insisted upon discrete categories and social stereotypes in interpreting India, they were led to a selective reinforcement of hierarchies. Allies were supported partly for what they could provide by way of social control. Moreover, because the surrogate forces were assumed to arise out of 'natural', social authority, any credence given to other voices in society was interpreted in the administration as weakness or folly. At times even aspects of British power, such as the police, were subject to the same critique. On the other hand the support for collaborators was qualified by the need to maintain British supremacy and by the evolution of British practice and ideas. The regulation of social and economic relations was increasingly thought of as a prerequisite of public order. This was not merely an attempt to enlist a wider range of the population by ties of interest; rather (as will be argued) it changed the nature of the state.

In second place in the imposition of order were the government institutions. The Indian bureaucracy was supremely a system of control as well as effectuation. Information flowed in and business was disposed of according to established routines within each office. Each separate function was allocated to a particular official, and tasks left written trails which could be traced by the supervisors. Standardised reports and returns recorded the conduct of business at lower levels and matters of routine, in marked contrast with the exchanges of extensive minutes and papers which contributed to decision-making at the top. If the Indian empire rested on paper, it did so by bulk in its upper reaches, and through duplication at its base.[4] For the Indians involved in the system there

[131]

were naturally rewards, including those supportive of social status. At all levels the patronage of government was used positively to attract support, but a far looser hold was kept over the wider activities of government, or society at large, than over the officials. The reason was partly that British rulers held their own administration first and dearest in their attention; the Raj was in that sense designed for its employees. On the other hand, a European officer might or might not be at the mercy of his *sheristadar* or head clerk. But certainly the clerk himself was a great man in the district, helping to determine among other things what requests or information would be entertained by the government. This too was an element in the maintenance of control. At all levels the petty functionaries of the state helped to define the exercise of power and to keep order in society. The police were merely one among many such agents, and for most of the British period far less important than executive officers, such as the land revenue staff. In short, the Indian bureaucracy provided a framework of control, over and above its administrative functions, partly because officials had definite responsibilities for public order, and partly by virtue of their symbolic and legitimising functions with regard to imperial rule.

These strategies were reinforced by the goals and perspectives of the British in India. Originally the East India Company had conceived of its responsibilities mainly in terms of guarding its investment. Its inevitable strategy was to conciliate Indians to its rule and to bind its potential supporters by ties of interest. But the East India Company was also an occupying power. It could not afford to trust too wholeheartedly to the common allegiance of the Indian elites, nor to reinforce the weapons of independent authority in their hands. It needed a standing army, not just to guard against external enemies and to increase its territories but also to protect it against lawlessness. This task could not be left solely to local elites because they too had at times to be coerced. Thus practical and political exigencies always limited the impact of British assumptions about India. Yet it was important too that the government was held to have a 'civilising mission', already evident in the prescriptive elements of the permanent settlement of Bengal's land revenue in 1793, but more obvious in the rhetoric of Evangelicals and Utilitarians as they justified British rule through allegations of Indian decadence and barbarism.[6] The state, as the major instrument of European influence, took on a theoretical responsibility not only for economic advancement but also for the moral order.

More specific interpretations were important to policy at different times. In the later nineteenth century there were two apparently opposed but partly complementary tendencies. One stressed the inadequacy of Indian institutions and the need for government intervention in (at least from J. S. Mill onwards) virtually any aspect of life;[6] another emphasised the need, while introducing 'equity and morality', to create 'the least possible disturbance of the practices, prejudices, and organic institutions of Indian society'.[7] The permanent settlement was an early example of the tendency to interfere; some of the reaction against it illustrated the fear of change. The first tendency is seen also in the mid-century enthusiasm for free markets, public works and 'modern' law and administration; the second appeared in the subsequent social conservatism of the supporters of tenancy reform and the opponents of land transfer. By the end of the century a majority of British administrators were very far from an unthinking condemnation of Asiatic institutions, but on the contrary made them an essential reference point in policy formation.[8] With a greater emphasis upon tradition, the British now expected a whole range of Indian behaviour to be determined by the past, and dangerous to change. They elevated *mentalité* into a guiding principle of government. But what the strategies shared – and was one reason for the growth of the state and its power – was the idea of India as a divided and divisive culture. To the orientalists it was so because of the supposed influence of caste, community and historical experience. To the early missionaries and reformers it was so because of potential individualities repressed by superstition and social tyranny but yet uncharted by civil laws and government. To the conservative interpreters of Sir Henry Maine it was so because of the necessary contribution of separate communities to the maintenance of social order.

British strategies for controlling India thus rested upon ideas of Indian backwardness which supported both a preference for 'appropriate' policies and a goal of reform. There was a conscious stress upon the supposed difference between East and West: European fairness, legalism and rationality were contrasted with the arbitrary despotism and superstition native to India. European agency was naturally preferred, as far as possible, and progress identified with British administrative, social and economic improvements upon the existing institutional inadequacies, which were traced to Indian 'backwardness'. According to John Strachey, for example, Indian law had once been so complex and diffuse as to be virtually unknowable, even under the East India Company; thus the police were oppressive and corrupt, and the courts seemingly acted out forms and ceremonies rather than offering justice. But such too was the government provided in Bengal – to people who understood only 'personal rule of the roughest sort'. By contrast, in the Punjab a better solution had been found by subordinating personal rulers, the British collector-magistrates, to a set of definite and rational rules.[9] Then after 1861 the Indian penal code embodied these virtues more generally; it comprised the English criminal law 'freed from all technicalities and superfluities' and modified only in 'surprisingly few' particulars to meet Indian conditions.[10] Centrepiece of the British judicial and penal structure, the code outlined the system of courts and defined the lawful activities of the police, including the manner of their investigations, their powers of arrest and the means which they should fulfil their obligations to keep the peace and protect the public. Because it was codified the law was supposed to be readily accessible not just to lawyers – and certainly the codes were ideal for the burgeoning army of Indian pleaders – but to the average member of the ICS. Generally the Indian law codes were held to 'approach the highest standard of excellence', in the Benthamite sense – that is, in 'form, intelligibility, and in comprehensiveness'.[11] They stood in stark contrast, in British imagination, to the awful anarchy of Indian society.

On the other hand, policy repeatedly had to be accommodated to Indian conditions, as, for example, in the assertions that European prestige was crucial for British dominion. The social distance demanded for British officers, buildings and institutions reflected the mutual isolation alleged for Indian categories; Europeans deliberately located themselves in an Indian milieu, trying to co-opt its social order and value system, so as to establish their own place at the top of the hierarchy. We have just noted for law and administration, lying beside rationalism in that most European of interventions, an assumption that 'All oriental people have a strong predilection for personal Government', preferring orders 'not from a man but from an office'.[12] The British faced a complex dilemma: they needed (and often wished) to co-opt what they interpreted as the 'natural' order and tendency in India; on the other hand they also criticised them as inadequate to the 'higher' goals now espoused. British security and prestige depended equally, they thought, upon innovation or improvement (the supposed 'benefits' of Western rule) and upon conservation or accommodation (its 'fairness'). They could escape neither of these perceptions, and could not reconcile them. When looking beyond the indigenous forms to the creation of new institutions, they found themselves hampered by 'native shortcomings'. For example, officials claimed repeatedly that subordinates, as in a police force, were *bound* to be unreliable and oppressive. These views were derived from racial and even linguistic prejudices, but were reinforced by the frauds and forgeries frequently found in government offices. Clerks and record-keepers were discovered in collusion with friends and patrons; embezzlement was common and it seemed very likely that there was a much larger problem in the extortion of bribes by Indian officials, especially the police. This did not necessarily affect the revenue and might help tie collaborators and employees to British rule, but ultimately it represented disloyalty to the system and to the definitions of public concern which the British proclaimed. It might also alienate more powerful supporters, whose concerns swam into greater prominence as British perception of social change was heightened. It was particularly invidious, in British eyes, that exactions might be demanded by those of relatively low status from the respectable and the high-born.[13] Yet the abuses were believed to arise out of society and its norms, which had to be replaced by an improved order. Whatever the realities of imperialism, many thought the honour and security of the Raj depended upon avoiding force and introducing new standards in public life, or – according to Lord Curzon in a celebrated speech to the corporation of Bombay in 1900 – upon 'native confidence in British justice'. Hence 'the man who either by force or by fraud shakes that confidence is dealing a blow at British dominion in India'.[14] (The other side of this coin was a sensitivity to dishonesty and misconduct not just by government servants but by any Europeans: if they were to represent a superior race, then they had to act the part.)[15] Such ideas indicate a complicated interplay of conservative and modernising impulses, a tangle which genuinely could not be resolved. The ideas were relevant to decisions about the policing of India, both because they affected the nature and operation of the police, and also because they help explain the limits upon the role of the civil force in subjugating the people and maintaining order. They offer answers to the question: why did the Indian police not develop more quickly?

Another consequences to be identified here is the preference for executive government. One argument, adopted from Denzil Ibbetson, went like this: Indians did not and should not govern themselves; they were allowed as much freedom as was compatible with good administration; the rule they best understood and appreciated was the 'personal rule of a strong and upright ruler'; though they objected to government interference as such, there was no reason to extend personal freedoms merely to comply with an abstract principle. Another argument could be as follows. The Indian was 'docile as a rule' but 'liable to fierce bursts of passion'. What was suitable for England was not so for India. Riots and disturbances proved the case. Hence it was 'not difficult to establish the position that a strong executive is required to keep even the more pacific portions of India in order'.[16] It followed, as in Strachey's view, that it was desirable that the District Officers should retain close control over the police, as provided by law and as maintained in practice in the United Provinces. Strachey deplored the tendency in some areas for the powers to become so limited that the police were 'virtually a separate department, administered by the District Superintendent, under the orders of the Inspector-General of Police, at the headquarters of the Provincial Government'.[17]

One problem with this position lay in theoretical scruples about the proper separation of powers. Revenue matters were largely debarred from all civil courts after 1822, except for some appeals with regard to sales or arrears, allowable after amendments to the law in 1859 and 1880. But a collector, in his capacity as a magistrate, though he had nothing to do with civil suits, could try all but the most serious criminal offences, passing sentences of rigorous imprisonment of up to two years. He also had general powers of arrest and investigation, being responsible for recording statements, issuing search warrants, binding persons over to keep the peace, and so on. He was supposed only rarely to interfere with detection and prosecution, or with the internal discipline and organisation of the police, but in other respects he was the hand of the force. In that sense the superintendent of police was formally his assistant. The arguments for such a system were most secure in the mind of a Punjab paternalist such as Denzil Ibbetson. He explained in 1906 that, although there was an obvious objection in theory if the magistrate were involved both in the police enquiries and with trying the resultant case, in practice a collector was far too busy to take any notice of police enquiries 'except in the most serious cases, which are triable only by the Court of Sessions'. This was not entirely true. But the reasoning undoubtedly affected the police, and was also seen very clearly in respect of the judiciary, incidentally qualifying its contribution to British 'fairness'. The general attitude was that far less damage (to Indian contentment, and hence to order and British interests) could be done through court work than on the executive side.[18]

The police and the system

The part played by civil policing in the British system of control was limited by British ideas about India, by British goals and by the nature of the police. Each of these will now be considered more fully, beginning with the impact of the ideas. Just as the British regarded recruitment to different services, or political structures, or public and private morality, all to be related (among Indians) to inherited occupations and aptitudes within a pervasive hierarchy, so too they held that there was no sense of common citizenship in India. Instead obligations were felt primarily towards those castes and communities with which the Indians were said to identify. Thus the British perceived many crimes to be committed by gangs, not individuals; and thus too they considered concepts of wrong to be assessed by Indians against the status and security of specific groups and not according to abstract or public values; an objective truthfulness might be demanded of Indians but should not be expected while a new court system or foreign laws of evidence lay outside the existing moral order and in conflict with older loyalties, which produced, instead, an subjective truth. In less rarified forms, such attitudes defined the expectations in police work too. Supposedly there were hereditary groups, for each member of which it was, according to Strachey, 'his trade, his caste – I may say his religion – to commit crime'. The emphasis on gangs was first associated with Sleeman's campaign against *thagi*, and became further institutionalised in the Criminal Tribes Act of 1871, around the same time as a framework for the development of the police was laid down.[19] Some of the methods of that developing force also reflected a British predilection for conspiracy theories, to explain crime or indeed popular and political protest, which was based once again upon a view of India as a mix of secretive cells to be penetrated and kept in isolation from each other. The British police officer expected family or caste ties and the authority of the patron or social superior to enforce 'morality' (as defined by the prevailing culture) but not necessarily to assist 'law'. These sactions promoted *an* order but not 'justice'; they reflected social interdependence but not principle.[20] Ibbetson described the 'peculiarities of the Indian code of ethics' slightly differently:[21]

> A decent man will not testify in support of a false charge, unless it is against an enemy by whom he has been injured so deeply as to be absolved from all restrictions, or so intolerable an evil-doer that the village must be rid of him at any price. But in support of what he knows or believes to be a true charge, he will conscientiously swear to any number of circumstantial lies ... The result is that there is hardly a single case that comes into Court ... that is not supported by evidence that is partly false.

The strengthening of these aspects of British ideas of India in the later nineteenth century elevated the social order until in some minds its preservation constituted the first duty of the government itself, the main preoccupation of great officers of state from the Viceroy down. This change ran in tandem with the British desire to create a more effective police force, but also greatly reinforced the sense that social order was too important a matter to be left to policemen alone.

There is, secondly, a popular view of the British in India as ruthless exploiters, subordinating Indian welfare and economy to imperialist demands. Such a rule would indeed have had the need to develop its coercive force, so as to repress the protests which the exploitation aroused. But (though, of course, the British did repress protest) the regulation of Indian law suggests an agenda and a forbearance which relate to British assumptions more than to economic demands. They largely left alone the laws of inheritance, the family and social relations, though these were important for the accumulation of capital, the transfer of land and the availability of labour and, therefore, arguably, for the development of Indian rural production in the interests of Lancashire. The British did intervene to codify the laws relating to evidence, procedures, limitations, contract and trusts; but they also deliberately excluded certain usages and customary rights, and in several cases restricted the application of the civil codes by specific legislation, inhibiting market forces in pursuit of social goals. Except for property law, intrinsically mixed with revenue policy and a major cause of litigation, the British civil laws in India affected Europeans and their enterprises far more than they influenced indigenous behaviour. Often the criteria justifying an enactment included either the fact that it protected or could be accommodated within Indian society, or the assertion that an existing practice in India was repugnant to humanity. The latter implied once again the notion of British rule resting in part upon popular acceptance due to its equity. Usually this meant refraining from the disturbance of existing interests, but *in extremis* it could imply intervention to outlaw some oppression or corruption which was permitted, it was supposed, by the dominance of the Brahmans, the divisions of society, and the ignorance and superstition of the people.

Important limitations upon the role of the police related also to the nature and standing of the force. In the villages and rural areas the petty, semi-official agents of civil policing had a very limited coercive value for the state. On the lowest rung of the formal ladder of control, the *chaukidar* or village watchman remained in the last resort an official of the community or its elites, despite all the attempts to incorporate him, by selection and training, even by remuneration, into a unified state apparatus; while the subordinate attached to the loosely controlled *thana*, or local police post, remained notorious as party to local networks of power and oppression, and a most imperfect instrument of the state. Some of the obstacles which stood in the way of developing this system were general to the administration. The usual view of Bengal was, to adopt the descriptions of its Chief Secretary in 1907, that on the one hand there were no village communities or local institutions other than those of British creation on which to devolve petty civil and criminal powers, though there were 'leading Indian gentlemen' who should be consulted as often as possible; and that on the other hand the British civil service was weaker and more distant than elsewhere, but still overworked and too frequently transferred from one post to another. These conditions had consequences for the police. First, their tasks at the lower level were far more general than in other provinces. In Bengal the sub-divisional officer (not usually a member of the Indian Civil Service) was the most local of the state functionaries who were integrated into a single bureaucratic structure. He had virtually no local staff. If he wanted information, he asked the local police: if he took action, other than by issuing a written order, he relied upon the police once again. Thus, despite measures undertaken in the 1860s to establish an independent civil force which was only formally responsible to the civil power, the district police remained effectively subordinated to the district magistrate. Secondly, the very senior levels of the police did not constitute a separate service. Until the first IPS appointment in Madras in 1919, inspectors-general were drawn from the ICS, and in Bengal even more than elsewhere the convention that they should stay in post for three years – far longer than the average – was in practice a condition which very often the government itself had to break. In all the specialist departments there was the danger that a person might be appointed without the requisite experience; but a superintending engineer or a medical officer was sent to the province by the Government of India from a cadre of specialists, and achieved promotion, very often, by transfer to another province. The police were less clearly professional – they did not enter the service with a technical qualification – and more obviously provincial in the pattern of their careers, partly of course because many of their skills and much of their knowledge had to be local. Moreover, even the supervising of the police was shared; a district collector would tour for several months each year, visiting *thana* posts as well as state *kachharis*, villages and estates, whereas a district superintendent of police, though he would inspect *thanas*, travelled mainly to investigate the most serious crimes.[22]

The differences between the police and other departments in India may thus be explained in terms of practicalities, but attitudes also played a part. There was some recruitment to the police of the literate and 'respectable' classes, eager for government employment. But in general the social status of the police was low, in both British and Indian eyes. At the lower levels, their manpower was sought among groups thought to show a traditional aptitude for the work, among 'turbulent' people long employed as guards or armed retainers, among castes of watchmen and others professing *kshatriya* (warrior) status, among 'criminals' whom it was hoped to reform.[23] To some extent this perpetuated worries about the need for European supervision. Suspicion of Indian subordinates, for which financial strains prevented a remedy, restricted British expectations in several spheres of government. Moreover, though the landed interest possibly declined, in British eyes its power remained supreme and 'traditional'. Many policies sought to preserve its strength quite explicitly as a means of maintaining order which was more appropriate to India than that provided by the police, with their much canvassed shortcomings of command and, at the lower levels, of honesty and fairness.

Professionalising the police

The main lesson of the discussion so far is that a professional police force emerged only to the extent that there was a reduction in the use of a wider range of state institutions as part of a system of control, and that in India such a development was slower and more uneven than in Britain. Certainly it was relatively incomplete even by 1920, though the police had gained greatly in organisation and prestige. The professionalising of the police lagged behind that of other state departments, but the British nonetheless sponsored an administrative revolution in Indian life. Paternalist and personal autocracy gave way to specialist, reforming or incorporating institutions. Even for the police there was an appearance of steady progression. The change had three elements. First, discipline and organisation began to be substituted for ethos and social type as the basis of management. Second, state institutions were identified with a particular branch of knowledge, or as embodying a skill with its own science. Thirdly, there was a corresponding shift of emphasis, from the performance of limited duties and from coping with crises as part of a generalist executive, towards the assumption of an absolute and exclusive responsibility for one aspect of state activities.

In the case of the police, the development was from a series of special units to combat *thagi*, enforce excise or forest laws, or protect state property, towards the establishment of a single force carrying out such duties while also being equated with the state as its principal coercive arm. A Police Commission in 1860 built on reforms already introduced in several provinces, most notably Madras, and provided for a command structure and an organisation based on areas of responsibility. At first the senior officers were mainly seconded from the army, but by the 1880s a civil background was becoming more common. In 1893, following the recommendations of the Aitchison Committee on the public services, the first open examination was held in London for entry into the Indian police. A further stage in raising the status of the service (in British eyes) was reached early in the twentieth century when it was provided that assistant superintendents, the officers in charge of police circles, should be European and normally recruited in Britain; also constituted was a subordinate or provincial police service, from which in exceptional circumstances members could be appointed to posts otherwise reserved for officers from its imperial, effectively European, counterpart. At these supervising levels the police force was thus intended to parallel the structure of the civil service itself.[24]

The motives behind this change were plain. The Government of Bengal considered, in 1901, that:

> In no branch of the administration ... is improvement so imperatively required as in the police. There is no part of our system of government of which such universal and bitter complaint is made, and none in which, for the relief of the people and the reputation of Government, is reform in anything like the same degree so urgently called for. The evil is essentially in the investigating staff. It is dishonest and tyrannical ...[25]

The argument here was that the very expansion of government responsibilities increased the dangers of abuse, especially when, as in Bengal, European supervision was weak. The police were being expected to take up a 'modern' task – the investigation of crime – within an unreformed institutional framework. The result, according to the Police Commission of 1903, was corruption:

> in every stage of the work of the police station. The police officer may levy a fee or receive a present for every duty he performs. The complainant often has to pay a fee for having his complaint recorded ... More money is extorted as the investigation proceeds ... The station-house officer will sometimes hush up a case on payment of his terms; he will ... levy fees from shopkeepers and others for services rendered, or to obviate vexatious espionage. He has a specially rich vein in cases concerning disputes about land, water or crops ... The illicit gains in some police stations in Bengal in connection with chur (or alluvial) lands are almost incredible.

Worst of all, perhaps, were the effects on the whole community:

> A body of police comes down to the village and is quartered on it for several days. The principal residents have to dance attendance on the police all day long and for days together. Sometimes all the villagers are compelled to be in attendance, and inquiries degrading in their character are conducted *coram populo*. Suspects and innocent persons are bullied and threatened into giving information they are supposed to possess. The police officer, owing to want of detective ability or to indolence, directs his efforts to procure confessions by improper inducement, by threats and by moral pressure ... All this is done to secure evidence in support of the view which the police officer from time to time holds regarding the case. If in his opinion enough of evidence is not thus obtained to secure a conviction, he will not hesitate to bolster up his case with false evidence ... When an investigation fails, the complainant is sometimes finally bullied or threatened into acknowledging that a mistake has been made and that the case is 'false'.

These complaints naturally contributed to the preference for other methods of control, but they also invited a remedy. The answer which the Police Commission recommended was to improve the standing of the force, by better pay and training, by effective supervision (ultimately by Europeans) and by the establishment of a career structure such as to encourage a better class of recruit to the intermediate levels.

The modernity of these views and proposals did not, however, remove some of the underlying assumptions about the best way of controlling the police and securing public order in India. As early as 1793, when village watchmen were declared subject to the orders of the police, the British system had supposedly denied the *zamindars* and the 'old village system' (as the Police Commission called it) any legal role in the use of coercion. But we have noted that the watchmen were not really incorporated into the state's system, and moreover that the *zamindars* remained broadly responsible for laying information and arresting wrong-doers. The Bengal Act VI of 1870 supposedly reformed the defects of these arrangements − it was particularly concerned to ensure the payment of village police − but substituted for stronger state control a greater trust in the self-regulation of the village community. Again, this was throught wanting, and after a further inquiry in 1883 an amending Act was eventually passed in 1892, to make district magistrates responsible for the appointment and level of wages of the *chaukidars*. Avowedly the intention was to secure the best men in these posts and to incorporate them into a single police force; later *daffadars* or supervisors were introduced to control the work of ten or twenty *chaukidars*. The village *panchayats* or committees which had hitherto supposedly been in charge were now dismissed as people of 'low calibre' unsuited to a supervisory role; they were still, however, to pay, if necessary through a government agent appointed to extract the *chaukidari* tax. The 1903 commission criticised the tendency of these changes and reasserted the supremacy of the local community, whose co-operation, it argued, was 'absolutely essential'. It wanted District Officers to take a greater interest than hitherto, hoped that the tax would not continue to fall so heavily upon the poor, and did not suggest that a village should *control* its police. But it insisted that, 'whether by employing landholders or leading *ryots* separately or as members of *panchayats*', steps should be taken to foster the existing village agencies of police work: 'the village police ought not to be separated from the village organisation and placed under the regular police'. The commission wanted to see, 'not a body of low-paid stipendaries or subordinate police scattered over the country, but the utilisation of the village agency itself'.[26]

This reassertion of the village community clearly contradicted the alternative tendency towards professionalisation. As already explained, the issues were complex. Some officials thought the growth of bureaucratic methods *worsened* dishonesty and oppression, and that indigenous elites had to be recruited, for example through committees of 'responsible villagers'. Others relied on a sufficiency of European administration and feared intervention in village life. Intellectual fashion and financial stringency too contributed to the apparent uncertainty.[27] Thus it was that the development of the police could be understood only in the context of the system of a whole. But none the less, as private coercion was confined and public concern expanded, the tasks of the police inevitably increased. They were given urgency not only because of this expansion of the state but also because new organisation among the Indians often presented a threat to public order and later a challenge to British rule. It thus became necessary to develop a professional and preferably a paramilitary police force, on hard-headed imperialist grounds.

The police and politics

Attempts to develop the police reflected a broad variety of influences and priorities. The preceding discussion has sketched an agenda for the ordering of rural society which went far beyond the establishment and improvement of the civil police. But these strategies had some inherent weaknesses, which worsened or became more obvious as time went on. By the early twentieth century there were indications that the 'reforming' system of government itself was under stress, expressed on the one hand in fears about public order and British security, as during communal riots, or in reaction to popular discontent and violence, and on the other hand in a sense that, because of economic and nationalist criticism and administrative inadequacies and bottlenecks, it was becoming ever more difficult to hold the first line of defence, which remained the 'cultivation of harmonious relations with the people ... the elimination of all causes which produce hostility and discord, ... [and] the exposure of misrepresentations which interfere with a good understanding'.[28] One major strain was administrative, especially the pressure on the District Officer. His old tasks became more onerous, many new ones were imposed upon him, and his work was increasingly politicised. As a strategy for maintaining order, generalised control headed by a European District Officer became less and less practical – the very effectiveness of government undermined it – while the expansion of government and arguments about devolution, specialisation and indeed Indian 'improvement' slowly weakened the belief in a system of control centred upon Europeans. Hence the police were expected to expand their role; by the 1920s law and order had become a subject reserved to the officials and not transferred to Indian Ministers.

The evolution of the British system of control reflected specific problems and failures in British rule. After the strains placed upon the administrators themselves, the next most important of these were connected with Indian reactions. This brings us to politics, for the development of Indian nationalism and the retreat of British control were both associated, paradoxically, with the growth of the Indian state. Its interference increased through administrative reform and law, and in education and public health, but equally as it admitted responsibility for the conditions of labour or the development of agriculture and industry, or claimed an Indian view of the use of the army, of foreign relations and of fiscal policy. Its acts of commission invited Indian reactions; its omissions encouraged nationalists to argue that Indians would do better. The unravelling of British control from the late nineteenth century undoubtedly depended upon political change, and the politicising of one area after another of government and of life in India. Here too the system may be said partly to have undermined itself. We have seen how the British wanted to reform India but also feared the consequences of change; it might be added that they often did both at the same time. In 1884, for example, Lord William Bentinck wrote of general education as his 'panacea for the regeneration of India' but, a little later, that the 'great curse of our rule' was 'a constant interference with the long-established native system of Indian society and the introduction of our own fancies and schemes, ... coupled with *our own* ignorance'.[29] Taken as a whole, British rule was equally vacillating. What made the difference over time was not just confidence in British *knowledge*, but also the growing capacity of the administration both to organise and to deploy the assumptions it made and the information it amassed about India. In short the imperfections of the British view became ever more significant and potentially damaging to the British connection as the intervention of the government increased, even when the intentions were conservative.

Moreover the state's perspectives on Indian society and the resultant strategies of control played a particular part in this mobilising of the nationalist challenge. The key here was the British assumption about Indian disunity, which persisted from the history and caste-based descriptions of James Mill, through the economic and social policies of the nineteenth century, and into the emphasis upon an Indian Muslim 'nation' and other socio-political divisions in the twentieth. At one level, so long as self-determination was refused, Indian division was irrelevant to political boundaries as the British saw them; but at another level it was crucial to British ideas of control. Obviously the identity and political ambitions of the Muslims were the most important example during the twentieth century; the British took measures designed to court and to use sympathetic religious figures. More generally (as said) the rulers expected 'community leaders' to assist in keeping order. Equally the castes, languages and races which they identified – some say invented – also provided outlines for their understanding of how India was to be managed.[30] Police, like other officials, were recruited in accordance with such categories. Thus the very institutions of the British contributed to a process of segregation; this was the case even with the provinces themselves. Just as the partition of Bengal in 1905 outraged most of the Hindu *bhadralok* ('respectable' classes) and gratified sections of a nascent Muslim middle class, so too were significant feelings brought into the open among the educated and professional classes in Bihar and Orissa by the reversal of the partition and the creation of a new province in 1912. This is an unfamiliar but instructive example of the forces unwittingly encouraged by British ideas. In Patna the *Beharee* wrote of its 'unbounded joy' at this 'day of national rejoicing', heralding the 'regeneration of Bihar'; but in Cuttack the *Star of Utkal*, citing the choice of capital and the probable membership of the executive council, saw the new province as a plot to benefit the Biharis at the expense of the people and resources of Orissa and Chota Nagpur. A key to these feelings was, of course, that they did not reflect nationalisms so much as justify a sectional concern for employment – in this case initially unavailing.[31] Yet the British made use of such feelings to balance appointments, and also to maximise their own control and avoid alternative local concentrations of power. Especially after 1857, members of the intermediate civil services, and of the police and army, tended not to be deployed in their home areas. The implications for practical control were very evident in the British notions of India's divisions, and are well known. Yet – less obviously – it was a vulnerable order which not only relied on identities but also called new ones into being. The British, depending on the categories and on disunity, were also helping to build social and political blocks which could combine against them.

The nationalist challenge had a mixed impact on the police force. The expansion of government was partly an attempt to recruit supporters for the state. To supplement the collaboration of educated and intermediary groups, new institutions were devised, such as district boards, and for these and other reasons new opportunities for power appeared alongside those associated with revenue. Even in the twentieth century strategies of control were being suggested by an expansion of local self-government and Indianisation, which may be regarded as weakening the British hold. But in terms of the perceptions of the officials they may also be considered a perpetuation of the old mixed strategies of control; thus they repeated the effect of limiting the development of the police. Specifically this implied a preference for control by the civil executive (as opposed to the police, the army or the judiciary), and in turn a tendency for policing to be identified as an instrument of that executive, and with the perpetuation of the Raj. Thus, rather than in police work more generally, it was in intelligence gathering and in the suppression of political violence of dissent that the professionalism of the police came to be concentrated. All subdivisions of effective state knowledge and action were to an extent diverted by the concentration upon the political struggle in the twentieth century, and by Indianisation of personnel and objectives. If the police gained in prominence mainly because of the dangers of terrorism and the challenge of political agitation, then they were not fully incorporated into a model of national government. The timing of more effective improvements in the police did indeed correspond very closely first with the point at which nationalist activity was seen as popular and permanent, and secondly with the stage at which the British began a considered attempt to combat it by 'political' as well as repressive means.

The more cosmetic changes to the police set in train after 1861 were still condemned as inadequate in 1903. But then, even in 1912 the Home Department did not consider monthly political reports to be essential – implying that they were not seeking to direct overall government policy towards Indian politics. Reports and supervision were thought appropriate only to an 'acute' situation.[32] In other words, popular agitation was regarded as an occasional, untypical problem. It is not surprising, therefore, that there was as yet no great seriousness about reconstructing the police as an instrument for the suppression of Indian politics. Attempts at a concerted policy using the police were made in Bengal after 1905, but, in common with the courts, they were regarded as having proved totally inadequate to the task. Thus the main trend in dealing with 'sedition' until the first world war was towards increasing recourse to executive powers. This was characteristic of the operation of the Press Act of 1910 and of detentions and deportations, in which legal sanctions and indeed attempts to appease public opinion were relegated to the margin.[33] The Rowlatt or Sedition Committee report of 1918, allegedly based on the relatively successful wartime containment of terrorism, was the most fully articulated expression of this view of Indian politics and revolutionary conspiracy, and of the need to suspend or supplement the normal powers and procedures of the legal system and the civil police; even then the excuse was the exceptional nature of the problem. But the Rowlatt Act and the disturbances which followed, the most serious since 1858, helped to discredit this approach for the British, just as, for most Indians, it (or rather General Dyer's atrocities in the Punjab and the subsequent popular support he received in Britain) provoked a sea change in their attitude to British rule. Thus the exception became the rule, and thus had to be met by law, at least in theory. The greater prominence of a civil though armed police dated from after the first world war, largely because it accompanied other attempts to protect the British cause through constitutional rather than despotic means and by regulating political activity while maintaining the support of 'moderate' Indian opinion.[34]

The rate and manner of the professionalising of the British Indian police were therefore very closely related to the exigencies of colonial rule. And yet this influence seems to have been affected in particular by a preference for alternative means of policing. The use of the army is an obvious example, but also significant were the elements of coercion and control inherent in civil administration. The example of Bengal demonstrates moreover that it was not the *strength* of these alternatives which was crucial: it was a favourite truism almost throughout British rule that the local agencies of the government were weaker in the permanently settled areas than in any other parts of British India – indeed, they consisted on a day-to-day basis of little more than *chaukidars* and constables. But Bengal was also slower in developing its police. The preferences of the rulers must therefore have been partly intellectual in origin.

Was the situation in India purely the product of imperialism? Surely it was also the result of specifically Indian conditions. The emphasis on ideas in the foregoing account suggests as much. The British are now thought to have got a great deal wrong in their image of India; it was falsely stereotyped, over-generalised and often racist or Eurocentric. But, however distorting their lens, it was undoubtedly trained upon the country and its people. Policies did result from a kind of dialogue between India and Europe. States impose order through their power but also through their conformance and acceptability. India was not (is not) a proto-Europe. Any Indian state therefore had to appeal to Indian notions of rule and social order. Europeans could not claim popular allegiance by means of an appeal to mythical history or culture, in the manner of a *raja* with his convenient genealogy and his social roles. They had no direct access to metaphysical or supernatural sanctions. But they did their best to invent a place and even a history for themselves within the existing perceptions and identities of India; and all the time they had to make accommodations. They believed in a single secular sovereignty, but tried to enlist the support of social and religious leaders. They advocated individual rights and social equity, but endorsed caste and community. They diffused power among many hands, though they believed it should be unitary and held only in theirs. Even at this level of generalisation these points remind us that the Indian police force was not merely a transplanted limb of the English police, and not a body made entirely in the image which the British rulers had of it, as an ideal. It was not even, very quickly, a 'modern' arm of government with specific responsibilities and professional methods and organisation. It was not any of these things because it was imperial, certainly, but also because it was Indian.

Notes

The following abbreviations are used: *H.* Proceedings of the Government of India, Home Department (National Archives, New Delhi; India Office Library, London). Citations give branch, series (A–D), number and date, and include 'keep withs' found only in 'file' volumes in New Delhi. Proceedings pre-1859 or post-1921 are differently cited. *PCR* Records of the Commissioner of Patna Division (Bihar State Archives, Patna). Citations give *basta*, collection, file and year. *Poll.* Political (Branch). *R & A* Proceedings of the Government of India, Revenue and Agriculture Department. See H. above. *Rev.* Land Revenue (Branch).

1 This is discussed for India in David Arnold. *Police Power and Colonial Rule: Madras, 1859–1947* (Delhi, 1986), which also provides the best account of the subject, applying in large part not just to Madras but to the whole of British India. This chapter will not seek to cover the same ground.

2 These paragraphs were based on the minutes of evidence taken before the *Select Committee on the Affairs of the East India Company*, vol. IV (House of Commons, 1833), the *Circular orders of the Superintendent of Police in the Lower Provinces, 1837–54* (Calcutta, 1854), *Reports on the State of the Police of the town of Calcutta for 1859–60 to 1861–62* (Calcutta 1861–62) and Sarmila Banerjee, *Studies in Administrative History of Bengal, 1880–1898* (New Delhi, 1978), chapters VIII–XI. See also Uma Dasgupta, 'Crime law and the police in India, 1870–80', *Indian Economic and Social History Review*, X, 4 (1973); Basudev Chatterji, 'The Darogah and the countryside: the imposition of police control in Bengal and its impact, 1793–1837', *Indian Economic and Social History Review*, xviii, 1 (1981); David Arnold, 'Bureaucratic recruitment and subordination in colonial India: the Madras Constabulary, 1859–1947', in Ranajit Guha (ed.), *Subaltern Studies: writings on South Asian history and society*, IV (Delhi, 1985).

3 See especially Ranajit Guha, *Elementary Aspects of Peasant Insurgency in Colonial India* (Delhi, 1983), and 'The prose of counter-insurgency', in R. Guha (ed.), *Subaltern Studies*, II (Delhi, 1983).

4 See B. B. Misra, *The Bureaucracy in India* (Delhi, 1977), pp. 1–37, and *The Administrative History of India, 1834–1947* (London, 1970); Arnold Kaminsky, *The India Office, 1880–1910* (New York, 1986); David Dilks, *Curzon in India*, I (London, 1969), pp. 221–4.

5 For an introduction to the question of British attitudes and interventions throughout the nineteenth century, as discussed in this chapter see Ronald Inden, 'Orientalist constructions of India', *Modern Asian Studies*, 20, 3 (1986); David Kopf, *British Orientalism and the Bengal Renaissance* (Berkeley, 1969); O. P. Kejariwal, *The Asiatic Society of Bengal and the Discovery of India's Past* (Delhi, 1988); C. H. Philips (ed.), *Historians of India, Pakistan and Ceylon* (London, 1961), notably essays by Philips, Das Gupta, Basham, Ballhatchet and Furber; E. T. Stokes, *The English Utilitarians and India* (Oxford, 1959); Francis G. Hutchins, *The Illusion of Permanence* (Princeton, 1967); Clive Dewey, 'Images of the Indian village community', *Modern Asian Studies*, 6, 3 (1972), and 'The rehabilitation of the peasant proprietor in nineteenth-century economic thought', *History of Political Economy*, 6, 1 (1974); David Lelyveld, *Aligarh's First Generation* (Princeton, 1978), chapter 1.

6 See, for example, Sir John Strachey, *India: its administration and progress* (London, 1903), pp. 209–10 and *passim*.

7 Sir Alfred Lyall, *The Rise and Expansion of the British Dominion in India* (London, 1894, 5th ed. 1910), pp. 381 ff.

8 The best analysis of this change has been that by Clive Dewey, for example in his 'The Official Mind and the Problem of Agrarian Indebtedness in India, 1870–1910', Ph.D. thesis, Cambridge University (1972).

9 Strachey, *India*, pp. 91–110.

10 *Ibid.*, p. 97, quoting James Stephen, *History of the Criminal Law*, III (1881), p. 332.

11 Strachey, *India*, pp. 95–6 (quoting Henry Maine, 'India', in *The Reign of Queen Victoria*, I, p. 503), and, by contrast, see pp. 365–8: Indians 'traditionally' expected to use torture to obtain evidence; thus one purpose of the code of criminal procedure was to protect the people against the police.

12 See 'Memorandum on social and official intercourse between European officers and Indian Gentleman', Ranchi, 1913, and other papers, H. Poll. B1–30 February 1914. On a broader perspective in regard to language and the ordering of knowledge, also relevant elsewhere in this chapter, see B. S. Cohn, 'The command of language and the language of command', in R. Guha, *Subaltern Studies*, III (Delhi, 1985). On the general question of prestige, display and British authority see Cohn, 'Representing authority in Victorian India', in Eric Hobsbawm and Terence Ranger (eds.), *The Invention of Tradition* (Cambridge, 1983).

13 On frauds see PCR 335 19/4 (1881–82) and R&A Rev. B17 January 1902; on collusion – cases in Shahabad, Muzaffarpur and Hooghly – see PCR 355 14/6 (1891–92) and 366 12/1 (1896–97); on security bonds see PCR 354 8/1 (1891–92). Even collectorate *sheristadars* fell under suspicion or were dismissed; see three instances in Saran in 1868, 1874 and 1880, in PCR 341 14/1 (1884–85), and also PCR 358 1/27 (1893–94). On the administrative system of the *tauzi* (revenue accounts) department in a collectorate see *Empress* v. *Sitaram* (J. F. Stevens, J.), 28 March 1891, with PCR 355 14/6 (1891–92). On English ledgers see also PCR 359 12/22 (1893–94). Note also the criticism of the failure of superior – that is, British – officers to check the *tauzi* records: PCR 357 12/4 and 14/3 (1892–93), files which include further examples of extensive fraud and embezzlement.

14 See the Earl of Ronaldshay, *The Life of Lord Curzon*, 2 (London, 1928), p. 149.

15 For a discussion of several of these matters see Kenneth Ballhatchet, *Race, Sex and Class under the Raj: imperial attitudes and policies and their critics, 1793–1905* (London, 1980).

16 Ibbetson, 1 August 1903, and J. P. Hewett, 15 April 1902, H. Judicial A196–204 May 1906.

17 Strachey, *India*, p. 367.

18 See notes by Ibbetson, Thomas Raleigh and others, H. Judicial A196–204 May 1906. The last comment contrasts with the sanguine assessment of Strachey, mentioned above, on the accessibility of the legal codes to civilians.

19 See Sanjay Nigam, 'A Social History of a Colonial Stereotype: the "Criminal Tribes and Castes" of Uttar Pradesh, 1871–1930', Ph.D. thesis, University of London (1987). The quotation is from Strachey, *India*, p. 400.

20 See, for example, Sir Cecil Walsh, *Indian Village Crimes* (London, 1929).

21 Note, 1 August 1903; see note 16 above.

22 *Minutes of Evidence taken before the Royal Commission upon Decentralization in Bengal* (London, 1908), vol. IV, pp. 3–20 (evidence of E. A. Gait, 27 December 1907).

23 In the 1880s the Bengal police were recorded by religion and status, as follows:

Officers	*Men*	
European and/or Christian	3·9	0·4
Brahmans	20·5	15·5
Rajputs and Khattris	5·7	18·6
'High-caste sudras'	27·5	12·2
'Low-caste sudras'	4·9	7·5
Hindus of 'other castes'	10·7	12·6
Gurkhas and Nepalis	1·3	2·4
Hindu total	70·6	68·8
Sheikhs	1·3	1·4
Other Muslims	23·5	28·3

(Adapted from Beames Committee report: see Banerjee, *Studies*, p. 211.) These figures cannot be interpreted with any confidence; but it might be concluded therefore that a majority of the regular police were of high or middling ritual status; from other

F

evidence, however, their economic and political standing was mostly low. More generally see Rajat K. Ray, 'Evolution of the professional structure in modern India: older and new professions in a changing society', *Indian Historical Review*, ix, 1–2 (1982–83).

24 See J. D. Shukla, *Indianisation of all-India Services and its Impact on Administration, 1834–1947* (New Delhi, 1982), especially chapter II. See also Arnold, *Police Power*, chapters 1–3.

25 Sir J. Woodburn to Home Department, 12 December 1901, quoted in the *Report of the Indian Police Commission 1902–3* (Simla, 1903). The following quotations are also from this report. Its publication was initially refused by the Secretary of State, but insisted upon in India when it was found that details had leaked.

26 *Police Commission Report* 1903. A context for these suggestions was once again racial feeling – the superiority of the European and the inferiority of the Indian.

27 For the significant debates on the issues referred to here see H. Local Boards A2–5 February 1893, A6–20 September 1896 and A12–13 August 1903.

28 Note by McPherson, 9 July 1921, H. Poll. file 65/1921. See also *Beharee*, 27 October 1912, H. Poll. B108 December 1912; and PCR 341 14/15(4) (1885).

29 See C. H. Philips (ed.), *The Correspondence of Lord William Bentinck, Governor-General of India, 1828–1835*, I (Oxford, 1977), pp. xxv–xxxi and xxxix–xlii.

30 See, for example, David Washbrook, 'The development of caste organisation in south India, 1880 to 1925', in C. J. Baker and Washbrook, *South India: political institutions and political change, 1880–1920* (Delhi, 1975).

31 See *Beharee*, 6, 9 and 27 October, 3 and 6 November and 12 December 1912, and *Star of Utkal*, 14 December 1912, and compare *Behar Herald*, 6 November, *Star of India*, 29 November, and *Behar-Advocate* and *Kayastha Messenger*, 30 September 1912: H. Poll B57–8 November 1912, B108–10 December 1912, and B76–9 March 1913.

32 See Le Mesurier to Wheeler, 5 June 1912, and notes, H. Poll D9 July 1912.

33 Note the visiting committees set up for détenus: typically they comprised the district collector, the district judge, and local dignatories, including politicians and pleaders. See H. Poll B6 September 1918.

34 On this view of the constitutional reforms see P. G. Robb, *The Government of India and Reform: policies towards politics and the constitution, 1916–1921* (Oxford, 1976).

Acknowledgements

This chapter is an abridgment and adaptation (at the suggestion and with the assistance of David Anderson) of chapter 2 of P. G. Robb, *The Evolution of British Policy towards Indian Politics, 1880–1920* (New Delhi and Riverdale, forthcoming). I am indebted to my wife, Elizabeth, for her invaluable assistance with the collecting of materials, to the staff of archives and libraries in India and London, and to the School of Oriental and African Studies for financial assistance.

CHAPTER NINE

From military to tribal police: policing the Upper Nile Province of the Sudan

Douglas H. Johnson

The history of policing in the Sudan is the history of an incomplete transformation from an auxiliary military body to a civil force. It is a complex mixture of paramilitary, civil and tribal organisations; of civil and tribal courts administering different law; and of urban, rural and frontier duties, ranging from criminal investigation to the armed pursuit of nomad tax defaulters and frontier raiders. This survey of the evolution of policing in the southern province of Upper Nile is not intended to provide a case study of a 'typical' Sudanese province. In many ways Upper Nile Province lagged behind the rest of the Sudan in the development of its police force, establishing a criminal investigation unit as late as 1953, just before independence.[1] But the province contained within it all the varied duties expected to different bodies of Sudanese police during the Anglo-Egyptian condominium. Here we focus on police support in the civil administration of rural areas from occupation in 1898 to Sudanisation in 1954.

Both the police and civil administration in the Anglo-Egyptian Sudan evolved from the Egyptian army of reconquest and occupation, and the majority of the earliest personnel (British, Egyptian and Sudanese) were soldiers. The subsequent progress of civil administration was often measured by its rate of demilitarisation, with the gradual replacement of seconded officers by civilian administrators and the handing over of internal security duties to the police. In so far as police were increasingly recruited locally, their posting throughout the rural areas was supposed to be a sign of closer government contact with the people. The military character of administration survived longer in the southern provinces than in the north, and throughout the Anglo-Egyptian period most police were trained as an armed constabulary, frequently supporting the army in pacification and punitive campaigns. The continuity of personnel between the army and police, the military style of police training and organisation, meant that the police presence in the southern Sudan retained something of the aura of an army of occupation. As British civil administrators themselves became more involved in the rural areas the police began to appear as a barrier between the District Commissioner and his people. But civil administration needed some force behind it, especially with the creation of Native Administration courts in the 1920s and 1930s, so that judgements could be enforced. It was then that a parallel system of tribal police was created, completely divorced from the civil police, as the main policing arm in the rural areas.

Police organisation in the Sudan underwent three stages of development. Between 1896 and 1905 the country was divided into military areas, with a 'police administration' at the district level under the charge of Egyptian military *ma'murs* and Egyptian army police officers, supported by soldiers of the Egyptian army as police. Between 1905 and 1925 the organisation of both police and prisons was devolved to the provincial governors, who were responsible for the recruitment, organisation and 'interior economy' of the police in their provinces. Ex-soldiers were to be weeded out of the provincial police forces and replaced by local Sudanese. Police in the field were under the authority of a *ma'mur* and a British inspector. Even as the inspector's administrative duties expanded he was still expected to train police and supervise criminal investigations. This latter duty clashed with his magisterial role trying the cases he investigated, and the press of other administrative work often meant that the military training of police was neglected. As early as 1919 it was proposed to centralise the police and appoint British commandants in each province, and in the following year there were several high-level proposals to replace the army entirely with a British-officered police force. From 1925 on, following the formation of the Sudan Defence Force (SDF) and the expulsion of Egyptian military and civil personnel from the Sudan, police were reorganised under provincial commandants. In the north they became more of a modern crime-fighting force, while in the south they continued their paramilitary role, auxiliary to the Sudan Defence Force, but responsible to the District Commissioner (the retitled inspector) at the district level. Centralisation continued in the 1940s, when a police school was established in Khartoum to train NCOs and other ranks. This latter period coincided with the introduction of administrative devolution to the provinces.[2]

The evolution of policing in Upper Nile Province untidily followed these three stages of national development. Egyptian army *ma'murs* and sub-*ma'murs* continued to supervise the police in the outstations throughout 1905–25, and the link between the army and the police was never broken completely. Police were generally recruited from within the province, but, unlike neighbouring Bahr el-Ghazal Province, where locally enlisted police served in their home districts, the district representation was always unbalanced. Police in the rural areas continued largely to be strangers to the local population; thus they did not forge the hoped-for link between government and the people. Finally, the exigencies of the Ethiopian border, both before and after the second world war, forced the province police to maintain their paramilitary role. As in the other southern provinces during this last period, it was mainly the chiefs' police, subject to the chiefs' courts, who enforced the law in the rural areas.

Police and rural administration

The first government outposts in the Upper Nile Province between 1902 and 1906 were manned by Sudanese soldiers of the Egyptian army, and it was from them that many of the first police were drawn. Most officers were Egyptian, a few were Sudanese;[3] they were permanently stationed in outposts, with itinerant British inspectors supervising their work. Local people rarely saw a British official and came to know about government mainly through the police and army. The 1905 reorganisation of the police changed very little in the province. Police officers, retitled sub-*ma'murs*, remained in place. The province was supposed to recruit new police locally to replace transfers from the army, but the Governor of Upper Nile had an annual problem finding willing recruits. Food scarcity brought some hungry volunteers in 1905, but there was an inadequate supply of men of sufficient 'physical ability and sobriety' in 1906. There was less difficulty in recruiting by 1908, but until 1911 volunteers were still imported from outside the province. Throughout the pre-war period there were usually moderate annual increments in the province police establishment, but by 1913 the Upper Nile police force was well below the strength of its two southern neighbours, Bahr el-Ghazal and Mongalla Provinces.[4]

The army still had to provide a number of police. In other parts of the country, it was confidently asserted, 'the old idea that service in the Police was to be granted to worn out Sudanese [soldiers] as a kind of reward no longer prevails',[5] but in Upper Nile Province we find a number of old soldiers in far-flung outposts well into the 1920s. They are immediately identifiable by the Arabic names they acquired as slave soldiers in the Egyptian and Mahdist armies, but they included Shilluk, Dinka and Nuer, representing the three largest population groups of the province. As such they played an important role as intermediaries between government and its as yet unadministered subjects. Their numbers were always small. 'We have got a few old Shilluks and Dinkas who can, as a rule, be trusted to try to bring a tribesman in if he is sent for,' wrote the Governor in 1905. 'But they are few and far between ...'[6]

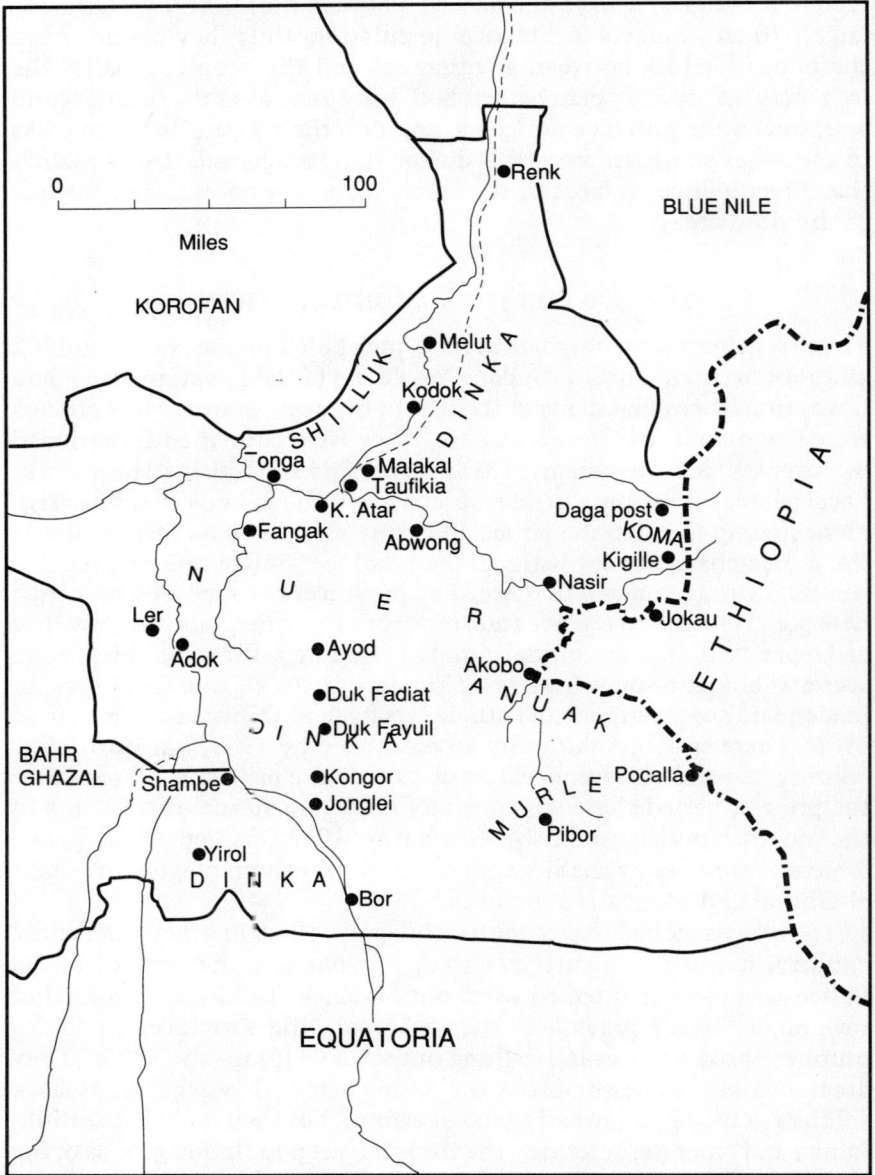

Upper Nile Province, showing some of the main police posts, *c.* 1904–55; boundaries approximate

Since no British administrator could speak any local languages until the 1920s, the government relied heavily on these few men as interpreters, but with mixed results.

Police interpreters were a constant feature of official contacts with local peoples throughout the first two decades of administration in the Upper Nile, acting as contacts with important chiefs, as official interpreters in punitive campaigns, and as assistants to itinerant British inspectors during routine court work.[7] Some sub-*ma'murs* and *ma'murs* also demonstrated a fluency in local languages which British administrators were slow to imitate. A few were themselves Sudanese and continued at a more elevated level the work of the humbler police interpreters. Some Egyptian officers displayed a competence which was quite contrary to their reputation among their British superiors, the most remarkable being Ahmad Muhammad Rajab. Appointed police officer at Fashoda in 1903, he learned Shilluk and is said to have married a sister of the *reth* (king). He was transferred to Abwong in 1904, serving as police officer and later sub-*ma'mur*. There he learned Dinka, a much more useful language administratively, as it was still spoken and understood by many Nuer, and so he became the main government intermediary with the Dinka and Nuer living along the Sobat and was indispensable to British officials on tour. Because of his competence in both Dinka and Nuer and his 'exceptional knowledge' of the customs of the two peoples, he was attached to the 1920 Gaajak patrol as assistant political officer. He left the province in 1924 when all Egyptian officials were expelled. Throughout his twenty-one years in administration not a single British official in the south came close to rivalling his knowledge of local languages or customs, yet because he was Egyptian he was subordinate to even the most junior, inexperienced or incompetent British administrator.[8]

It was this latter point which inhibited the development and use of 'native officers' and police in administration. The administration of the Anglo-Egyptian Sudan was supposed to be British in character, whatever it was in fact. The Governor of Upper Nile Province wrote as early as 1904 that it was 'practically impossible to permit *mamurs* & Police Officers to give administrative decisions amongst the tribes. Our one idea was to give interpretation to British honesty. Native officers capable of doing this are as yet few and far between.'[9] It became axiomatic among British authorities that ex-soldier interpreters and Egyptian and Sudanese officers were prone to corruption when unsupervised and were inevitably a barrier between the British rulers and their Sudanese subjects. This assertion was so axiomatic that it was rarely substantiated by documented examples.

The reality was often different. The Governor of Upper Nile was eventually forced to admit that 'administrative work has been done by Egyptian and Sudanese Officers which is of quite as high a standard as that achieved by more senior administrators ...'. Two years later, when the province government was trying to discover the details of customary law, the Governor realised 'that minor Officials who have so worthily been fulfilling their unobtrusive duty to the Province, manifest a facility in discussion on topics of tribal law and custom which is most encouraging to the cause of progress'. The Governor of neighbouring Mongalla Province was similarly impressed by some of his native officials. The Dinka ex-police quartermaster Fadl el-Mula Eff. Abdallah seemed to possess 'great intelligence, tact, and discretion ...'. He was appointed assistant superintendent of the Twic Dinka when Kongor was occupied in 1909, and it was thanks to his efficient administration that 'the Nuers and Dinkas have abstained from cutting each other's throats and cattle-raiding', and that law and order were introduced. 'No one,' the governor asserted, 'could have done it better.'[10]

British officials in the south continued to be dependent on native officials. It was, perhaps, more this feeling of dependence than any consistent inadequacy which fuelled British hostility. There were some spectacular failures. The intelligent, tactful and discreet Fadl el-Mula favoured his Dinka charges over the Nuer so much that the Nuer attacked his police at Duk Fadiat and he was removed at the insistence of an irate neighbouring Upper Nile Province administration.[11] But the successes were no less an influence on the direction of local administration, if less well publicised. Ahmad Muhammad Rajab made substantial contributions to the first published Dinka grammar and the first outline of Dinka law, though his British superiors received the credit. But even his success could be represented as detrimental. In 1927, when the creation of native courts became an administrative priority, there was only one Dinka chief in Melut judged capable of hearing simple cases. His authority, it was said, had been 'rather undermined' by Ahmad Muhammad Rajab:

> who by having a good knowledge of the Dinka language, and being a most impartial judge was invariably sought out to settle Dunjol cases in preference to their own Chief. Thus the Chief had little opportunity to prove his worth until Ragab Eff. left the Country ...[12]

It was the nationality, and thus the potential disloyalty, which limited the usefulness of Egyptian junior officers to the government. The policemen, the ordinary *najar*, were all Sudanese, many being ex-slave soldiers. In Upper Nile Province, unlike the other two southern provinces where irregular territorial units were raised, the old soldier element seems to have continued to be dominant in the police force until the 1920s. In many ways these old soldiers demonstrated a more constant loyalty to the government than newly recruited locals. It was in the nature of the institution of Sudanese military slavery that ex-soldiers continued to seek government employment on release from the army, even after lengthy and distant service.[13] Sa'id Abd al-Rahman, a Shilluk, served in the King's African Rifles for twenty-one years, won the DCM during the first world war, and joined the Upper Nile Province police as a captain in 1919. He helped arrest mutinous Egyptian officers in the Nuba hills in 1924, commanded the police garrison which took over the eastern district from the army in 1925, and was that great rarity, a Shilluk policeman. It was in this capacity, as late as 1930, that he was of most value to the government, despite his illiteracy and lack of knowledge of the Sudan Penal Code.[14] More recent recruits could not always be counted on for such extended loyalty. It was an ex-policeman, Ruop Joak, who fired the first shot in the Gaawar rising against the government in 1913, and who continued to advise the prophet, Dual Diu, against the government in the 1920s. Another Nuer ex-policeman, Kok Yai, scouted out the defences of Duk Fayuil in 1928, before joining Dual Diu's raid on the police force there.[15] It was against this background that the province administration decided in the 1920s to reduce the presence of the police in the rural areas and replace them with a tribal police force under the authority of government-appointed chiefs.

The small size of the police force before 1925 retarded, in part, the government's pursuit of crime, and hence its prosecution of criminals. With their small numbers (little more than 150 before 1920), the police in Upper Nile were mainly confined to major government centres to keep order among the immigrant population. In the first years of this century they only rarely ventured out into the rural areas. This weakness forced the government to limit its working definition of serious crime. The great majority of criminal cases, it was reported in 1909, were 'unimportant affrays', best left alone. Among the Shilluk and Nuer these affrays could develop into 'small internecine wars' if absolutely ignored, but experience taught that premature interference was often resented by both sides. 'The official's position resembles that of the referee at a football match between two Welsh colliery districts,' the deputy governor reported. 'If there is a really serious grievance, formal complaint will be made to the Government by the losing side, otherwise it is best to leave the quarrel to fizzle out.' Deaths caused in these open fights were, *faute de mieux*, left to tribal custom, as the government had insufficient force to ensure the arrest of the culprits. Yet cold-blooded killings were treated differently, if found out. In 1908 two Shilluk robbed and murdered a northern merchant. This crime, the first of its kind 'among the negroids', was discovered by accident, but the two murderers were soon caught and executed, tried under the Sudan Penal Code rather than tribal law, whose 'many absurdities interfere with a just settlement ...'.[16]

This feeling of impotence was frustrating to government officials. True, it was possible to report in 1911 that 'notwithstanding a plentiful absence of law, the Province rejoices in a fair measure of order ...',[17] but such order as could be rejoiced in was almost accidental. By 1910 province administrators had grown tired of visiting chiefs 'with a small escort of police, listening to cases, giving decisions which could not be insisted upon',[18] and a new, more aggressive policy of systematic tribute-collecting patrols among the Nuer south of the Sobat was adopted. It was a policy which further reduced the police presence in the rural areas, since the patrols were drawn from the local garrison of Sudanese soldiers and seasonally imported mounted infantry from the north. Police accompanied the civil inspectors only as their personal escorts. Government entered a new military phase and removed itself almost entirely from governing through a system of justice as well as through the rule of law. Tribute was assessed and extracted collectively from whole sections; non-payment was punished collectively; collective punishment was also sometimes inflicted in the pursuit of individual criminals. This policy had most unfortunate consequences on rural security and contributed directly to passive and active resistance among the Nuer.[19]

It was not until after the first world war that the province authorities tried to return to a softer approach, replacing the army with police in as many functions as possible. Police were stationed at the new outpost in the interior at Ayod in 1918. Inspectors toured their districts with escorts of police rather than army, and tribute was collected by policemen rather than soldiers. This helped to change local perceptions 'that crime by individuals must result in general and collective punishment, usually at the hands of a military force', and people in the rural ares became more willing to help officials detect and arrest criminals. There was even a case of a Gaawar chief co-operating in the arrest of his own son.[20]

Province mounted police were introduced in 1918 to round up cattle in tribute and court fines. The internal role of the mounted police, as opposed to the seasonal use of mounted infantry, was debated throughout the 1920s. Though the army garrison was progressively reduced in the province, in 1927 a new Governor delayed its final removal in order to secure more funds from the central government to increase local police and raise a new force of chiefs' police. He even suggested that the annual use of Muslim northern Sudanese mounted infantry for tribute collection would be preferable to exposing 'pagan' southern Sudanese police to the Islamising influences of Malakal and thus risk spreading Islam in the rural areas.[21] This atavistic preference for the army may have contributed to the last great pacification campaign in the Sudan. In 1927 the Lou Nuer leader, Guek Ngundeng, opposed the raising of a new tribal chiefs' police force and the construction of a motor road through Nuer country. The District Commissioner urged that mounted police arrest Guek and quickly remove him from his territory before he could organise effective resistance. The Governor refused to sanction the use of police, arguing that there were too few to spare, thus forcing the use of the army on a much larger scale. The army and Royal Air Force's ponderous attack on the Lou was one factor in spreading disaffection more widely among the Nuer. The mounted police might well have prevented opposition from coalescing. Throughout the military operations of the next two years province police, an 'irregular' force capable of living off the land, were relied on more and more for work the army was incapable of attempting.[22]

Financial problems following the Great Depression put an end to the use of the army in provincial administration. The post-1925 reorganisation meant that Upper Nile did not have to find all its own recruits, for police could come from other southern provinces. In 1930 southern police replaced northern police in all stations south of Malakal and in 1931, following budget cuts of 10 per cent, regular police replaced the army throughout the province.[23] By this time the role of the government police was confined to maintaining the District Commissioner's prestige and acting as a back-up force to handle any security problems. All other police duties were taken over by the chiefs' police of the new Native Administration.

Police and Native Administration

As early as 1905 it was recognised that constant interference by uniformed and armed police in village affairs would cause resentment, and in the north it was proposed that a system of village police be introduced to serve as a link between the people and the police proper.[24] No similar proposal for the creation of rural police in Upper Nile Province was made until 1916, when C. H. Stigand (then inspector in Nasir but soon to be governor) suggested that each Nuer chief should be required to send a relative as a *wakil* (deputy) to reside in the district station. In addition to this each section was to provide two riflemen to act as messengers between the station and the section. In time 'discipline and rough training' would be introduced and the riflemen would be used in lieu of mounted police as a mobile force 'available for rounding up "wanted" men and others ...'.[25]

This proposal had to await the formal creation of native courts before it could be implemented. A tribal police force had to be subject to a recognised tribal authority. Until the introduction of devolution in the south, following the Milner report of 1921, there were no such authorities fully recognised, co-opted and invested with specific judicial and administrative duties by the government. At least one District Commissioner began the informal appointment of young warriors as assistants to Nuer chiefs in his district as early as 1922,[26] but Native Administration police were not authorised until 1925. The first body so formed was the Shilluk *reth*'s police. They became the model for the recruitment of chiefs' police elsewhere in the province. It was intended to be 'a purely Shilluk organisation': only young men who were 'true Shilluks of good family' were chosen (ex-soldiers or ex-police being immediately disqualified); the recruits were trained together in order to create an *esprit de corps*; they were given a distinctive arm badge; and they were employed to enforce the *reth*'s judgements and further his authority among the tribe (no other Shilluk chiefs could hear cases). Within three years the *reth*'s police were able to make arrests, recover stolen cattle, stop small affrays and enforce the payment of fines, very occasionally needing the assistance of one or two government police.[27]

As chiefs' courts were established in other districts of the province the formation of chiefs' police followed apace. By 1927 there were chiefs' police for the Dinka of Northern District (Renk and Melut), the Shilluk of Central District (Kodok and Tonga) and the Dinka and Nuer of Southern District (Fangak, Abwong and Duk Fayuil). By 1930 chiefs' courts and chiefs' police were also established among the Nuer of Eastern and Western Districts, and the Anuak of Akobo. Only among the Murle of Pibor Post did the formation of chiefs' police precede rather than follow the establishment of chiefs' courts; as there was almost no litigation among Murle themselves, there were no court decisions to enforce.[28]

In each district the function of the chiefs' police was essentially the same. They were a means of introducing 'discipline' into the rural areas, hence their semi-military training, which taught them to line up, stand to attention and use obsolete rifles. Originally they resided in their own villages under the orders of their chiefs, but as the court system became more organised so, too, did the police. By 1935 in Lou district a special body of court police was established under the direction of the court president, assigned to court work only. By 1954 each Lou court had such a body of men, renamed 'post police' and commanded by their own *shawish* (sergeant). In 1943 a special body of police was set up in Western Nuer District, stationed at fixed posts (rather than their homes), armed with single-shot rifles and paid a higher wage than ordinary chiefs' police. In function they began to resemble more and more the regular police of the north. But the government was at pains to emphasise their distinctness from the province police. Initial opposition to the recruitment of chiefs' police among some groups of Nuer had stemmed from the fear that enlistment would lead to incorporation into the army and exile to the north. Thus, while distinctive clothes were handed out for use when chiefs' police visited the towns, in their own villages they were encouraged – even ordered – to wear nothing. They were to remain integrated within their own communities, not separated from them.[29]

Native Administration police were supposed to act as the main support of the chiefs' authority in the villages and were the chiefs' main contact with the District Commissioner during the rains. They were to come from 'good families' (which excluded 'detribalised' ex-policemen), and in most districts this meant that they came from the chief's own family. In fact the chiefs' police were often a training ground for future chiefs.[30] This was in contrast to the careers of old policemen, very few of whom retired to the rural areas in any administrative capacity. Perhaps the only exception was *bash-shawish* (sergeant-major) Farajalla Nuer, a Gaajak Nuer and former interpreter at Nasir and Akobo. Under his Nuer name, Kong Dungdit, he was made chief, not of his natal section in Nasir district, but of a group of 'scallywag' Lou near Akobo along the Anuak border. The government wanted someone to keep order in this turbulent and frequently disputed area, and found that a police sergeant-major suited its purpose better than the still nascent chiefs' police. Kong Dungdit prevented fights, arrested cattle raiders, organised the cultivation of cotton, collected taxes and fines on time, and kept his villages under a most un-Nuer-like 'close and strict control'. He treated his appointment as just another government posting. On retiring as chief in 1942 he did not stay with his former subjects but returned to his kinsmen among the Gaajak.[31]

The authority and independence of the chiefs' police grew with that of their chiefs. They shouldered considerable responsibility soon after their formation. Their general authority was, however, inhibited by sectional loyalties. In the Nuer and Dinka districts the police were selected by section headmen (but appointed by the DC), and in some districts (such as Bor) were reluctant to serve outside their home area. Headmen also hesitated to use their personal policeman to extract cattle fines from their own sections.[32] It was for this reason that in some districts units of court or post police were formed under the control of court presidents or executive chiefs. But sectional loyalties were still strong. In 1941 the Dok head chief (and former chiefs' policeman), Riek Dong, was attacked by a rival section. Riek repelled the attack with the rifles of four of his own police and two government police, but the attacking body of 700 men contained a number of headmen supported by their own police.[33]

The government seemed able to count on the loyalty of the chiefs' police to itself rather better than could the chiefs. Throughout the operations against the Lou prophet Guek Ngundeng and his Gun section in 1927–29 the government received constant reports on Guek's movements and active assistance from a number of chiefs' police from the Mor Lou, the opposing segment to Guek's Gun. Only two chiefs' policemen out of all the Lou Nuer were detained as political prisoners during the Nuer Settlement of 1929. As far as the District Commissioner was concerned, the Lou chiefs' police were 'more reliable than the Chiefs, [and] do not fear their people, being young bloods themselves ...'. In the neighbouring district of Nasir the chiefs' police were considered the best instrument for spreading government influence and knowledge of 'what Government work means' to the villages.[34]

District Commissioners regularly stressed the importance of the Native Administration police. They were 'really the backbone of the Native administration' (1929), they supplied 'an invaluable channel of communication between Chief and the District Commissioner' (1930), they played 'an important part in the Devolutionary scheme of things' (1934), and they were 'vital to the maintenance of public security' (1954). Their creation allowed for the reduction in numbers in the regular police establishment, and throughout the 1930s District Commissioners frequently proposed that the province should replace all government police with chiefs' police. This never became policy, but some DCs acted as if it had, running their districts without the aid of regular policemen.[35]

The parallel use of regular and tribal police was made possible – even necessary – by the parallel systems of law employed in the southern provinces. The regular police enforced the Sudan Penal Code, as applied by courts in the towns. The penal code covered such cosmopolitan crimes and vices as *araki* distilling, hashish and prostitution, and defined theft and murder differently from customary law. It was rarely applied in the rural areas, but, when it was, regular police were brought out from the towns, to which they were normally confined. When customary law was violated, it was the chiefs' police who apprehended criminals for trial by chiefs' courts.

Police and the frontier

The long frontier with Ethiopia required the continued presence of regular police. Frontier patrolling was a military duty which devolved to the police, especially in the second world war, when police participated with other military units in the containment of the Italians and the invasion of Ethiopia. Apart from that exceptional interlude the border with Ethiopia had to be patrolled to thwart Ethiopian incursions (by raiders and arms dealers), and to prevent Sudanese subjects from absconding into Ethiopia to escape government justice or taxation. Frontier security remained in the hands of the army until the 1920s. In 1921 two small police posts were established in Koma country at Kigille and Daga to protect the Koma from Nuer, Anuak and Ethiopian raids, and to interdict the firearms trade. In 1925 the police took over most of the army's duties in Akobo and Pibor. The year-round police presence at these posts and the regular frontier patrols of the mounted police did protect the border peoples from raids, but the arms trade was only deflected to other points along the border.[36]

The main problem with the border, as far as the Sudan government was concerned, was that it could be crossed by Sudanese people attracted to the periodically freer life under Ethiopian authority. This interfered with the administration of Nuer and Anuak courts, as those against whom judgements had been made would move into Ethiopia, outside the courts' jurisdiction, leaving unresolved feuds behind them. The most intractable border problem involved Anuak kingship succession disputes in the area south-east of Akobo. The Anuak king did not have the same power as his distant cousin, the Shilluk *reth*, but for all that the various families of Anuak nobles competed mightily (and sometimes bloodily) for the possession of the emblems of office, which alone conferred kingship. The border cut through the Anuak, leaving most Anuak in Ethiopia but most nobles in the Sudan. From 1921 the Sudan government tried to regulate succession to kingship, but retired kings frequently fled into Ethiopia rather than hand over the emblems. Rival nobles, too, would go to Ethiopia to obtain firearms and followers, and then return to attack reigning kings.[37] It was in the nature of this periodic border guerrilla warfare that the police, rather than the army, were best suited to deal with outbreaks of noble rivalry, and that Anuak policemen came into their own, on both sides of the law.

The plentiful supply of weapons from Ethiopia and the outbreak of war with Italy meant that many Anuak gained some practical military experience. A few saw service in *Bimbashi* with E. E. Evans-Pritchard's Anuak irregulars against the Italians in 1940–41. One, Agada war Akwei, became king of the Anuak in 1942. Another, Abula Agwa, joined the police after leaving Evans-Pritchard's service, but on his discharge became Agada's main rival. In 1944–45 there was a particularly bloody feud between Anuak nobles in which an ex-policeman was involved. A noble with at least one murder to his credit was the brother of yet another policeman stationed at Pibor. As a result of this feud, which threatened to spill over into the Ethiopian Anuak, a small police post was established on the border at Pochalla in 1945.[38] This post was at first commanded by a police sergeant with extensive frontier experience at Daga and Kigille, but it became clear that local knowledge was needed as well. An Anuak chiefs' policeman was permanently stationed at the post, and it was he who gave warning of Agada's involvement in a raid against an Ethiopian Anuak village in 1947. Other chiefs' police were relied on to help locate captives taken in that raid and to search for fugitive raiders. In 1950 an Anuak police corporal was placed in charge of Pochalla, and over the next few years a number of Anuak policemen and NCOs were posted to Pibor District.[39]

In the early 1950s Abula, aided by an ex-policeman, raised a small army of his own riflemen and threatened both Agada and the Pochalla police post. Abula easily evaded an army patrol sent after him early in 1952, but he overreached himself when he raided Pochalla in June that year. Though Abula attacked the thirteen police with seventy armed men of his own, the Anuak corporal organised the police defence (with police wives passing the ammunition) and repulsed Abula's force. The war between Abula and the government thus resembled (if it was not already) a large inter-Anuak feud. After Abula's defeat a police quartermaster from Malakal was sent with reinforcements to take charge of the border. Not being an Anuak, he saw the conflict in a slightly different light from the main participants and managed to negotiate Abula's surrender before the end of the year.[40] The experience of the Anuak and the border thus revealed the limitations of 'tribalising' police too much and demonstrated the continuing need for a more neutral regular police force.

Conclusion

The transition from military to tribal policing in the Upper Nile invites comparison with those two ideals of imperial policing, the Royal Irish Constabulary and the 'bobby on the beat'. Such an interpretation would, however, misrepresent the changing nature of policing in the Sudan. It is true that the Egyptian gendarmerie was modelled after the RIC, but the Sudanese police were not modelled after the Egyptian gendarmerie. They were organised on quite different lines and described in quite different terms.[41] The police were military in origin because they grew out of an army of conquest, but as pacification gave way to occupation, and occupation to administration, so the roles assigned to the police changed. It could be said that it was precisely the military origin of the Sudanese police that made the paramilitary RIC model unsuitable. The police had to establish a civil role for themselves in order to police the Sudan as something other than an army of occupation. There were many obvious advantages in the devolution of province security from the army to the police. Army units were constantly moved around and could be called away to other parts of the country for an emergency as well as for regular battalion rotation. The police, however, stayed in the province. They

[164]

were able to maintain greater continuity, and they also had a greater chance of establishing regular contact with the people.

The internal national tensions peculiar to the Anglo-Egyptian condominium undermined the efficiency of the police in the southern provinces. British administrators were ultimately suspicious of the influence (either benign or subversive) of Egyptian officials and Muslim, Arabic-speaking Sudanese soldiers. With the preservation of 'tribal' integrity as the cornerstone of Native Administration, the presence of regular police became a threat to the policies of British rule. In so far as the police were descended from the army they represented assimilation into a Muslim, urban culture. The regular police remained a foreign body within the province, despite being increasingly composed of southern Sudanese. First, it was the arm of the bureaucratic administration of the province, as opposed to the native court system. The provincial bureaucracy was composed almost entirely of foreigners throughout the condominium period, whereas the courts contained representatives of the people. Second, the primary duty of the regular police outside the towns was to keep order rather than enforce the law of the courts – that was the role of the tribal police. In addition the continuing frontier duties of the regular police meant that they never lost their military character.

At the beginning of this century the police were seen as one means of incorporating local people into the structure of administration, of making them a part of it rather than opposed to it. The same idea prevailed with the adoption of the policy of Native Administration, with a tribal police force replacing the regular police. The Native Administration police did establish new channels of communication between the province administration and the rural population. They also served to train and channel office-seekers into the hierarchy of chiefs' courts. But since the rural courts remained separate from, and to a certain extent subordinate to, the major civil and criminal courts of the urban areas, the chiefs' police remained supplementary to the regular police. The tribal bobby was never completely supreme on his own beat.

Notes

1 'The Upper Nile Province annual report for the period 1st July 1952 to 30th June 1953', Sudan Archive, University of Durham [SAD] 642/7/10.
2 'Remarks on the civil administration', *Intelligence Report, Egypt* 50 (28 August – 31 December 1896), App. M(3), pp. 60–1. M. W. Daly, *Empire on the Nile: the Anglo-Egyptian Sudan, 1898–1934* (Cambridge, 1986), pp. 71, 74, 309, 323. M. Coutts, 'Police', and 'Annual report. Prisons department 1905', *Reports on the Finance, Administration, and Condition of the Sudan, 1905* [hereinafter *GGR*]. Sarsfield Hall to Civil Secretary, 4 May 1919, SAD 678/3/44. *Report on the Administration of the Sudan for the Year 1949*, Cmd 8434, Sudan No. 1 (1952), p. 12.

3 See *Sudan Government Gazette*, 1901–05, and War Office, Egyptian Army, *Yearly Army List*, 1902–05.
4 See *GGR 1906–13*. In 1913 the provincial police forces were: Bahr el-Ghazal, 583; Mongalla, 284; Upper Nile, 150.
5 M. Coutts, 'Annual report. Central prisons department, 1906', *GGR 1906*, p. 439.
6 G. E. Matthews, 'Annual report. Upper Nile Province, 1905', *GGR 1905*, p. 157.
7 'Report by El Kaimakam H. H. Wilson Bey on a march from the Sobat (mouth of the Filus) to Bor', *Sudan Intelligence Report* [*SIR*] 128 (March 1905), App. A, p. 7. Tweedie to Governor, Upper Nile Province, 8 May 1914, Southern Record Office, Juba [SRO], UNP 14. Acting Governor, Upper Nile Province, 8 August 1920, Nasir, END 66.A.1. *Sudan Monthly Record* [*SMR*], n.s., 77 (May–June 1935), p. 6. 'Ben Assher', *A Nomad in the South Sudan* (London, 1928), p. 120.
8 Conversation with Zahir Surur Asadat, Retired Officers' Club, Omdurman, 5 March 1980. *Sudan Government Gazette*, 1902–24, and *Yearly Army List*, 1904–14. O'Sullivan, 'Lau Nuers', 1906, National Record Office, Khartoum [NRO], Dakhlia I 112/13/87. F. R. Woodward, 'Report on patrol in the Nuer country', *SIR* 153 (April 1907), App. A, pp. 6–7. Governor, Upper Nile Province, to Civil Secretary, 4 February 1920, NRO, UNP 1/13/117. See Borradaile's condescending remarks in 'Ben Assher', *Nomad in the South Sudan*, pp. 92–3.
9 G. E. Matthews to Wingate, 31 July 1904, SAD 275/5/38.
10 G. E. Matthews, 'Annual report. Upper Nile Province, 1906' and 'Annual report. Upper Nile Province, 1908, *GGR 1906*, pp. 725–26 and *GGR 1908*, p. 664. R. C. R. Owen, 'Annual report. Mongalla Province, 1909', *GGR 1909*, pp. 756, 765–6.
11 D. H. Johnson, 'Tribal boundaries and border wars: Nuer–Dinka relations in the Sobat and Zaraf valleys, c. 1860–1976', *Journal of African History*, 23 (1982), p. 193.
12 C. G. Cann to Governor, Upper Nile Province, 1 March 1927, Malakal UNP 1.B, copy in possession of the late Natale O. Akolawin. See H. H. Wilson, *English–Dinka Vocabulary* (Khartoum, 1906), p. 3; H. D. E. O'Sullivan, 'Dinka laws and customs', *Journal of the Royal Anthropological Institute*, 40 (1910), pp. 171–91.
13 D. H. Johnson, 'The structure of a legacy: military slavery in northeast Africa', *Ethnohistory*, 36 (1989), pp. 81–2, and 'Sudanese military slavery from the eighteenth to the twentieth century', in L. Archer (ed.), *Slavery and other Forms of unfree Labour* (London, 1988), pp. 146–7.
14 K. C. P. Struvé, 'Annual report. Upper Nile Province, 1925', *Reports of Governors of Provinces for the Year 1925* (Khartoum, 1926), pp. 410–11. (Cann) 'Handing-over notes, Shilluk district, 1930' SAD 212/14/40.
15 Interview with Kulang Majok (Gaawar Nuer), 13 April 1981. 'Note by Mr. Wedderburn-Maxwell on the Duk Faiyuil affair. August, 1928', NRO, Civsec 5/3/12, *Sudan Monthly Intelligence Report* 331 (February 1922), p. 4. P. Coriat, *Governing the Nuer: documents in Nuer history and ethnography, 1922–31*, ed. D. H. Johnson (Oxford, 1989), documents 1.3. and 2.1.
16 K. C. P. Struvé, 'Annual report. Upper Nile Province, 1909', *GGR 1909*, pp. 804–5. Matthews, 'Annual report, 1908', p. 663. F. W. Woodward, 'Annual report. Upper Nile Province, 1911', *GGR 1911, II*, p. 247.
17 Woodward, 'Annual report, 1911', p. 251.
18 Woodward to Civil Secretary, 28 October 1913, NRO, UNP 1/12/101.
19 Johnson, 'Tribal boundaries and border wars', p. 195. D. H. Johnson, 'Judicial regulation and administrative control: customary law and the Nuer, 1898–1954', *Journal of African History*, 27 (1986), pp. 64, 66–7.
20 'Note on military action and administration in the Nuer country', Intelligence Department, 23 November 1927, NRO, Dakhlia I 112/13/87. Struvé, 'Annual report, 1925', pp. 412–14. Coriat, document 1.1.
21 'Minutes of meeting in Kaid el 'Amm's office, 24.01.27', and MacMichael, 'Notes on conversation with the Kaid el 'Amm and the Financial Secretary', 31 October 1927, both in NRO, Civsec 1/2/6. 'Discussion, Khartoum, August 13 1927, between Kaid el 'Amm, C. A. Willis, governor UNP, J. D. Craig, acting civil secretary', NRO, Civsec 5/2/10.

22 Coriat, *Governing the Nuer*, introduction and document 3.2.
23 'Upper Nile Province Annals. Chapter 1', NRO, UNP 1/44/328.
24 Coutts, 'Police', *GGR 1905*, p. 175.
25 C. H. Stigand, 'Report on Sobat valley Nuers', May 1916, NRO, UNP 1/12/101.
26 Kulang Majok, cited in Coriat, *Governing the Nuer*, introduction.
27 Struvé, 'Annual report, 1925', p. 414. C. G. Cann to Governor, Upper Nile Province, 1 March 1927, Malakal UNP 1.B, copy in the possession of the late Natale O. Akolawin.
28 See C. A. Willis's collection of district reports and handing-over notes in NRO, Civsec 57/2/8, and SAD 212/14. C. L. Armstrong, 'Taking-over notes. Eastern district, Upper Nile Province', 8 April 1920, and 'Jekaing progress notes', 8 April 1930, both in NRO, UNP 1/51/4.
29 A. H. A. Alban, 'Note on the indigenous basis of the present administrative system', 26 June 1935, SRO, UNP 32.B.1. 'Lou Nuer District. Handing-over notes of Mr. P. L. Roussel', 1954, SRO, LND 48.A.2. Willis to Civil Secretary, 13 April 1928, NRO, Civsec 5/3/12. Coriat, documents 3.2 and 1.5.
30 See Car Poc in Coriat, *Governing the Nuer*, document 1.5; and Riek Dong in 'Upper Nile Province personality sheet No. 36', NRO, UNP 1/34/276.
31 E. C. Tunnicliffe, 'Akobo', 1930, NRO, Civsec 57/2/8 and SAD 212/14/88. *SMR*, 73 (January–February 1935), p. 8, and 77 (May–June 1935), p. 6. 'Upper Nile Province Monthly Diary', April–May 1937, SRO, BD 57.C.1. 'Upper Nile Province "Who's Who"', Malakal, UNP SCR 66.D.4.
32 R. T. Johnston, 'Handing-over report on Bor & Duk District', 13 April 1934, NRO, UNP 1/51/3 and SAD G/S 586.
33 [Wedderburn-Maxwell], 'Dok and Aak Nuer', 1 January 1945, P. P. Howell Mss., SAD.
34 Coriat, *Governing the Nuer*, documents 1.5, 3.2 and 3.3. Armstrong, 'Jekaing progress notes', NRO, UNP 1/51/4.
35 Coriat, *Governing the Nuer*, document 1.5. Tunnicliffe, 'Akobo', NRO, Civsec 57/2/8. Johnston, 'Handing-over report', NRO, UNP 1/51/3. 'Handing-over notes of Mr. P. L. Roussel', SRO, LND 48.A.2. Coriat to his wife, 2 July 1931, Rhodes House, Mss. Afr. 1684. W. Thesiger, *The Life of my Choice* (London, 1987), p. 269.
36 Struvé, 'Annual report, 1925', pp. 410, 413. C. L. Armstrong, 'Nasir district notes', August 1930, NRO, Civsec 57/2/8 and SAD 212/14/60–1. 'Upper Nile and Pibor District Monthly Diary', October 1923, NRO, Civsec 57/3/12. Maxwell, 'Report on eastern frontier district, Upper Nile Province', 6 July 1927, SRO, UNP G. Reports. Pawson, 'Handing-over notes', 1933, NRO, Civsec 57/2/9.
37 D. H. Johnson, 'On the Nilotic frontier: imperial Ethiopia in the southern Sudan, 1898–1936', in D. Donham and W. James (eds.), *The Southern Marches of Imperial Ethiopia: essays in history and social anthropology* (Cambridge, 1986), pp. 220–31.
38 J. N. Grover to Governor, Upper Nile Province, 26 November 1944 and 8 May 1945; D. M. H. Evans to Governor, Upper Nile Province, 17 December 1944, all in SRO, UNP 66.B.14/J.
39 J. N. Grover to Governor, Upper Nile Province, 8 May 1945; R. E. Lyth to Governor, Upper Nile Province, 8 February 1948; Abdin Farah for A/DC Pibor District to Governor, Upper Nile Province, 1 July 1952, all in SRO, UNP 66.B.14/J. Lyth to commandant, police, 5 October 1949, and 'Headquarters order on police promotions and transfers: dated 22nd February, 1952', both in SRO, PD 52.C.5.
40 R. E. Lyth, 'Report on the incident at Pochalla on 2/6/52', and R. E. Lyth to Governor, Upper Nile Province, 12 November 1952, both in SRO, UNP 66.B.14/J. Not that this voluntary surrender did Abula any good. He was tried and hanged for murder in 1953.
41 See War Office, General Staff, *Military Report on Egypt, 1906* (A.1103), pp. 203–6.

CHAPTER TEN

'Protectors and friends of the people'? The South African Constabulary in the Transvaal and Orange River Colony, 1900–08

Albert Grundlingh

This chapter analyses the role of the South African Constabulary (SAC) and British attempts to establish imperial dominance over the Transvaal and the Orange Free State. The focus is not only on the relationship between the conquered Boer population and the SAC, but also on the wider and vital structural function of the force within the context of the socio-economic and political imperatives of the colonial state after the Anglo-Boer war of 1899–1902.

The South African Constabulary had its origins in the war. After the British forces had captured the capitals of the Free State and the Transvaal in May and June 1900 and the Boer republics were annexed as British colonies, arrangements had to be made for the administration of the areas deemed to be under British control. The rudiments of a new administration were established with the appointment of a military Governor for each colony, assisted by a number of District Commissioners. The formation of a police force to add weight and authority to these developments was considered a priority, and in September 1900 Major General R. S. Baden-Powell was instructed to raise a force for police duties in the Transvaal and Orange Free State. The annexation of the republics, however, proved to be premature. Hostilities continued as the Boer forces changed their tactics from conventional to guerilla warfare. This largely ruled out regular police work and until the declaration of peace in May 1902 the SAC was employed as a military force under the British commander-in-chief, Lord Kitchener. During this time SAC units were engaged in several field operations and also did duty on the blockhouse lines.

Sir Alfred Milner, the British High Commissioner, regretted that the force was being used not for the protection of the 'settled population', but rather as part of the army involved in sweeping the country. Although Milner realised that while the war continued it was impracticable to distinguish between the civil and military work of the SAC, he nevertheless thought that Kitchener had erred by turning the constabulary into regular army units and had ignored other possible functions of the force.[1] This view was shared by the War Office, who pointed out to Kitchener:

> that the Constabulary cannot be utilised to the best advantage if employed merely as mounted troops moving in flying columns from district to district. The aim and duty of the Constabulary – should be to achieve prolonged, continuous and effective occupation of definite areas. Within their allocated areas the Constabulary should be perpetually active, familiarising themselves with the inhabitants of the country and rendering it untenable by small bodies of enemies or rebels. Occupied areas should contribute to the pacification of the country.[2]

In the event it was exceptionally difficult to create such areas where civil administration could be introduced without fear of disruption from Boer commandos. It was only in the Bloemfontein district that a 'protected area', patrolled by the SAC, could be established with a modicum of success. A cordon of posts surrounded the Free State capital for a radius of twenty-five miles and within this area farming operations were resumed. The SAC was assisted by a number of surrendered Boers who had defected to the British side – the so-called 'joiners' – and although this combined force managed to repulse a few Boer attacks, its hold on the area was at best tenuous.[3]

During the war the SAC consisted of 7,500 men, a large proportion of whom had been recruited in Canada and Australia. To some extent official thinking on the nature and composition of the constabulary was influenced by the example of a semi-military Canadian force, the North West Mounted Police. With the conclusion of hostilities the composition of the SAC altered upon the departure of some Canadians and Australians, and recruitment had to continue in Britain and South Africa. The SAC was specifically billed as a rural police force and accordingly attempts were made in Britain to attract men from a farming background. It was hoped that the experience of such men would be valuable when dealing with the predominantly rural Boer population. A considerable number of ploughmen, farm workers and other members of the rural underclasses in Britain thus found their way into the SAC.[4] Judging from a middle-class perspective, Emily Hobhouse, the prominent Boer sympathiser, was appalled that the British enlisted ordinary farm labourers to police the Boers. While in South Africa she commented on the SAC, 'Where on earth was such a low, rough, almost criminal-looking crew raked together? ... Poor South Africa! Will no nice English people ever come out here?'[5]

The notion of police work as a distinct career with a particular professional identity emerged in Britain only during the latter part of the nineteenth century. but gradually policing did begin to offer working-class men some degree of social mobility.[6] For those who enrolled in the SAC, a police career meant a regular income (5s to 7s for a constable), which compared favourably with the cyclical fluctuations in agriculture and the spectre of seasonal unemployment. Moreover, enrolment in the SAC also held out the prospect of acquiring land; members of the constabulary were promised and given preferential treatment in taking up land, and later some of the men pooled whatever savings they had in order to purchase farming property in partnerships.[7]

With the cessation of hostilities the SAC retained much of its semi-military character. Units were pushed out and scattered over the Transvaal and the Orange River Colony to replace army personnel who had been withdrawn. A network of police posts and patrols was established, to ensure that the farms in each district could be visited on a regular basis. By the beginning of August 1902 twenty-eight districts, sixty-one sub-districts and 210 posts were occupied. The Inter-colonial Council, established to bring about closer co-operation between the Transvaal and Orange River Colony, was responsible for the administration and funding of the force. Baden-Powell remained in charge of the constabulary until April 1903 and was followed by Colonel J. S. Nicholson, who did duty until August 1905. He, in turn, was succeeded by Colonel R. S. Curtis, who served up to the disbanding of the force in June 1908, which followed the abolition of the Inter-colonial Council once self-government had been granted to the two colonies. The number of men in the force gradually decreased from a peak of 9,482 in July 1902 to 1,733 in May 1908 as less intensive patrolling of the country districts was required and the administration of the SAC began to wind down. The constabulary was replaced by the Transvaal and Orange River Colony Police. Although some members of the force were retained, after self-government it was attempted to enroll more local men from the respective colonies.[8]

Much of the work of the SAC for the first six months after the war centred around the repatriation of the Boer population. Repatriation was a mammoth task, involving the transportation and resettlement of more than 200,000 men, women and children. This population had to be helped until it was able to support itself, for the scorched-earth policy of the British army had virtually reduced parts of the countryside to wasteland. The devastation was such that few farmhouses were intact. The SAC had to report on the progress of resettlement and was instrumental in conveying the needs of destitute families to the repatriation department. It also had to assist the magistrates in restoring civil administration in the rural areas. Moreover the SAC was expected to perform a range of other duties not normally pertaining to a police force, such as the exhumation and reinterment of persons killed during the war, the compilation of census data, the registration of voters, the distribution of letters, the inspection of stock and the destruction of locusts.[9] In the initial phase after hostilities, crime detection and prevention were very much of secondary concern to the constabulary.

The nature of its work brought the SAC into regular contact with the recently subjugated Boer population. It was therefore considered an important agency for promoting the image of the new regime, particularly so, it was explained, 'at a period when every man worthy of the name of Englishmen must do his utmost to prove that our administration is an improvement on that of our precedessors'.[10] In true imperialist fashion the SAC was seen to be the standard-bearer of a new and better order, entrusted – as Kitchener interpreted it – with 'the great and noble task of embodying in the eyes of the burghers of the Transvaal and the O.R.C. the character and behaviour of their British fellow-subjects, of whom they must be for some time the most conspicuous exponents'.[11]

Very little, if any, of this vision was ever successfully implemented. The SAC had to deal with a sullen, subject people who had lost their political independence and much of their material possessions in a devastating war which had left a legacy of emotional bitterness towards the British. Moreover the constabulary was often unfamiliar with the customs of the country, and the language barrier proved to be a formidable obstacle. The vast majority of the men in the SAC were fluent in English only, and were unable to communicate with Boers, who spoke only Dutch.[12] To obviate the problem a concerted attempt was made to enlist a number of Dutch-speaking members. Few 'bitter-enders' – those Boers who fought till the conclusion of hostilities – were, however, prepared to join a British police force. Consequently the authorities had to fall back upon Boers who had collaborated with the British during the war. Approximately 400 of these 'joiners' enrolled in the two colonies.[13] Baden-Powell had hoped, optimistically, that the collaborators would form 'a link with the people',[14] but it was hardly a move calculated to endear the SAC to the Boer population at large. The collaborators were intensely hated and openly despised by the 'bitter-enders', who refused to have any contact with them. In 1905 an SAC officer was forced to admit, 'I do not think you would get a good class of Boer to join the Constabulary. The farmers do not like the Boer policemen. They would sooner deal with the English policemen, if both parties could understand each other'.[15] The policy of enlisting erstwhile collaborators in the police had a further negative effect in that the hostility towards the 'joiners' was also directed against the SAC.[16] The constabulary, ostensibly a neutral force, thus become tainted by association.

Even without the presence of collaborators in its ranks the Boers would still have regarded the constabulary with a measure of distrust.

Since the SAC had been used as a military unit during the war to fight against the republican commandos, the Boers found it hard to accept it as a peace-keeping force, upholding law and justice, after the war. On a symbolic level this was reinforced by the khaki uniform – the uniform of the British army – worn by the constabulary; it blurred the lines between peace and war and made the Boers less likely to view the SAC in a favourable light. As one officer reported, 'the Boers thought we are here as spies, wearing khaki; they have got very tired of khaki; they regard us as soldiers'.[17]

The constabulary, as the representatives of a new judicial and administrative system, also had to cope with a Boer population whose notions about the dispensing of justice in the rural areas differed somewhat from those the constabulary was expected to implement. Some Boers fondly harked back to informal and uncomplicated concepts of justice which, they claimed, had held sway in the former republics. 'The people here,' the Resident Magistrate of Potchefstroom testified in 1905:

> have been accustomed to a field-cornet with two or three policemen under him, and if any complaint occurred, the field-cornet would send a policeman out to investigate the difficulty. In many such cases the complaints would be settled on the spot; at the present time the farmer does not get that satisfaction.[18]

In comparison with the republican administration of justice the British system was found to be much too cumbersome and bureaucratic. One Boer explained the difference as follows:

> I wish to point out how it was in former days. If two neighbours had a difference, whether about the trespassing of cattle or on account of ploughing in another's field, or such like, the Field-cornet acquainted with the circumstances managed to settle the differences and keep the people out of the office, but as it is now these people have to go to the office, summonses have to be issued, the Government and the people are put to expense, and a great deal of dissatisfaction arises.[19]

Boer disgruntlement with the SAC found expression in wide-ranging and much publicised criticism. The SAC was accused of being inefficient and unable to track down cattle thieves and other offenders, of wrongfully and arbitrarily impounding animals, of harassing Boer families suspected of being in unauthorised possession of firearms, and of intimidating teachers who had set up Christian National Education schools in opposition to imperialist government schools. In addition the force was considered far too large and expensive.[20] Much of this criticism stemmed from a more general political resentment at the imposition of British administration after the war. The constabulary was viewed as a military force of occupation, raised 'solely for the purpose of spying on the Boers' and organised to act decisively in the event of a Boer insurrection.[21] This view was reinforced by the fact that the SAC attended and monitored Boer public political meetings, and also used plain-clothes agents to report on more informal political activity amongst the Boers.[22] 'If you went to many of the farmers,' one Boer explained, 'and asked why the South African Constabulary was in existence, they would tell you that the force was here to watch the Boers.'[23]

Along with other issues such as education and compensation for war losses, dissatisfaction with the constabulary became a convenient rallying point for Boer politicians. At the Brandfort Congress of 1904, which was to mark the beginning of post-war political mobilisation of the Boers in the Orange River Colony, the alleged incompetence of the SAC was discussed at length.[24] To many Boers the constabulary symbolised the inadequacies and vindictiveness of British rule, and such grievances were skilfully exploited by the leadership to rekindle political activity in the former republics.

Although Boer criticism of the SAC served as a focal point of political mobilisation, to some degree the complaints may have been justified. However, it would be decidedly misleading to accept such protests at face value and to conclude that the SAC afforded the Boers no protection. After all, the Boers were not likely to heap praise on any agency of their conquerors in the post-war period. It is necessary to move beyond the litany of Boer complaints which often masks the more important and wider structural function of the SAC in the post-war society which was being engineered by the new British rulers. Of particular significance in this respect is the role of the SAC in dealing with Boer and African producers in the countryside.

As a result of Kitchener's drives during the war, many white landlords had been forced to abandon their farms, which African cultivators occupied with alacrity. On this land they often planted crops, kept cattle and built new dwellings. Financially some of them benefited from the larger tracts of land at their disposal and the higher wartime prices being paid for produce. They assumed that after the war they would be allowed to retain possession of the land they had occupied and in certain districts, especially in the western Transvaal, Africans refused to budge with the post-war return of Boer families. To complicate matters further, Africans had acquired large numbers of Boer cattle during the war under the guise of custodianship, through independent looting or on the instruction of British officers. In the post-war period, with cattle in short supply, they were naturally reluctant to part with what they considered was rightfully theirs. These developments, which gave rise to considerable tension and turmoil in the countryside, struck at the heart of the Boer landowning class. Control of the land and possession of cattle in the former republics were of vital importance in defining the Boers as a ruling class; now, under a different administration and through the circumstances brought about by the war, the position of the Boer ruling class was under a distinct threat from the rural underclasses who, as former squatters, tenants or peasants were determined to hold on to the gains they had made during the war. The situation had all the ingredients of open class conflict.[25]

While the British military, under the exigencies of war, readily countenanced the position of Boer landlords being undercut by African cultivators, the civil administration after the war felt obliged to reverse the process. Despite promises of a more equitable dispensation for Africans under British rule, it was never seriously contemplated that black and white should be put on a remotely equal footing, especially with Milner as Governor of the two colonies. The administration was more concerned to reconcile Afrikaners to British rule, which, among other considerations, involved acceptance of the pre-war pattern of relations between landlord and tenant in the rural areas.[26] Moreover, given the imperatives of British policy to reshape the Transvaal along the lines of a modern capitalist state, the creation of a large proletariat was essential. This, in turn, called for the destruction and dispossession of a peasantry that showed signs of independence. The existence of a flourishing peasant economy, enabling peasants to sustain themselves without recourse to wage labour, would have run counter to a basic requirement of the new capitalist society envisaged by the British. What was needed was a class of landowners 'who conquered peasant lands and parcelled them out under the feet of their original inhabitants'.[27] Boer landlords, who had done just that in pre-war days, thus had to be rehabilitated to their former position of eminence, which meant the restoration of land, cattle and labour, and the disarming of Africans.

It is in this context that the immediate post-war role of the SAC should be viewed. The tasks and functions of the constabulary were clearly spelt out as being responsible for the 'maintenance of peace and order – by a sufficient display of force to overawe the unruly or disaffected' or if it need be, 'for the suppression of disorder, risings or breaches of the peace by the application of force'. Moreover, the constabulary also had to see to the 'effective control and conservation of property'.[28]

After the war SAC reinforcements were rapidly despatched to areas where Africans were reported still to be armed, and behaving 'above themselves' by refusing to work for their ertswhile landlords.[29] From the Orange River Colony it was reported that the 'native during the first few months of the peace were very much disinclined to work, owing probably to ... the accumulation of wages paid to them during the war'.

In addition they were 'at first, somewhat defiant of authority'. This situation, however, was remedied by the 'Constabulary being able to assist the farmers' in rounding up and coercing black workers back into service.[30] The interventionist presence of the constabulary was furthermore essential for allowing Boers to return to their farms, particularly in the western Transvaal, where the Kgatla held sway. Until December 1902 not a 'single Boer had dared to come back', and it was only in 1903 that a few, 'relying on the South African Constabulary', summoned up the courage to do so.[31] In other districts the SAC was also required 'to bring the Natives into a state of order' and to protect the property of Boers, which enabled the 'repatriation of the Burghers to proceed without delay or danger to them'.[32]

The task of disarming the over 50,000 Africans who had acquired arms during the war (the vast majority having served on the British side) was undertaken by the Native Commissioners, who, anxious to prevent any uprising, initiated a cautious policy of diplomatic overtures to chiefs, informal persuasion and the lure of financial compensation for firearms returned. However, for this policy to be effective it had to be backed by stiff legal penalties and the knowledge that the SAC was waiting in the wings, ready to enforce the policy by military means if necessary. To a people who had just witnessed the might of the British army in operation against the Boers, the threatened use of force was a powerful inducement to surrender any arms in African possession. In October 1902 it could be reported that the disarming of Africans had progressed satisfactorily and that 'the constant presence of the Constabulary is having a good moral effect on the ... Natives'.[33]

Clearly, the constabulary played an important role in the restoration of the Boer landlords. Indeed, one historian has argued:

> If the British Administration (with its coercive apparatus) had left the returning Boers and the agrarian workers to their own devices on the farms, if it had not intervened in the class struggle between them, then the Boer landowners – the fundamental rural ruling class of the Transvaal – may have been unable to restore its existence.[34]

It was only occasionally that some Boers were allowed to acquire arms and organise sorties independently of the SAC in order to repossess land and livestock.[35] For the most part, Boers were reliant upon the coercive machinery of the state – the SAC – to protect and promote their material interest in the immediate post-war period.

After the Boers had been settled on the land, the constabulary paid greater attention to ordinary police duties. It had to deal with a wide variety of offences, the most common being drunkenness and disorderly behaviour. The profile of offences committed by Africans differed markedly; the overwhelming majority of cases related to breaches of municipal regulations, vagrancy and contraventions of the pass laws. In relation to the overall population ratio, very few whites were prosecuted for the first two of these offences, and the pass laws of course did not apply to whites.[36] It is clear from the offences committed by Africans that the main thrust of police work was directed not towards preventing or solving crimes like theft, housebreaking or assault but towards the preservation of the colonial social order and the concomitant fulfilment of the perceived needs of the upper classes. Many of the municipal regulations, which proliferated in the post-war period and ensnared many Africans, were designed to maintain the 'white character' of the towns by not allowing Africans permanent residence and acting against 'loiterers'. At the same time they also aimed at satisfying the labour needs of the white inhabitants by having an abundance of labourers available in overcrowded locations at a safe distance from the towns.[37]

The SAC was essentially a 'white man's' police force and the members were not required (except possibly in cases of unrest which might have spilt over into white areas) to patrol African locations.[38] The policing of African communities was of concern only where white interests were affected; crime amongst blacks living in the locations did not merit much attention. This explains to a great extent the woefully small black police force (given the large numbers residing in locations) of 932 men in 1908 who were supposed to police all the locations in the two colonies.[39] In the outlying areas the various 'traditional' chiefs were responsible for law and order.

The underclasses were the main policing target of the SAC, and the numerically much smaller educated African elite had less occasion to come within the orbit of the constabulary. This, however, does not imply that the SAC had any greater respect for the educated stratum of black society. Sol Plaatje, the noted author, journalist and later politician, had more than sufficient justification for being upset with the way in which he was treated when he had to visit the police station at Lichtenburg in the western Transvaal on official business. Upon entering the office, a constabulary officer yelled at him, 'Take your hat off, you damned, bloody, dirty black swine! And always wait till you are spoken to!' In a letter to the Attorney General of the Transvaal, Plaatje, familiar with colonial laws and regulations, pointedly remarked that in the Cape Colony such conduct would have been a distinct contravention of the Police Offences Act, No. 27 of 1882. He could also not refrain from adding in a sarcastic note:

I am not sure whether or not I am 'damned', but of the following I am quite certain, viz., (1) that I had no bloodstains on me at the time (2) I was not dirty, while I need hardly add that (3) I am not a pig.[40]

[176]

The educated elite was optimistic that the British administration would generally improve its social and political standing, and to Plaatje it must have been particularly galling to find that the attitude of police officials of the new Milnerite regime was just as offensive, if not more so, than that of the police of the former republics.[41]

Although the character of the SAC gradually changed from a semi-military force to that of a regular police force, the authorities still viewed the constabulary as an important military deterrent. The 'fear of a native rising' particularly preyed on their minds, and an essential task of the SAC was to act as a first line of defence, sufficiently powerful to overawe possible belligerents and to prevent large-scale 'native disturbances'.[42] There was no hesitation in calling on the force in 1906, in the wake of the poll tax rebellion in Natal, when there were widespread fears that Africans in the Transvaal would stage a similar insurrection. From the northern Transvaal it was rumoured that Mphephu, the Venda chief who had been conquered by the Boers only in 1898, was contemplating taking up arms 'to avenge the many wrongs which he and his people had suffered under the late regime'. No such revolt took place, but the rumours were taken sufficiently seriously for a mobile SAC column to be despatched to the area immediately.[43] On other occasions the help of the SAC was also invoked to dispel the 'fear of native risings' in the eastern Transvaal.[44]

Another extraneous service carried out by the SAC in 1905–06 was to prevent the desertion of Chinese labourers who had been imported to work in the gold mines of the Witwatersrand. Between 1903 and 1907, 63,695 Chinese were shipped to the Rand to compensate for the shortage of African labourers, who, in the immediate post-war period, had refused to work at a reduced wage rate and had also resisted the imposition of new mining techniques, necessary for the extraction of low-grade ore. Importing Chinese labourers was more expensive than using black labour at the reduced rates, but this disadvantage was offset by the longer contract period insisted upon for Chinese labourers (three years as against six months for African labourers), and their greater efficiency because they had little option but to accept the new mining techniques. They were also less likely than Africans to desert, because they had no base outside the mining compounds. The fact that some of them did desert bears testimony to their sheer desperation to escape the apalling conditions under which they had to live and work.[45]

Partly owing to a public outcry against the 'perpetration of outrages' by Chinese deserters in the Witwatersrand area, but mainly because the mounting number of Chinese who had deserted threatened the cost-effectiveness of the labour experiment, the mine owners sought tighter controls. One way was to approach the state for help and to rely on its coercive apparatus. The required assistance was readily forthcoming and the SAC was called in. A cordon of sixty posts was strategically established around the Rand; the areas between these posts were regularly patrolled and all houses, disused shafts, caves and other possible hiding places were searched in order to track down deserters. A 'very considerable number' (3,994) were apprehended, and the attempted desertions from the compounds showed a significant decline.[46]

The duties of the SAC also extended to the collection of taxes from Africans in the rural areas. In comparison to the haphazard system which had prevailed in pre-war republican Transvaal, taxes were collected much more vigorously and methodically under the British administration. A particularly high rate of taxation applied in the Transvaal, which Milner tried to justify by arguing that Africans now experienced the 'benefits' of British rule. Therefore 'taxation should be in proportion to the services and benefits bestowed upon them by our Government'. Such a vague and dubious argument does very little to conceal the more compelling reason for the high rate of taxation: the dwindling labour force on the mines in the immediate post-war period had to be augmented, and one way of trying to effect this was to tax Africans to such an extent that they were forced into work. Sir Godfrey Lagden, Commissioner of Native Affairs, was quite frank about this, and bluntly averred that it was essential to 'tax highly in order to produce labour'.[47] Initially the SAC was not asked to collect taxes, but a shortage of staff in the Native Affairs Department in certain districts necessitated their use. There were widespread complaints about the way in which the SAC collected taxes. Whereas officials of the Native Affairs Department went about their task in an organised way and with much circumspection so as to avoid antagonising reluctant taxpayers even further and to minimise the risk of an insurrection, the constabulary did not share the same sensibilities. Through sheer administrative incompetence it often forced Africans to pay the same tax several times over, and they were also inclined to be heavy-handed in their dealings with taxpayers.[48] The Native Affairs Department would have preferred to do without the help of the constabulary, but in order to spread the net of taxation as widely as possible they continued to rely on the SAC in certain districts.

The wide-ranging functions of the SAC should be seen against the background of the new state which the British attempted to establish after the Anglo-Boer war. The specific nature of the state was, in turn, an outcome of the underlying and deeply embedded causes of the conflict. As recent historiography has revealed, the actual causes of the war should be sought not so much in the role of capitalists as individuals or in vague, general British expansionist aims but more precisely in the structural form which capitalism had to assume in the Transvaal. Although the

Kruger government had tried in its own way to create favourable conditions for capitalist growth, it had been hamstrung by a variety of factors and proved unable to fulfil the needs of the mining industry to a sufficient extent. By the late nineteenth century Britain's central position in the international money market was being increasingly challenged by American and German competition and it became important for Britain to supplement its gold reserves. It would be an oversimplification to view this as the only consideration which led to the war. But it is reasonable to argue that no imperial statesman in the tense 1890s could ignore the importance of the South African gold-mining industry for Britain, and allow that industry to be threatened by a regime incapable of guaranteeing its vital interests. Consequently the Transvaal state had to be reshaped to make it more amenable to the demands of mining capital and to bring that state within the political and commercial orbit of the British Empire.[49]

In the post-war period, then, the state had to provide conditions in which the mining industry could prosper. This involved several areas, but most notably the bureaucracy had to be transformed: a modern, efficient civil service was required and especially a well run Native Affairs Department, an uncorrupt judiciary and an effective police force.[50] The latter was particularly important in view of the notoriously unreliable police force, known as the ZARPS (ZAR police), which had epitomised the republican government's inability to cope with the demands of an emergent modern state. In the light of this, it is not surprising that the SAC was an active agency for ensuring the smooth functioning of a new, more efficiently run capitalist social order.

As an essential part of the coercive apparatus of the state the SAC was partly instrumental in altering the balance of class forces in the countryside. It also acted as a deterrent to African uprisings and readily assisted the mine owners in maintaining repressive labour practices. In addition it contributed to the proletarianisation of Africans through the part it played in tax collection, and in its actual policing duties the underclasses were its main target. The SAC not only provided extensive policing, to an extent unknown in the former republics, but more than anything else it was a vital element in the government's social engineering designs. In this way the constabulary actively helped to shape the contours of the new society which emerged after the war.

It was, nevertheless, necessary for the new administration to project the constabulary as a force which served the interests of all classes in society. Thus Lord Selborne, Milner's successor, proclaimed in 1908 that the SAC 'had a record of unstained honour and public utility, and its fame will long remain in South Africa'.[51] Similarly, Joseph Chamberlain, Secretary of State for the Colonies, had told the House of

Commons in 1903 that the constabulary was a 'great civilising and uniting influence', actually fulfilling that time-honoured and mystical task of all police forces as 'friends and protectors of the people'.[52] However, to move beyond the obvious rhetoric and to give some meaning to Chamberlain's statement, it is necessary, in view of the preceding analysis, to replace 'people' with 'upper classes' – those classes who wielded power in the rural areas, the towns, and in the mining industry on the Witwatersrand. The essential point will then have been made.

Notes

The following abbreviations are used: *Cd* Command Papers. *CS* Archives of the Colonial Secretary (Transvaal). *CSO* Archives of the Colonial Secretary (Orange River Colony). *CT* Archives of the Colonial Treasurer. *FA* Free State Archives Depot. *FLD* Archives of the Foreign Labour Department. *GOV* Archives of the Governor. *HC* Archives of the High Commissioner. *LD* Archives of the Law Department. *LDE* Archives of the Department of Lands. *Lt. Gov.* Archives of the Lieutenant Governor. *SAC Papers* South African Constabulary Papers. *SNA* Archives of the Secretary of Native Affairs. *TA* Transvaal Archives Depot.

1 Milner to Chamberlain, 3 December 1901, TA, HC 2/45.
2 St John Brodrick to Kitchener, 15 June 1901, TA, HC 2/45.
3 A. M. Grundlingh, *Die 'Hendsoppers' en 'Joiners': die rasionaal en verskynsel van verraad* (Cape Town, 1979), pp. 171–4; Milner to Chamberlain, 3 December 1901, TA: HC 2/45; *Times History of the War*, V (London, 1907), p. 261.
4 Compare *Times History of the War*, IV (London, 1906), p. 496; *Times History*, V, pp. 82–3; TA, GOV 1165/70/10, Review of the South African Constabulary, 1900–1908, p. 1; TA, SAC Papers, Box 70, Attestation forms.
5 R. van Reenen (ed.), *Emily Hobhouse: Boer War Letters* (Cape Town, 1984), p. 89.
6 R. Reiner, *The Politics of the Police* (Brighton, 1985), p. 45.
7 Inspector of Lands to Under-secretary for Lands, 25 April 1906, TA, LDE 164/305; Milner to A. Jameson, 28 April 1904, FA, CSO 449/344/04.
8 Review of the South African Constabulary, pp. 2, 9, 31, TA, GOV 1165/70/10.
9 *Times History*, VI, pp 42–3; Review of the South African Constabulary, pp. 2, 32, TA, GOV 1165/70/10.
10 Memorandum on the South African Constabulary, June 1902, TA, HC 2/45.
11 Kitchener to Baden-Powell, 17 June 1902 (copy), TA, GOV 1165/70/10.
12 Report of the South African Constabulary Commission, Minutes of evidence, Evidence of Maj. G. D. Gray, Bloemfontein, p. 372, 31 August 1905, TA, HC 5/47.
13 Grundlingh, *'Hendsoppers' en 'Joiners'*, p. 284; A. P. J. van Rensburg, 'Die Ekonomiese herstel van die Afrikaner in die Oranjerivierkolonie', *Archives Yearbook for South African History*, 30, I. (1967), p. 193.
14 *Cd. 1551, Papers relating to the progress of administration in the Transvaal and Orange River Colony*, p. 196, Report by Baden-Powell, December 1902.
15 Report of the South African Constabulary Commission, Minutes of evidence, Evidence of Capt. O. Wood, Heidelberg, p. 305, 28 August 1905, TA, HC 5/47.
16 Col. E. Pilkington to H. Goold-Adams, 11 July 1902, FA, CSO 114/1776/02.
17 Report of the South African Constabulary Commission, Minutes of evidence, Evidence of Maj. J. Douglas, Pretoria, p. 250, 25 August 1905, TA, HC 5/47.
18 *Ibid.*, Evidence of J. B. Skirving, p. 285, 28 August 1905.
19 *Ibid.*, Evidence of J. du Plessis, Pretoria, p. 278, 28 August 1905.
20 *Friend*, 3 March 1905, 17 January 1903; *De Volkstem*, 22 February 1905; Report of the South African Constabulary Commission, Minutes of Evidence, Evidence of H. F. du

Plessis, Ventersburg, p. 276, 28 August 1905, TA, HC 5/47. C. M. Du Plooij to Lawley, TA, Lt. Gov. 90/95/62. H. E. James to Director of Agriculture, 25 April 1906, TA, TAD 599/2134/06.

21 *De Volkstem*, 22 February 1905 (quotation translated from the Dutch).
22 Van Reenen (ed.), *Hobhouse: Boer War Letters*, pp. 221, 251; Cd 1551, Report of Baden-Powell, December 1902.
23 Report of the South African Constabulary Commission, Minutes of evidence, Evidence of J. Marais of Pretoria, p. 404, 1 September 1905, TA, HC 2/45.
24 Cf. *Officieel Verslag van de Brandfort Kongres*, pp. 68–71.
25 P. Warwick, *Black People and the South African War, 1899–1902* (Cambridge, 1983), pp. 164–5; J. Krikler, 'The Transvaal agrarian class struggle in the South African war, 1899–1902', *Social Dynamics*, 12, 2 (1986), pp. 4–7.
26 D. Denoon, *A Grand Illusion: the failure of imperial policy in the Transvaal Colony during the period of reconstruction, 1900–1905* (London, 1973), pp. 96–7.
27 Krikler, 'The Transvaal class struggle', pp. 11–12.
28 Memorandum on the South African Constabulary, 11 March 1902, TA, HC 2/45.
29 South African Constabulary report, 'B' division, undated but probably August 1902, TA, CS 119/8850.
30 Report on the South African Constabulary, July 1902 to July 1903, FA, CSO 396/754/04.
31 E. F. Knight, *South Africa after the War: a narrative of recent travel* (London, 1903), p. 273.
32 Review of the South African Constabulary, 1900–1908, p. 6, TA, GOV 1165/70/10.
33 Report on the South African Constabulary, 7 October 1902. See also Krikler, 'Transvaal class struggle'. TA, Lt. Gov. 89/94/3.
34 Krikler, 'Transvaal class struggle', p. 11.
35 Warwick, *Black People*, p. 166; Krikler, 'Transvaal class struggle', p. 15.
36 Cf. Report on the South African Constabulary, 30 June 1904 (statistical table of offences with which accused persons were charged), FA, CSO 516/6773/04.
37 Cf. C. J. P. le Roux, 'Die verhouding tussen blank en nie-blank in die Oranjerivierkolonie, 1900–1910', *Archives Yearbook for South African History*, 50, 1 (1987), pp. 152–3.
38 Colonel R. S. Curtis to Military Secretary, 5 December 1905, TA, SNA 525/49/05.
39 Native Police Strength, 1908. TA, CT 222/84/28.
40 S. Plaatje to Attorney General, 30 April 1904, TA, LD 727/2288/04.
41 For Plaatje's general disillusionment with the British administration see B. P. Willan, *Sol Plaatje: a biography* (Johannesburg, 1984), p. 117.
42 Selborne to Secretary of the Intercolonial Council, 29 April 1907, TA, HC 2/45.
43 Native Commissioner, Pretoria, to Native Commissioner, Pietersburg, 22 May 1905, TA, SNA 526/9/06.
44 R. S. Curtis to Selborne, 27 March 1907, TA, HC 2/45.
45 P. Richardson, *Chinese Mine Labour in the Transvaal* (London, 1982), pp. 8–46, 173–5; S. Marks and S. Trapido, 'Lord Milner and the South African state', in P. Bonner (ed.), *Working papers in Southern African Studies*, 2 (Johannesburg, 1981), p. 70.
46 Commissioner of Police to Deputy Commissioner of Poflice, 14 September 1905, TA, LD 1133/1416. Commissioner of Police to Secretary, Law Department, 13 March 1906, TA, FLD 25/47/06.
47 These quotations and other information on taxation were taken from D. R. Burton, 'The South African Native Affairs Commission, 1903–1905: an analysis and evaluation', M.A. dissertation, University of South Africa (1985), pp. 124–6.
48 Report of the South African Constabulary Commission, Minutes of evidence, Evidence of W. Windham (Acting Commissioner of Native Affairs), pp. 177–80, 22 August 1905, TA, HC 5/47. See also T. Smuts to A. Lawley, 31 October 1904, TA, Lt. Gov. 126/110/76. H. R. Pattison to Colonial Secretary, 18 February 1903, FA, CSO 228/1334/03.
49 Marks and Trapido, 'Lord Milner', pp. 52–81; C. van Onselen, *Studies in the Social and Economic History of the Witwatersrand, 1886–1914*, 1, *New Babylon* (London, 1982), p. 23; Krikler, 'Transvaal class struggle', pp. 11–12.

[181]

50 Marks and Trapido, 'Lord Milner', p. 68.
51 Selborne to Inspector General, 14 May 1908 (copy), TA, GOV 1165/70/10.
52 Extract from a speech by Chamberlain, 1903, TA, GOV 1165/70/10.

CHAPTER ELEVEN

Policing, prosecution and the law in colonial Kenya, c. 1905–39

David M. Anderson

The subject of law and order looms larger in the history of Kenya than in that of any other British colonial possession in Africa. This fact arises not merely from the 'Mau Mau' Emergency of the 1950s, which drew direct attention to the problems of social control and the methods of law enforcement employed and condoned by the state; even from the early years of the century, law and order had been a near obsession with certain sections of the European settler community, who made the 'protection' of European persons and property from the threat posed by the 'native' majority a constant political issue which no colonial governor could afford to ignore. The protection of that settler community (who numbered no more than 21,000 before 1939) was the responsibility of the Kenya Police, a body whose institutional history has been partially charted through the semi-official study by W. R. Foran.[1] But, given the importance of policing as an element in the establishment and main-tenance of colonial control in Kenya (as elsewhere), and the surely critical role of policing as a principal agency through which an alien system of law was administered among the African population, it is perhaps surprising that historians have paid little attention to the Kenya Police or to policing in Kenya.[2]

A major reason must surely be the difficulty in isolating the police and the functions of policing from the broader fabric of colonial rule. All agents of colonialism and all elements of the colonial administration were, in some senses, involved in policing. The history of colonial policing in Kenya was integral to the broader history of the colonial experience, and it is important that the activities of the colonial police should be seen in relation to the wider pattern of social controls enforced by the colonial state. The first aim of this chapter is therefore to examine the ways in which the particularities of local conditions affected the pattern and practice of policing in Kenya, and especially to set policing within the context of the operation of the legal system. The second aim is to give a brief account of the activities of the Kenya Police – their handling of crime, their success in bringing prosecutions and obtaining convictions, and the nature of the punishments inflicted upon offenders.

Policing and the law

The Kenya Police were typical of most colonial forces in British Africa, comprising an establishment of European inspectors and assistant inspectors, with some Asian juniors, and an entirely African rank and file. In the early 1900s, while the pacification of Kenya (or the East African Protectorate, as it was then named) was still incomplete, the role of the police was as much military as civilian. The 'frontier' tradition of this early period lived on in the ethos of the force until the 1920s. Training in weaponry and military-type drill took priority, and the European recruits attracted to the force in those early days tended to be drawn from a military background.[3] From 1905 efforts were regularly made to recruit men from the Royal Irish Constabulary, but this yielded only a handful of suitable candidates; two were accepted in 1905, and one in 1906.[4] A few cadets were recruited in London, but the vast majority of European officers in the Kenya Police transferred in from other colonies, especially from southern Africa. These were seldom men of the highest quality, and even Foran's praise of their activities can hardly disguise the fact that the early Kenya Police were officered by a motley crew.[5]

Concern over the condition of the police in Kenya contributed significantly to the decision by the Colonial Office in 1907 to inaugurate a new training course specifically for serving colonial police officers and new recruits for the colonies. Taught under the auspices of the RIC, and based in Dublin, this rather rudimentary course was modelled on an earlier programme of training developed for police serving in the West Indies. Officers bound for Africa studied tropical hygiene and sanitation, the identification of fingerprints, and the use of weights and measures.[6] If this programme of study had any effect in improving the performance of the Kenya Police, then the results were slow to manifest themselves.

The few early inspection reports which survive are critical of officers and rank and file alike, painting a grim picture of ill discipline, poor training and aged equipment.[7] No one was much impressed by the Kenya Police, and many held strong opinions as to how the force might best be developed. Writing in October 1907, Colonel E. H. Gorges, an officer in the King's African Rifles with nearly ten years' experience in eastern Africa, described the Kenya Police as 'an armed mob ... of partially trained men'. Unless placed under the command of a soldier, he went on, 'they will go from bad to worse and may be a source of danger to us in the future'.[8] Most soldiers shared Gorges's view that the military should have control of the police, whilst colonial officials in London were inclined, even as early as 1907, to push towards a civilian police force under a separate command and distinct from the military.[9] Matters of finance lay at the root of this debate. In 1908 the East African Protectorate was garrisoned by 1,100 troops, more than half of whom were based in Nairobi. The 2,200 armed Kenya Police were responsible not only for policing duties but for the military defence of much of the country. In outlying districts the police were the only 'show of strength' immediately available to the administration. They were certainly inefficient, but they were also relatively cheap. To have fewer but better trained police was the aim of colonial officials such as Popham-Lobb in London; but this implied a wider, and more expensive, role for the King's African Rifles, bringing them out of their centralised barracks and into the rural areas.[10] It was a view shared by the representatives of Kenya's European settlers, who desired to limit the interference of meddlesome police officers in their day-to-day affairs whilst wishing to be comforted by a stronger military presence.[11] Parsimony prevailed: the reforms of 1908 brought slight improvements in training and in the inspectorate, but the police continued as a quasi-military force.[12]

By 1910 the establishment of the force stood at more than 2,000 men, of whom around fifty were Europeans. The force was reduced in size during 1911, following a government order which restricted the activities of the Kenya Police by placing responsibility for the policing of the 'Native Reserves' in the hands of the district administration.[13] This measure, part of a wide-ranging set of governmental cost-cutting reforms, limited the effective jurisdiction of the Kenya Police to the larger urban centres and the White Highlands (the land occupied by European settler farmers). In 1912 the actual strength of the force stood at 1,623, but the steady expansion of police activities brought the figure back up to the 2,000 mark by the early 1920s.[14] (See table 11.1) In essence the Kenya Police operated only in the 'European' parts of the colony, although they were responsible for the control of Africans resident within those areas. This division of jurisdictions remained intact until the 1940s, when the Police Ordinance was amended to allow the Kenya Police to operate in certain specifically designated Native Reserves.[15]

The much more extensive lands occupied by the bulk of the African population, the Native Reserves, were under the control of administrative officers – the Provincial and District Commissioners and the District Officers. In each district the administration established its own Tribal Police, at first on an informal basis but later formalised under the Tribal Police Ordinance.[16] As their name suggests, these units comprised African recruits. Up to the mid-1920s Tribal Police tended to serve in their own districts, often being recruited through the agency of the

Table 11.1 The strength of the Kenya Police Force, 1925–38

Personnel	1925	1926	1927	1928	1929	1930	1931	1932	1933	1934	1935	1936	1937	1938
European officers	79	96	112	113	127	133	121	113	98	101	105	105	106	112
Africans and Asian rank and file	2,145	2,087	2,044	1,974	2,036	2,042	1,661	1,651	1,629	1,660	1,730	1,741	1,886	1,919
Total	2,224	2,183	2,156	2,087	2,163	2,175	1,782	1,764	1,727	1,761	1,735	1,846	1,992	2,031

Source. Police Department annual reports, 1925–39

local chief. This rather haphazard system was improved by agreements to 'second' African constables from the Kenya Police to the Tribal Police, serving in the Native Reserves under the command of the district administration. The District Officer (DO) or District Commissioner (DC) was effective head of the Tribal Police in any district, but it was common to find Tribal Policemen assigned to particular locations without any formal supervision or command. Additionally, District Commissioners could, and frequently did, request that detachments of Kenya Police be deployed to their district. Many such police 'garrisons' became a permanent feature of district administration. The 'secondment' of police constables to the Native Reserves under this scheme was strongly disliked by the senior officers of the Kenya Police, who considered that the discipline of African corporals and constables deteriorated when they were placed in country stations under the nominal command of administrators who had no direct experience of police training and methods. In the mid-1920s up to a third of the total establishment of the Kenya Police was on secondment of this sort, although the proportion decreased in the 1930s.[17]

The pattern of policing was further complicated by the 'Special Districts' of Kenya's arid north. In these areas the administration was supported by the military, although small numbers of African constables were also seconded to serve there. These areas continued to be treated, in effect, as 'frontier territories' throughout the inter-war years.[18] Finally, it is important to note that Kenya's officially gazetted Forest Reserves were the responsibility of the Forestry Department, which employed its own police force of Forest Guards. While the Kenya Police had jurisdiction over these forest areas, in practice they left it to the Forest Department, except for occasional 'sweeps' through the forests (first initiated in the 1920s) in search of stolen livestock. From the mid-1920s onwards the principal aim of the Forest Department was to keep Africans out of the gazetted forests, and to restrict the use of forest products; therefore the policing function of the Forest Guards was real and active.[19]

Unfortunately, criminals did not always restrict their activities to the jurisdiction of a single police force. Indeed, many of the most prevalent forms of crime were committed against the property of Europeans in the 'White Highlands', by persons who then fled to the Native Reserves. In these circumstances the Kenya Police could not normally pursue the fugitive beyond the limits of their jurisdiction except when in 'hot pursuit', and so had to hand the case over to the DC, or chief, and the Tribal Police.[20] While there was usually no lack of co-operation from the DC in such circumstances, the response of an African chief was often more fickle.

Cases of cattle theft offer perhaps the best illustration of the difficulties that 'split' jurisdiction created for effective policing. The common pattern in such cases was for cattle to be stolen from a European farm, run through the forest and then into the Native Reserve. If the Kenya Police were fortunate enough to track the thieves to the Native Reserve boundary, the chief of the location through which the thieves had entered the reserve was expected to take up the chase (with Tribal Police, if they were available, or with any other retainers he could muster). Many African chiefs required some 'encouragement' on this score, and it was provided for by legislation. As well as setting down harsh punishments for cattle theft (a fine ten times the value of the stock stolen), the Stock and Produce Theft Ordinance of 1913 gave the DC power to extend this as a collective punishment to any location whose chief or inhabitants failed to co-operate in the tracking and/or apprehension of a stock thief known to have entered the location.[21]

Two points need to be stressed here. Firstly, while the Kenya Police (and indeed the Kenyan settlers) valued this legislation as essential in dealing with stock theft, it was difficult to implement. To guard against the abuse of collective punishment, all such cases were subject to careful rules of procedure and had to be confirmed by the judiciary in Nairobi and also by the Governor, before being sent to London for final approval. Accordingly, successful prosecutions were rare.[22] Stock theft therefore became something of a political issue for the Kenyan settlers who were so often its victims, and a sore point for the Kenya Police, matters to which I will return later. Secondly, stock theft also became a political issue for the DCs in whose district thefts were prevalent, and who were made responsible for galvanising the local chiefs into their 'policing' role. Matters were complicated further still by the strong suspicion that the Tribal Police could not be trusted to report or apprehend stock thieves, and by the realisation during the 1930s that many Tribal Police were themselves implicated in stock theft cases.[23]

The rather messy division of police jurisdictions was mirrored by an equally complex and ambiguous arrangement in the operation of legal codes. At face value things were straightforward enough. The law of the East African Protectorate (subsequently Kenya) was initially based upon Indian codes. Between 1897 and 1908 thirty Indian Acts came into force, including the Indian Penal Code, the Criminal Procedure and Civil Procedure Codes, and the Evidence Act. After 1902 most locally drafted ordinances were based upon Indian legislation, although they frequently made allowance for 'local conditions'.[24] While a majority of both the local professional judiciary and the lay magistrates (the DCs and DOs) seem to have been happy with the operation of the Indian codes, it is clear that the Legal Adviser at the Colonial Office from 1917 to 1931, Sir John Risley, and his successor, Sir Henry Bushe, saw the codes as a

compromise, and favoured (wherever possible) the enactment of provisions that were closer to English law.[25] But the preference for Indian
codes among officials in Kenya was based upon practicality rather than
principle. As a Colonial Office official minuted in 1906, 'The great
advantage of Indian law is that it is codified and English law is not –
hence it is possible for it to be administered in the East Africa Protectorate, as in India, by persons having no legal training'.[26] Here was the
critical factor in the administration of the law: the bulk of the judicial
work fell upon untrained lay magistrates, the DCs and DOs of the
colonial administration. Only by persistent pressure brought to bear
upon the office of the Kenya Attorney General through the 1920s did
the Colonial Office succeed in 1931 in persuading the Kenya government
to accept a new penal code, modelled closely on the English law of
criminal procedure. Thereafter the character of the law in colonial Kenya
moved increasingly towards English codes and practice.[27]

A commission of inquiry into the administration of justice and the
procedures of policing in East Africa, held in 1933, highlighted in its
report (the Bushe report) the over-dependence upon the DC as magistrate
as the fundamental weakness of the East African legal system, and
recommended reforms that more closely resembled the practice and
procedures of the English system.[28] The Commissioner of Police,
R. G. B. Spicer, held that the powers of justices of the peace were all too
limited. 'In no respect,' wrote Spicer in his report for 1925, 'does a JP
in Kenya furnish a link between the police and the locality'.[29] Formal
restrictions on the types and extent of punishments dispensed by JPs
tended to undermine the impact of prosecution, while the frequent
alteration of punishments on review and confirmation of magistrate's
court cases exposed the inadequacies of many JPs in administering the
law effectively and with due regard to legal procedure.[30] These factors,
which we will now consider in more detail, led to tension between the
police and the administration, and led the police to support any measures
that would widen the powers of the magistracy.

A third set of 'codes' (if we may term them such) were woven into the
legal fabric of colonial rule in Kenya, and had an important bearing upon
the actions of magistrates: customary law. The order-in-council governing the enactment of the penal code in Kenya (and indeed applicable
to all three East African territories) stated that in all cases involving
Africans, whether civil or criminal, the court should 'be guided by native
law so far as it is applicable and is not repugnant to justice and morality',
and shall 'decide all such cases according to substantial justice without
undue regard to technicalities of procedure and without undue delay'.[31]
These clauses can be (and indeed have been) shown to be so vague as to
be virtually meaningless, and in practice there is no evidence that they

were ever used to promote customary law in the colonial courts during this period. But many DCs and DOs, acting in their capacity as magistrates, interpreted the clauses as amounting to an effective 'loosening' of the strictures of court procedure, and this had important implications for the practice of policing and a considerable bearing upon the African perception of the powers of the police.

All DCs and most DOs held the power of magistrates, of which there were three classes, in both Native Reserves and Settled Areas. All magistrates' courts had the power to hear criminal cases of all categories, with the exception of murder, rape and one or two other specifically named offences. The classes of magistrate determined the power of sentence that could be delivered.[32] The difficulty for the DC lay both in his ignorance of and inexperience with the legal codes and in a double confusion of his roles: one political, the other judicial.

Firstly, in his capacity as magistrate the DC was expected to administer justice with recourse only to the evidence presented before him in the court. Yet he could not help but be aware of a range of factors pertaining to any case that might influence his decision, without those facts being 'evidence' as such. Most obviously, queried Bushe and his fellow commissioners in 1933, was it not likely that a DC/magistrate would pass sentence with one eye on the legal codes and the other on the political climate in his district? This was certainly indicated by the pattern of case confirmations conducted by the Supreme Court judges. Of all magistrates' cases requiring confirmation during the early 1930s, the sentences in some 20 per cent were reduced upon review, and the evidence presented before the Bushe Commission indicated that members of the judiciary felt the harshness of many sentences had more to do with politics than with the weight of evidence put before the magistrate. More surprisingly, perhaps, the statements of administrators tended to bear this out, DCs arguing that the latitude to act in this way was an essential part of the maintenance of law and order in their districts. The harshness of sentences passed by DCs and DOs during the 1920s and 1930s is strikingly apparent when compared with similar cases dealt with by Resident Magistrates.[33]

This point lay at the heart of the debates that evolved in Kenya during the 1930s between those who advocated the DC as the best protector of African interests in legal proceedings (because he knew the district, knew the people, knew the language, and could bring all this local knowledge to bear on the case) and those who proposed a shift towards a more formalised judicial procedure that respected the basic tenets of English legal practice with regard to evidence and procedure. This struggle between the 'administrative view' and the 'judicial view' has been characterised by other writers as basically to do with differing conceptions of 'substantial justice'.[34] A less charitable interpretation might suggest it was a dialogue of the deaf: between judges on the one hand who could not sacrifice the accepted principles of English law to the peculiarities of Africa, and district administrators on the other who were less concerned with justice *per se* than with the wider issue of law and order. But the apparent polarity between the administration and the judiciary may itself be an oversimplification of a more complex debate. There were administrators, among whom one should number the Bushe commissioner Philip Mitchell (then serving in Tanganyika), who saw the need to improve the training of administrators in legal matters. The failings of a DC as magistrate were mechanical rather than conceptual: procedure was more often the pitfall than was any notion of justice.[35]

To the DC, slackness in court procedures which allowed evidence that an English judge would rule as inadmissible, or flaunted the Evidence Act by permitting an African witness to give his evidence in his own way at an early stage of the proceedings (and perhaps omit cross-examination at a later stage), might be defended as a means of administering justice 'without undue regard to technicalities of procedure'. This had a very direct bearing upon policing because the adherence to strict court procedures impinged upon the collection and presentation of evidence and prevented the Kenya Police from utilising witnesses in a manner which the witness could comprehend and properly exploit on behalf of the prosecution. To this extent the police supported the administrative officers in their efforts to 'adapt' procedure to local circumstances. On the other hand, the frequent review of sentences and overruling of prosecutions on the basis of technical irregularities in procedures in magistrates' courts was a constant irritant to the police, who felt that it served to undermine the authority of the law in the eyes of Africans.[36]

The second set of confusions surrounding the role of the DC concerns his policing function: the DC was magistrate, yet also head of the Tribal Police, and so might find himself having investigated and collected evidence for a prosecution over which he subsequently presided in his role as magistrate. Could the proper rules of court procedure and admissibility of evidence be followed in such circumstances? The members of the Bushe Commission thought it unlikely, and here again saw the dangers of 'substantial justice' giving way to local politics.[37]

The division of jurisdiction and duplication of function between the Kenya Police and the district administration highlight the need to situate policing within the wider legal framework of the colony. The choice of legal structures, and their operation in practice, may ultimately have a considerable bearing upon the activities of the police. It might be argued that we cannot understand the function of any police force without understanding the law they seek to enforce.

Crime and prosecution

Any attempt to compile a picture of crime in colonial Kenya must confront the problem of sources. Records of the subordinate courts do not survive, except as aggregate statistics incorporated in the annual reports of the Police Department and Judicial Department. Supreme Court records, and those of the Appellate Division, are more readily available but deal with only a very small portion of total criminal cases. The aggregate statistics available to us have many shortcomings, and offer a rather blunt instrument for measuring the shifting pattern of crime and the changing nature of policing. The discussion which follows is accordingly generalised and selective, but does serve to indicate the broader trends. It also reveals some of the political pressures with which the police had to contend.

The 'frontier tradition' of the Kenya Police can really be said to have come to an end with the appointment of the new Commissioner of Police, R. G. B. Spicer, in June 1925. Reviewing his new command, Spicer was appalled by the complacent attitude of the force to rising levels of crime, the failures in detection of crime, and the backwardness and inappropriateness of many policing methods employed in the colony.[38] Spicer's new broom swept clean: by the time of his transfer to take charge of the Palestine Police in 1931 the professional standards of the Kenya Police had improved remarkably.

Among the more notable initiatives introduced by Spicer were night patrols in urban areas and on the settler farms, and the reorganisation of the Criminal Investigation Department. Night patrolling began in Nairobi towards the end of 1925, and had a very rapid impact upon levels of arrest and subsequent prosecution, especially in relation to cases of housebreaking, robbery, illegal residence and vagrancy. In 1926 in only 38 per cent of robbery cases reported were prosecutions obtained: by 1927 the figure had risen to 69 per cent. Figures for housebreaking over the same years were 36 per cent and 50 per cent respectively.[39] When extended to the farms, night patrolling also brought an improvement in prosecution levels for produce theft and for offences against the Native Registration and Labour Ordinances. While welcomed by the European inhabitants of the towns, night patrols on the farms met with a mixed reception, some European farmers finding themselves the victims of this increased police surveillance, being prosecuted for contravention of the various labour laws. With an attitude perhaps shared by colonial police forces elsewhere, the Kenya Police were reluctant to be involved in prosecutions under the labour ordinances, and while contravention of these laws was widespread it is probable that only a small portion of the real total came before the courts.[40]

[192]

While night patrolling had an immediate and measurable impact, the reorganisation of the CID was more significant for the longer-term development of policing work. Until 1925 the CID had devoted much of its time to dealing with immigrants and passport details, managing only a small amount of intelligence-gathering and virtually no work of criminal investigation. Spicer reversed these priorities by organising the department into three wings, Intelligence, Crime and Immigration, giving the latter the minimum resources and ensuring that record-keeping and reporting procedures were overhauled to provide the basis of the proper work of criminal investigation.[41] It is clear both from the Police Department reports and from the comments of administrative officers in other departments that these changes saw a great improvement in the efficiency and success of police operations, a trend that continued through the 1930s.

Statistics on crime and prosecutions for the period 1925–36 bear this out. It must be remembered that the Kenya Police handled only those cases occurring within the Settled and Urban Areas, and that the aggregate figures for cases reported to the police set out in table 11.2 do not give a complete picture of criminal activity in the colony as a whole; but they do indicate the improvements in the policing of the 'European areas' of Kenya. In terms of the number of true crimes reported, it is clear that there was a sharp and sustained increase at the start of the 1930s. The period 1931–36, when the number of cases reached a peak, coincided with economic depression and severe financial retrenchment in the colony, one consequence of which was a reduction in the numbers of police (see table 11.1). With the level of crime rising, and the number of police falling, we might therefore expect to see a decrease in the percentage of successful convictions obtained for cases reported over these years. However, the level of convictions remained steady as a percentage of total true cases – at over 60 per cent. There may have

Table 11.2 Cognisable crime in Settled and Urban Areas, under the penal code, Kenya, 1926–36

Type of case	1926	1927	1928	1929	1930	1931	1932	1933	1934	1935	1936
Cases reported	3,942	3,594	3,231	4,023	4,171	5,162	5,686	4,892	5,476	4,510	4,609
True cases	3,475	3,182	3,010	3,769	3,982	4,977	5,370	4,610	5,281	4,351	4,458
Brought to court	2,259	2,451	2,385	2,884	3,067	3,889	3,924	3,265	3,695	3,120	3,030
Convictions	1,946	2,091	1,958	2,368	2,614	3,329	3,453	2,869	3,243	2,795	2,701
Convictions in true cases (%)	56	65	65	62	65	66	64	62	61	64	60

Source. Police Department annual reports, 1925–36, and Judicial Department annual reports, 1923–36.

been fewer policemen on the ground, but the bulk of the losses had been absorbed by reducing the number of constables seconded to the Native Reserves. Levels of policing in the urban areas dropped less dramatically in this period than the aggregate figures might suggest, and there was very little reduction in the number of European inspectors in the force. When resources were limited, the Police Department invariably gave priority to the protection of European persons and property. Over the same period the increased professionalism and efficiency of the police undoubtedly contributed to the improvement in the overall proportion of cases being brought to trial.

However, these aggregate figures can be broken down to examine particular types of crime, allowing a more careful analysis of convictions in this period. Table 11.3 offers a summary of total convictions in subordinate courts for the periods 1922–29 and 1930–39 respectively. The total number of convictions increased considerably over this period, but the increase is not evenly distributed over all types of offence. The number of convictions for offences against property increased significantly, as did convictions under the Stock and Produce Theft Ordinance. But it was an increase in convictions for minor offences that accounted for the bulk of the rise. In 1922 minor offences accounted for 61·8 per cent of total convictions; by 1939 the figure had risen to 81·6 per cent.[42] Although these figures include prosecutions initiated by DCs and other sections of the administration, it is clear that minor offenders dominated the work of the Kenya Police, and dominated the proceedings of the subordinate courts.

It was primarily through prosecutions of this type that colonial policing and colonial law made its impact upon Africans. Taking 1937 as a sample year, we can get some idea of the offences for which Africans were most commonly convicted. In that year more than 6,000 Africans were prosecuted for being resident in townships without permission and for failing to produce a pass; 4,772 for failing to pay their hut and poll tax; nearly 4,000 for offences against the Native Registration Ordinance; 2,216 for contravention of the Liquor Ordinance; 1,790 under the Diseases of Animals Ordinance; 1,535 for trespass; 1,245 for vagrancy; and 1,485 for offences against the Traffic Ordinance (although it is interesting to note that this was one law that seemed to be contravened by everyone, irrespective of race – 1,412 Asiatics and 1,020 Europeans were also convicted of traffic offences in 1937). In the same year 4,122 Africans were convicted of offences against property (including stock and produce theft), and only 956 of offences against the person.[43]

Whilst minor offences made up the bulk of police work in court, a much greater proportion of time and resources was expended upon serious crime.[44] This was the area where police activities were under close

Table 11.3 Comparative total convictions, subordinate courts, Kenya, 1922–39

(a) 1922–29

Convictin	1922	1923	1924	1925	1926	1927	1928	1929
Against person	930	974	977	963	972	938	1,037	910
Malicious injury to property	128	143	156	144	197	220	208	173
Stock and Produce Ordinance	532	534	775	732	723	712	756	917
Against property	1,806	1,809	1,973	1,915	2,033	2,385	2,149	2,537
Highway and revenue, town and municipal, native registration, hut and poll tax	9,575	9,951	11,060	9,117	12,505	18,083	18,021	22,449
Employment of Natives Ordinance	2,187	1,839	1,387	1,533	1,417	1,620	1,312	1,492
Resident Native Labour Ordinance	–	–	–	79	751	1,050	844	901
Other	323	381	232	367	347	534	368	404
Total	15,481	15,631	16,560	14,850	18,995	25,542	24,695	29,783

(b) 1930–39

Conviction	1930	1931	1932	1933	1934	1935	1936	1937	1938	1939
Against person	1,231	1,130	1,049	1,046	1,034	948	1,120	1,001	948	925
Malicious injury to property	208	220	152	125	144	120	186	189	86	120
Stock and Produce Ordinance	787	820	1,441	1,141	1,118	639	610	878	793	999
Against property	2,783	3,175	3,192	3,178	3,846	3,004	2,911	3,313	2,973	3,322
Highway and revenue	10,948	13,742	15,004	13,567	16,476	17,453	17,766	18,212	18,180	21,436
Town and municipal	8,275	9,991	8,927	6,00	9,231	7,211	7,264	9,905	7,198	7,921
Native Registration Ordinance	5,067	5,682	5,289	3,532	4,003	5,041	4,797	4,405	4,702	4,917
Hut and poll tax	4,417	4,637	7,583	11,837	10,616	9,263	12,172	4,772	6,793	3,729
Employment of Natives Ordinance	1,614	2,434	1,626	1,417	2,095	1,082	1,447	1,195	1,754	1,593
Resident Native Labour Ordinance	903	1,260	1,363	1,095	1,280	1,023	1,003	1,104	798	872
Other	488	820	425	546	622	829	796	1,173	700	718
Total	36,723	43,911	46,051	44,353	50,465	46,613	50,072	46,147	44,925	46,552

public scrutiny. In Kenya the dominant position of the European settler community dictated that it was their concerns to which the Kenya Police were expected to respond: indeed, such was self-evidently the intention of the colonial government in restricting the jurisdiction of the Kenya Police to the Settled and Urban Areas. In the view of most Europeans, the police were there to protect settlers and settler society from the African masses. Evidence of this attitude was to be found almost daily in the pages of the colony's newspapers during the early 1930s, when the increase in serious crime caused alarm among settlers.[45] The anxieties of the European community were a factor which the Commissioner of Police could not afford to ignore. This point had been brought home to Commissioner Spicer very forcibly in 1925, when one of his first duties was to sit as a member of the stock theft commission of inquiry. Complaints of the inadequacies of the police and the shortcomings of the judiciary in their treatment of stock thieves was an almost constant refrain among settlers who gave evidence to this commission.[46]

The crimes which inevitably generated the loudest outcry from the European public were offences against European property, especially housebreaking and stock theft. The total number of such crimes may appear rather small (see table 11.4), but the value of the property stolen was frequently high. The Kenya Police went to considerable lengths to be seen to be combating these particular crimes, regularly producing statistics of police successes in these areas to counter European accusations of rising crime waves and inadequate policing.[47] However, the police could not disguise the fact that they were less successful in obtaining convictions in cases of serious crime than in minor offences. In this they were little different than police forces elsewhere: rates of conviction for serious offences climbed to around 40 per cent in the late 1920s, but slipped again in the early 1930s as levels of crime increased sharply and police numbers fell back.[48]

Stock theft was obviously a rural crime, but to a significant extent so too was housebreaking. Surprisingly perhaps, only one in six housebreakings reported between 1927 and 1931 took place in Nairobi.[49] The police presence on the farms was much less overt than in the towns. The establishment of 'farm patrols' during the early 1930s in areas where stock theft and burglary were particularly prevalent had little impact upon the level of crime, and placed police resources under severe strain. By the early 1930s these crimes were no longer undertaken simply by opportunistic individuals: professional and well organised gangs of criminals were known to be operating throughout the Settled and Urban Areas. The police adopted new methods to meet the challenge, setting up special units to deal with these crimes, and using surveillance techniques with known criminals.[50]

Table 11.4   Incidence of stock theft and housebreaking, cases reported,
Settled and Urban Areas, Kenya, 1922–38

Year	Housebreaking	Stock theft
1922	573	189
1923	503	185
1924	492	192
1925	580	232
1926	475	224
1927	373	170
1928	334	173
1929	543	269
1930	525	254
1931	739	317
1932	998	406
1933	928	429
1934	1,097	376
1935	741	332
1936	704	340
1937	869	353
1938	886	423

Source. Police Department annual reports, 1925–38.

There was a clear sense among the police and the judiciary of the emergence of a 'criminal class' in Kenya by the 1930s. A combination of economic depression and drought certainly contributed to the increase in crime between 1930 and 1936, but it was also apparent that crime was becoming more professional. In the Kikuyu areas police intelligence had identified gangs of housebreakers,[51] while in the Western Highlands investigations suggested that a large proportion of stock thefts were being conducted by highly organised gangs.[52] The rapid acceleration of recidivism also caused much concern at the time, and there were wider debates among Europeans about the impact of detention and imprisonment upon convicted Africans. Many District Commissioners held the view that the prisons, and to a lesser extent detention camps, acted as 'universities of crime' rather than having a salutary and deterrent effect upon offenders.[53]

While there is no direct evidence that this concern in any way affected the decisions reached by magistrates presiding in subordinate courts, there were notable changes in the pattern of sentences passed between 1927 and 1939. Over this period those sentenced to be fined accounted annually for between 60 and 69 per cent of those convicted. However, between 1933 and 1936, when the economic recession was at its worst in Kenya, the number of convicted persons imprisoned or detained for failure to pay fines increased dramatically, amounting to more than 35 per cent of all those convicted in 1933 and 34 per cent in 1936, as compared with a figure of only 11.5 per cent in 1927. As we have already noted, this period coincided with a general increase in the level of crime, and an increase in convictions. The net result was a substantial increase in the population of the prisons and detention camps, resulting in a crisis for the Prison's Department.[54] Further research is needed to establish whether the subsequent reduction in the proportion of those convicted who were sentenced to terms of imprisonment (from 25 per cent of total convictions in 1927 to 12·6 per cent in 1939) was in direct response to the overcrowding of the prisons or reflected a gradual process of liberalisation in the subordinate courts.

Conclusion

Policing, in its broadest sense, was the cutting edge of colonial rule in Kenya. The enforcement of colonial laws ostensibly brought order and regulation to the lives of Africans. This regulation of life became more pervasive as colonial rule went on, and was to reach its height in the era of 'development' after 1945, with the promulgation of numerous by-laws and local orders that legislated for almost every aspect of African daily life. The law, and the various authorities who policed it, gradually hemmed Africans in: much anti-colonial feeling was stimulated after 1945 by the incursion of state regulation into the lives of ordinary people, by the interference of the colonial government that increasingly came to believe in its right to engineer a new social order. The thrust of such policies was not the clamp-down by the police upon 'serious crime', but rather the ever widening realm of minor offences. The trends can be seen already emerging in the late 1920s and 1930s, as both the district administration and the Kenya Police became more efficient organisations, better able to enforce legislation. The history of policing in Kenya must therefore be closely linked to the history of the judiciary, and of the law itself: the three were bound together as a single mechanism for sustaining the authority of the colonial state.

Notes

1 W. R. Foran, *The Kenya Police, 1887–1960* (London, 1962).
2 For anecdotal accounts of policing in Kenya see W. R. Foran, *A Cuckoo in Kenya: the reminiscences of a pioneer police officer in British East Africa* (London, 1936), and Major J. H. Rayne, *The Ivory Raiders* (London, 1923). A. Clayton and D. Killingray, *Khaki and Blue: military and police in colonial Africa* (Athens, Ohio, 1989), pp. 109–35,

contains a brief survey of policing in colonial Kenya based around the reminiscences of nine former officers and also drawing heavily upon Foran. See also James B. Wolf, 'Asian and African recruitment in the Kenya Police, 1920–50', *International Journal of African Historical Studies*, VI, 3 (1973), pp. 401–12.

3 Foran, *Kenya Police*, pp. 3–35.
4 'RIC men for the BEA Police', 30 March 1905, Public Record Office, Kew (PRO), CO 533/9; Chamberlain (Inspector General, Royal Irish Constabulary) to Secretary of State for the Colonies, 17 October 1906, PRO, CO 533/23; Foran, *Kenya Police*, p. 19.
5 Foran, *Kenya Police*, especially pp. 14–20; see also Major Pope-Hennessy (Staff Officer, KAR) to Captain Crauford (Gordon Highlanders), 6 February 1908, PRO, CO 533/52.
6 'Police training in Dublin', memo. by Popham-Lobb, 11 January 1908, PRO, CO 533/52; see also the despatch from Lord Elgin to Hayes Sadler, published in *The Official Gazette* (Nairobi), 15 August 1907. For a longer list of the 'skills' provided in Dublin see Foran, *Kenya Police*, p. 39.
7 'The East African Police', report by Popham-Lobb, 5 February 1908, PRO, CO 533/52, summarises the reports of the inspectorate for earlier years.
8 Colonel E. H. Gorges to Major Pope-Hennessy, 20 October 1907, PRO, CO 533/52.
9 'The East African Police', report by Popham-Lobb, 5 February 1908, PRO, CO 533/52.
10 *Ibid.*
11 *Legislative Council Debates (East African Protectorate)*, 1717 (1907–08), comments by Baillie and Delamere.
12 Foran, *Kenya Police*, pp. 36–42; Antrobus to Treasury, 28 May 1908, 'Scheme for reorganising the EAP and Ugandan Police', PRO, CO 533/52. See also Lord Elgin to Hayes Sadler, published in *The Official Gazette* (Nairobi), 15 August 1907.
13 'Government Circular No. 12, 15 February 1911'. For a comment on this see Police Department Annual Report, 1926, p. 22.
14 East African Protectorate Annual Report, 1912/13, PRO, CO 544/5.
15 See David Anderson, 'Stock theft and moral economy in colonial Kenya', *Africa*, 56 (1986), pp. 399–416.
16 'Tribal Police Ordinance', *Laws of Kenya: Statutes and Ordinances, 1948* (Nairobi, 1948).
17 See Police Department Annual Report 1925, p. 40, for criticism of this practice.
18 The special character of these areas is well conveyed in the Native Affairs Departments Annual Reports 1927–34 (Nairobi, 1927–34). See also Foran, *A Cuckoo in Kenya*, and Rayne, *The Ivory Raiders, passim*.
19 See David Anderson, 'Managing the forest: a conservation history of Lembus, Kenya, 1903–63', and references therein, in D. M. Anderson and R. H. Grove (eds.), *Conservation in Africa: people, policies and practice* (Cambridge, 1987).
20 Police Department Annual Report 1925, pp. 22–3.
21 'Stock and Produce Theft Ordinance, No. 8 of 1913', *Laws of Kenya, 1948*, c. 206.
22 Case papers on collective punishments have survived, some to be found in PRO, CO/533, others in the Kenya National Archive, Nairobi (KNA), Attorney General (AG) Deposit 5.
23 Anderson, 'Stock theft', pp. 409–11.
24 H. F. Morris and James S. Read, *Indirect Rule and the Search for Justice: essays in East African legal history* (Oxford, 1972); Y. P. Ghai and J. P. W. B. McAuslan, *Public Law and Political Change in Kenya: a study of the legal framework of government from colonial times to the present* (Oxford, 1970); James Read, 'Crime and punishment in East Africa: the twilight of customary law', *Howard Law Journal*, 10 (1964), pp. 164–86.
25 This is covered in considerable detail in the *Report of the Commission of Enquiry into the Administration of Justice in Kenya, Uganda and the Tanganyika Territory in Criminal Matters, May 1933, and Correspondence arising out of the Report* (HMSO, 1934), hereafter cited as *Bushe Report*. Morris and Read, *Indirect Rule*, p. 119, argue that this feeling developed from 1923.
26 Minute by Ellis, Despatch 326, 8 June 1906, PRO, CO 533/4.
27 Much of this is drawn from Morris and Read, *Indirect Rule*, chapter 4. However, it should be noted that the India Evidence Act was not replaced until 1963, and even in its then revised form remained largely unaltered. H. F. Morris, *Evidence in East Africa* (London, 1968).

28 *Bushe Report, passim.*
29 Police Department Annual Report, 1925, p. 20.
30 Figures for the confirmation of cases, and amendments to punishments, are given in all Judicial Department Annual Reports.
31 See *Bushe Report*, para. 47, for a brief discussion of this.
32 Class I magistrates served in Settled Areas, Class II and Class III in Native Reserves. Until 1921 circuit judges travelled the colony. Thereafter, the Resident Magistrate system was expanded to take in Nakuru, Eldoret and Kisumu as well as Mombasa and Nairobi. Details are to be found in the Judicial Department Annual Reports, 1921–38.
33 *Bushe Report*, paras. 46–8.
34 Morris and Read, *Indirect Rule*, introduction.
35 *Bushe Report, passim.* For a colourful account of a District Commissioner at work as a magistrate see Henry Seaton, *Lion in the Morning* (London, 1963), pp. 15–17, 22–24.
36 This issue is a recurrent theme in the annual reports of both the Judicial and the Police Departments over the period.
37 *Bushe Report*, paras. 47–9.
38 See Spicer's remarks in the Police Department Annual Report 1925, *passim.*
39 Police Department Annual Report, 1927, statistical appendices.
40 Anthony Clayton and Donald C. Savage, *Government and Labour in Kenya, 1895–1963* (London, 1974), especially chapter 4.
41 Police Department Annual Report, 1925.
42 Calculated from the Police Department Annual Reports for 1922 and 1939.
43 Police Department Annual Report, 1937, statistical appendix.
44 For examples see the descriptions of police work contained in the department's annual reports, 1925, 1930 and 1937.
45 See the *East African Standard*, especially January to May 1930 and March to August 1934.
46 The report of the 'Stock Theft Commission' has not survived, but papers are to be found in KNA, PC/Nyanza. 3/18/1, and subsequent files.
47 See the carefully prepared figures in the Police Department Annual Reports, 1925–36.
48 Judicial and Police Department Annual Reports, 1925–35.
49 Police Department Annual Report, 1931.
50 Police Department Annual Reports, 1937, 1938 and 1948.
51 Police Department Annual Report, 1927, gives the earliest example.
52 Anderson, 'Stock theft', offers a detailed analysis of this.
53 See Read, 'Crime and punishment', *passim*, and, for a more recent discussion of related issues, Erasto Muga, *Crime and Delinquency in Kenya* (Nairobi, 1975).
54 See Prison Department Annual Reports, 1932–38, and for the figures see the statistical appendices to the Judicial Department Annual Reports for the same period.

Acknowledgements

The insights which this chapter may offer owe much to discussions about colonial policing with David Killingray and Richard Rathbone, and about colonial Kenya with John Lonsdale, Richard Waller and David Throup. I am also grateful to Andrew Roberts and Ed Steinhart for their comments on an earlier version.

PART III

Policing the colonial city

CHAPTER TWELVE

'Whisky detectives' in town: the enforcement of the liquor laws in Hamilton, Ontario, c. 1870–1900

James L. Sturgis

'The ambitious city'

On 13 August 1878 in the city of Hamilton, Ontario, a case of suspected arson came before the Police Magistrate. It concerned a planing mill owned by one Robert Addison. On the morning of Sunday the 11th, according to Addison's testimony, he had gone to the factory, where he had satisfied himself that everything was in order and that the furnace doors were closed. He then proceeded to a tavern where he met a carpenter named John Brass, with whom he drank a whisky. The two moved on to Farr's tavern, where they had three more drinks together before rounding off the morning with at least one whisky at Kramer's. Acknowledging that he was not sober by the time he set off for home, Addison's estimate was that he had consumed at least six drinks. While he was at home sleeping off the effects of his morning's intake, it was alleged, Brass, disappointed at not being given a job in the mill by Addison, had set fire to it.[1] For the purposes of this chapter, the point of the episode is less the frequency of arson as a means of revenge in the nineteenth century than the ease with which the individuals concerned were able to purchase and consume alcoholic drink. The fact was that in Ontario in 1878 the law forbade the selling of alcohol on Sundays. This study, then, will focus on explaining why such drinking behaviour occurred and, more important, why there were difficulties in enforcing the liquor laws in Hamilton during the late nineteenth century. There are several obstacles which are immediately encountered, not the least of which is the lack of comparative studies. One very respected authority has recently reminded us that even in the United States, where temperance history has its greatest centrality and recognition, the analysis of liquor law enforcement has yet to be begun.[2]

The incident described above took place during the decade of crucial importance in the development of new attitudes towards drinking in the province. Many of the freewheeling and permissive attitudes and practices of earlier pioneering generations still prevailed. However, as farming became more intensely commercial, combined with the effects of the rise of industrialism and urbanism, the old ways came under more frequent and intense attack from a rising band of temperance advocates. Increasingly prominent in this onslaught were the ministers of the major Protestant Churches, especially the Methodists and the Presbyterians. Also to the fore were the women's organisations, such as the Women's Christian Temperance Union (WCTU), which had been much inspired by the brave example of the women of Ohio in their crusading attempts to close down the saloons. They were joined by a new breed of secular and professional temperance organisers, such as F. S. Spence, who took a leading hand in forming the Dominion Alliance for the Total Suppression of the Liquor Traffic in 1875. What all these groups shared was an outlook which placed increasing emphasis on the use of the law as a means of social control. In their opinion the evils of the drink trade were so enormous in individual and social terms that only the state itself could, either by introducing national prohibition or by local option, cure them. The advocacy of moral suasion or gospel temperance could still be heard but the new orthodoxy regarded such preventive measures as supplementary and incapable on their own of reversing the wet tide. As a result the decade saw frequent attempts, some in force for only short periods of time, to enforce a ban on all sales of liquor and beer at the local level.[3]

The only attempt by the prohibitionists to introduce local option in Hamilton happened in 1881, via the terms of federal legislation in the form of the Canada Temperance Act of 1878. The results of the vote on 13 April produced a serious setback to their hopes when only 1,161 supported while 2,811 opposed this legislation.[4] A provincial plebiscite in 1894 again showed Hamilton in opposition, as did a federal plebiscite in 1898, when 2,844 voted in favour of prohibition and 4,376 against.[5] It was not until 1902, in another provincial vote, that prohibition won a favourable response. It might be said that Hamilton was drifting in the direction of the prohibitionist camp, but not with any marked conviction. Indeed, the disastrous vote in 1881 induced temperance workers in the city to fall back upon more traditional methods of reclamation of the individual by gospel temperance. For many years the leader of the Hamilton Temperance Club was Daniel Black Chisholm. A lawyer by training and a convert to Methodism in 1854, he was president or director of several leading life insurance companies, as well as having an interest in several tenement buildings in the city. After serving as Conservative MP for Hamilton from 1872 to 1874, he abandoned his political career in federal politics after a legally contested election in 1875.[6]

Hamilton developed in the years after 1846, with the location of the Great Western Railway there in the 1850s providing a spur to industrial activity. One consequence of its industrialisation was the increase in the number of firms which employed over 150 workers. The 1871 census showed Hamilton to have five such industries, which, in Ontario, put it in second place only to Toronto. Naturally enough, the population of the city grew apace, from 25,000 in 1870 to 52,000 in 1900. From a situation in the 1850s when every class of person was able to walk to work, the expansion of residential areas in outlying parts accompanied an increased clustering of similar types of occupational groups. The working classes became predominant in the northerly parts of the city near the tracks and in the low-lying land of the bay, whilst the better-off established themselves nearer the mountain. Ethnically, Hamilton retained a very British character throughout the period. In 1871 the English segment of the population represented 28 per cent of the total, followed by Canadian-born at 19 per cent, Scots 17 per cent, Irish Catholics 15 per cent and Irish Protestants at 11 per cent. Americans and Germans made up the largest of the minority groups. The fact that by 1890 Hamilton contained 31,649 Canadian-born citizens as against 15,596 foreign-born was evidence of its steady rather than spectacular growth.[7]

In keeping with its incorporation and growth as a city was the development of Hamilton's Police Department, which mirrored the gradual evolution of professionalism in other cities on the continent. If Eric Monkkonen's criterion for the starting point of the new police is taken, then it was in 1880 that a standard uniform for both summer and winter wear was decided upon by the governing body, the Police Commissioners.[8] However, as early as 1857 the twenty-nine members of the department made it the largest unit of the civic bureaucracy. Economic recessions and civic parsimony kept numbers in check in succeeding years to such effect that in 1876 the force numbered only two sergeants, two detectives and twenty-eight constables. By 1892 the numbers had risen to fifty, which included four detectives.[9] The method of controlling the police inevitably partook of certain features of the London Metropolitan Police, as was also true of many American cities. However, unlike the latter, where a greater concern for democratic control led eventually to serious problems of patronage and bribery, Hamilton tried to sidestep such problems by substituting in 1872 control by a committee of the city council for an independent Board of Police Commissioners. Composed of the mayor, the police magistrate and the senior county court judge, the board handled the administrative duties of the police, including the drawing up of regulations and the disciplining of the force. In doing so Hamilton adhered to the same pattern which Toronto had established in 1858.[10]

The pay of the police was a constant source of friction. Often it was only the pressure of public opinion, concerned about the proper levels of public security, that induced the commissioners to be more generous. In 1885, as a result of a public deputation, the levels of pay per year were raised to: sergeants and detectives, $725; first-class constables, $584; second-class constables, $492.[11] Such remuneration put policemen roughly on a par with skilled workers. After provincial legislation in 1875 the police commissioners lost their former responsibility for the licensing of premises. This duty was taken over by a Board of Licence Commissioners, appointed by the government. In addition, the new regulations provided for a licence inspector who now became the key enforcement agent. In Hamilton, however, the police commissioners retained overall control, since the inspector operated as a detective within the force. The commissioners also made certain that the chief of police and his entire force were made responsible for the enforcement of the liquor laws, stipulating, in particular, that the chief was to inform them of any infractions of the law.[12]

The Mowat machine

Hamiltonians in search of a drink had a wide range of sources from which to choose. The tavern, in company with its downmarket and shabbier associate, the saloon, functioned, as elsewhere, as a vitally important social organism – a centre of warmth and conviviality, a meeting and hiring place, and a cheap location for food and shelter. Although the licensed grocery stores were supposed to confine their activities to those of an off-licence, they had a well earned reputation for encouraging a great deal of illegal sampling and tippling on the premises. Not to be outdone, drug stores, although legally entitled to dispense liquor for medicinal purposes, found ample possibilities for illicit sale as well. Besides the opportunities for illegal vending by licensed establishments, such as selling liquor in forbidden hours, there were, of course, those places which never pretended to come within the threshhold of the law. It has to be said, however, that the legal framework within which liquor was sold was of a fairly rudimentary kind. Among the clear stipulations were those which prohibited sales near public works or on polling days or to Indians. The law which caused the greatest difficulty of enforcement was one which antidated confederation in 1867. As early as 1859 the legislature in Canada West had outlawed the opening of all outlets between 7 p.m. on Saturday and 8 a.m. on Monday. The manner in which these laws were obeyed was revealingly depicted in a speech in 1868 by E. B. Wood, the Provincial Treasurer, in the legislative assembly of Ontario. It was his opinion that the early closing law on a Saturday and the ban on Sunday drinking were 'universally violated', and that those who sold within the law were outnumbered by those who did not.

Such was the state of public opinion that steps taken to control the illegal vendors were often defeated; he cited an instance in Woodstock the previous year when a riot broke out after a successful conviction. Leaving aside the threat of public disorder, a conviction would almost certainly lead to an appeal being lodged in which in nine cases out of ten the jury would side with the accused.[13]

Self-respecting temperance advocates could not be expected to be satisfied with this state of things. When the Liberals assumed power in 1872, they exerted more and more pressure for change upon a government which they regarded as favourably disposed to their cause. The head of the party and Premier from 1872 to 1896 was Oliver Mowat, a man who could be said to have discovered the formula for political longevity in Ontario. He combined a reforming instinct with a shrewd appreciation of the value of patronage and seizing the main electoral chance. Mowat liked to hug the recognisable shores of public opinion and in any difficult narrow passage to seek out the middle way. A teetotaller himself, he calculated in the early days of his administration that changes in the liquor laws were necessary in order to fulfil the expectations of Liberal and temperance activists throughout the province. The result was a series of measures brought in by the Provincial Treasurer, Adam Crooks. It was unequivocally laid down that police officers had a duty to enforce regulations. The kind of evidence required to bring about a conviction of illegal selling was relaxed so that it was no longer necessary to catch someone in the actual act of drinking. Because municipalities, fearful of losing needed revenue, had not responded to earlier enabling legislation allowing a reduction in the number of licences, Crooks passed legislation which tied a maximum number of outlets to size of population. This was coupled with a rise in the licence fees. Except in so far as these measures emanated from a Liberal government, thought to be anxious to curry favour with temperance forces, they were not in themselves partisan. What was clearly controversial was the step taken to put the decision-making as to who would get a diminished number of licences in the hands of the previously mentioned licence commissioners.[14] One of the predictions made at the time by the opposition spokesman, William Macdougall, was that provincial appointment would lead to blatant political patronage.[15] That such a view was borne out by subsequent events had been attested to by, among others, Professor P. B. Waite, who points out that it became potentially damaging for a licence holder to become too closely identified with the Conservative Party.[16] In other words, respect for the law was seriously impaired by the political coloration which it took on.

John Mackenzie, who was licence inspector in Hamilton during the 1880s and early 1890s, was alleged to have worked actively in the Liberal interest. It was the Conservative newspaper, *The Hamilton Spectator*, which reiterated this charge. As the Mowat machine rolled on from one electoral triumph to another the complaints became more bitter and insistent. In 1888 the newspaper charged that the 'whisky commissioners', its none too delicate rendering of the licence commissioners, were attempting to root out all Conservative licence holders. Mackenzie was named as being particularly zealous in this regard. It also claimed that mere groggeries could be legalised if the owners were of the correct political persuasion.[17] On the other hand, as another newspaper claimed in 1898, a respectable place, such as the Mountain View Hotel, could lose its licence because it became widely known that the owner was a Conservative.[18]

The most detailed and incriminating accusation was levelled against John Mackenzie in 1889. The case concerned James E. Lottridge, a brewer, who also controlled the mortgages of nearly 50 taverns and saloons in the city. When the Liberals gained power Lottridge had begun to move away from his former Tory allegiance, at first locally and eventually nationally as well. Under oath he had declared that he was only going 'where my interests are'. It then became common practice for Lottridge, in company with Mackenzie, to canvass practically the entire group of licence holders. In return for such loyalty Lottridge was able to retain his existing licences as well as getting inside information as to when general inspections were to be carried out.[19]

Mackenzie's disciplinary record within the police force lends itself to the interpretation that he may indeed have had influential friends. For misdemeanours, such as drunkenness, ordinary members of the department might expect to be granted a second chance but they would be pressing their luck if another offence were to occur. It is instructive to compare this with the elasticity with which Mackenzie was treated. On 11 March 1884 it was reported that, when drunk, Mackenzie had drawn a revolver in a threatening way against a constable. The next month he was fined for being inebriated and using abusive language. In July the chief reported to the board that Mackenzie had been guilty of 'improper conduct' but the only action taken was to assert that 'an error of judgement' had been made. In September 1885 Mackenzie was publicly charged with having beaten up a man named McGrath and arresting him without a warrant. Eventually, having been defended by the city solicitors, the charges against him were dropped. Then in 1891 another member of the force reported Mackenzie for being drunk, using profane language and threatening to handcuff the constable concerned. Mackenzie's denial was upheld by the commissioners, who considered that the inspector was 'suffering from the effects of too much quinine and was not himself that day'. The next year, with the weight of the evidence

[207]

of five constables against him, he was fined $10 for being intoxicated. Despite this record of misconduct it was not until August 1894 that action was taken. Even then he was not dismissed but, instead, demoted to constable.[20]

'The whisky detectives'

Ontario inherited its legal system from England and suffered the same difficulties of a system which lacked a public prosecutor to bring cases before the courts.[21] Temperance forces constantly lamented the fact that, even after the reforms introduced by Crooks, the public were not willing to try to rid themselves of the nuisance and insult of illegal drinking by initiating court action. Increasingly the task was taken on by the new police forces, which, however capable they were of dragging endless cases of drunken or disorderly persons into court, had their effectiveness in this regard severely reduced by the very fact of their uniform. The problem of the licence inspector was similar. He would soon become known to the relevant layers of society so that his face was as much a signal to others as the policeman's uniform. Take, for instance, what happened to inspector R. F. Keays on a Saturday night in May 1876. At about 10 p.m. he had hidden himself away to the rear of a saloon belonging to Samuel Easter, where he observed an unusually heavy traffic of callers being silently admitted through the back door. Keays's curiosity got the better of him, and as he moved closer, the door was immediately locked and a bell rung. Easter then contested Keays's right of entry long enough to allow his intended customers to make good their escape.[22]

The stratagem adopted by the police and inspectors in Ontario to deal with such limitations was the recourse to paid informers who, in recompense for their efforts, were paid half the fine of anyone who was convicted, which usually amounted to at least $10. These individuals, who in the folklore of the time were regarded with opprobrium, were the so-called 'whisky detectives'. Rarely can a calling of any kind have had so much odium attached to it. One of them, George Albert Mason, became so notorious that when he pitched up in London in 1872 his presence led to a near riot.[23] In the opinion of *The Hamilton Spectator*:

> whenever a witness appears in court to give evidence concerning infractions of the liquor law, especially if that witness is a professional informer, the public display more sympathy for the defendant than for the witness. One reason for this partiality is the bad character of some of the most noted informers.

The editorial added that the public strongly suspected that anyone who depended on such work would not cavil at the convenience of perjury.[24] Nevertheless, the province had made a stand on the question of illegal selling and was determined to reduce its prevalence. In Hamilton the amount of money spent on paid informers rose from $132.57 to 1875 to $1,006.75 in 1878. In four different months in the latter year the total figure exceeded that for the whole of 1875. After 1875 there was also an additional bonus of $4 for each case, whether successful or not, for the inspector on top of his annual salary of $700.[25]

One of the 'whisky detectives' who plied his trade for a time in Hamilton was named William Wilson. As an accomplice in the task of gaining sufficient information to bring about conviction he had made an arrangement in November 1878 with a lesser known individual, a woman by the name of Potter. In an obvious attempt to impair her credibility as a witness, a hostile newspaper report alleged that she was a bigamist whose real name was McDonald. Nevertheless, her claim that she had successfully purchased a bottle of beer after 7 p.m. from a grocer was corroborated by Wilson, who had stood outside with notepaper in hand. The result was a fine of $20.[26].

Wilson was also involved the same year in what appears to have been something of a vendetta by Inspector Keays against William Aitcheson, a forty-year-old grocer. Two convictions of illegal selling in December followed hard on the heels of a similar charge brought against him in October.[27] This latter case led to a judgement that Aitcheson had transgressed the law by taking an order for liquor outside his shop.[27] Aitcheson wrote to the press to complain that the case had arisen because he had accepted an order for a gallon of brandy off the premises from a man who lived five miles away. It was his firm opinion that it was common practice for leading retailers to send pedlars from door to door selling liquor. And even if the practice were to stop, what about the wholesalers, who recognised no limits to where they might solicit for business?[29] This outburst led to an attempt by Wilson to cash in on his vulnerability. Within two months Aitcheson was in court again, this time with a charge levelled by him against Wilson. Aitcheson alleged that by means of a ruse he was tricked into having a meeting with Wilson at a house near his shop. Wilson asked him if he had any reason to suspect that Keays was hostile towards him. When Aitcheson gave a noncommital reply, Wilson volunteered the opinion that Keays hated him 'like the devil'. After informing Aitcheson that he had evidence on three separate counts of illegal selling against him, Wilson offered the view that 'the old man', Keays, had 'gone for you quite enough lately'. Everything could be settled satisfactorily if Aitcheson paid $30. When this had been done Wilson gave the grocer the information as to who the new 'whisky detectives' in

[209]

town were. However, Aitcheson had, prior to this, taken the precaution of informing a police officer, who now appeared on the scene and arrested Wilson. He later upheld Aitcheson's testimony in court.[30]

As such an episode demonstrated, those against whom charges were levelled could often be as inventive as the detectives themselves. In late 1879 two individuals, Alfred Page and George Langley, sought convictions against a number of hotel keepers and liquor dealers. The two men, while waiting to give evidence in court, were suddenly arrested on a warrant from St Catherines, alleging perjury against a shopkeeper there. As they were being escorted to the railway station a large crowd followed close behind, hooting and barracking them. The result of this legal manoeuvre was that when the cases came up in Hamilton they were dismissed, since the witnesses were behind bars in the neighbouring city. Page and Langley were strongly of the view that it was influential interests in Hamilton who had engineered their disappearance.[31]

Working on the margins

John C. Weaver has typified the change which came over many North American cities at the turn of the century as one which incorporated new criteria of bureaucratic efficiency and institutional reform. This stage replaced one where the predominant ethos on the surface was moral purity but which underneath was characterised by political fixing and shady dealings.[32] In the upper reaches of society this kind of atmosphere could expose law officers to the temptations and dangers of various combinations of treating, bribery and political arm-twisting. At the other end of society there were more traditional dangers of a too cosy collusion between law enforcers and disreputable or quasi-criminal elements. After all, the unsocial hours and the nature of their work separated the police from the ordinary public, giving them more in common with those who operated on the margins of society.[33] In this respect the detective was more under suspicion than the ordinary policeman on the beat. In 1883 a group of distillers, brewers and hotel keepers, parading under the name of the Ontario Trades Benevolent Association and claiming 2,500 members, gave evidence before a federal special committee in Ottawa. Their animus was directed against the unlicensed establishments which, they charged, hired 'runners' after 7 p.m. on Saturday to entice as yet unsatisfied drinkers into their often squalid premises. Interestingly, they asked that the police be given responsibility for dealing with such illegal sites rather than 'the irresponsible detectives', many of whom, they claimed, were of the criminal class themselves.[34] What follows in the way of elucidation of working at the margins can be little more than a searchlight playing upon the darkness.

The kind of twilight world within which police and detectives worked and socialised can be gleaned from several incidents concerning so-called houses of ill repute. The attitude of the law toward prostitutes was, to say the least, punitive.[35] In 1873 an instruction had gone out to the police that they were to inspect such places weekly and report on who frequented them. Later this was amended to stipulate that detectives were to undertake such duties fortnightly.[36] Houses where sex was for sale also experienced a demand for liquor and this, not surprisingly, led Inspector Keays to attempt to gain convictions against the owners via the well trodden route of the paid informer. But who of an even semi-reliable kind could one get to provide the information? Keays's chosen instrument on one occasion in 1878 proved extremely faulty. It was with the evidence provided by someone who appeared in court under the name of Lorenzo McBride that Keays brought separate charges against two women and a man for illegally selling beer. The usual tactic of the defence in such cases was to try to discredit the witness. Thus, during interrogation in court, McBride was forced to admit that he had been in jail in Cayuga for theft and that a similar charge was pending in Toronto. Several witnesses made the highly likely point that McBride was not his real name. The defence lawyer tore what remained of McBride's reputation into shreds by suggesting that he had abandoned his family and had been driven out of his home town of Caledonia because his reputation was so unsavoury. In the circumstances Keays wisely decided to drop all charges.[37] Another side of the problem was police officers who consorted with prostitutes. In 1878 three constables, one a former licence inspector, were confirmed to have spent over two hours in a house of ill fame in John Street.[38] In 1884 a Detective Doyle barely escaped dismissal when charges of being drunk and in the company of a prostitute at the Glassblowers' Ball were brought against him.[39]

At another level the suspicion was that police officials could be hampered in their duties by political or social pressures. For instance, how did the police deal with 'a powerful political boss' of the predominantly Irish area of Corktown, 'Dude' Sullivan, who was also a licensed grocery store owner?[40] Or to what extent did the law turn a blind eye to the very prevalent practice of political parties depositing kegs of beer in inviting places for the convenience of electors on polling day?[41] That politics in a more general way could influence the action of the police was the opinion of the Rev. Father Geoghegan of Hamilton, who, in a public speech to considerable applause, stated that:

> Our policemen don't put themselves out to treat our boys with ordinary decency. I have seen policemen on Saturday night who could not notice men coming out of the side door of a saloon run at a lad who was catching a ball in the street, and threaten him with arrest. But the boys had no votes

which could control the aldermen who put the coat on the policeman's back, while the bar-room loafers had.[42]

Another perennial problem was the frequent practice of the police accepting or demanding free drinks at saloons or taverns. In March 1888 the police commissioners stated publicly that tippling by members of the police force had increased worryingly over the previous six months. The chief was instructed to warn officers against this practice, as were the licence commissioners to do likewise with the saloon keepers.[43] That the problem did not go away was evidenced by the fact that as late as 1909 the mayor told the police commissioner that, according to several very reliable citizens, it was common practice for policemen to demand free liquor at saloons.[44] That the police were less than dutiful, but positively unhelpful in bringing to court those guilty of infractions of the liquor laws, was the charge of the licence inspector in 1907, although he later thought better of the allegation and withdrew it.[45] In 1895 two aldermen demanded a public inquiry after having been informed by certain policemen that their superior officers discouraged them in any attempt to curtail the activities of illegal gambling places.[46]

Liquor laws and public opinion

America's 'noble experiment', Prohibition, was brought down by the inability to enforce it. When a substantial portion of the population did not support the law it was flagrantly flouted.[47] In Hamilton the licence and police commissioners were more and more uncomfortably squeezed between a minority of respectable and vociferous temperance advocates, usually with religious or business connections, and a less articulate but majority acceptance of drinking facilities, backed up by traditionally powerful and wealthy brewers and hotel keepers. As opinion polarised in the late nineteenth century, even the Mowat government found it testing of its ingenuity to ride the temperance and liquor horses at one and the same time. J. M. Gibson, MP for Hamilton and a Minister in the Liberal government, admitted in 1897 that they were caught between 'two fires'. The resulting heat was such that 'we have been obliged to make such important concessions to the advanced wing (which seems to embody nearly the whole of the Methodist denomination) that we have incurred the dissatisfaction of the liquor trade to a rather serious extent'.[48]

Hamilton's civic authorities were subjected to numerous pressure groups who urged a reduction in the number of licensed outlets and the strict enforcement of the law. Among such bodies was the Young Men's Christian Association, which in particular called for the upholding of the early closing law on Saturdays.[49] Another organisation of some note was the Evangelical Alliance, the origins of which lay in the No Popery outburst in Liverpool in the 1840s, but which in a Canadian setting paid increasing attention to the problem of drink. In 1875 its representatives asked for a curtailment on the issuing of any more licences.[50] In its struggle against the drink trade the organization adopted various measures such as appealing to all self-respecting females to do what they could to prevent the serving of alcoholic beverages on festive occasions, such as New Year's Eve. The treasurer of the organisation admitted in 1879, however, that, in contrast to the staunchness of its mainly ministerial members, laymen were too 'lukewarm' in their support.[51] From time to time the Hamilton Temperance Club criticised the police for the inadequate enforcement of the laws. The criticism was always met by the chief, as on one occasion in 1884, with a denial that the force was anything less than assiduous in its dedication to the upholding of the laws concerning drink.[52] After the formation of the Women's Christian Temperance Union in the city in March 1875, it too became a force to be reckoned with.[53] Its chief contribution was undoubtedly in creating public awareness of the issues surrounding juvenile smoking and drinking.[54] As parental concern increased in the 1890s the chief had to pay more attention to this new category of social problem.[55] Another powerful element which began to take a strong line on the need to reduce the number of licences was the leading manufacturers. In 1878 Edward Gurney, R.M. Wanzer, Adam Hope, L.D. Sawyer and F.C. Ker joined forces with 761 ratepayers to make such a demand. In particular, they wished to abolish all grocery outlets, arguing that such a step would reduce public charges for food and shelter. Some members of the city council were less than impressed with the temperance credentials of this group; one stated that 'those tipplers who had put their names to that petition, when their hearts were not there, made asses of them-selves'.[56] The self-interested motives of the leading men in this move were all too transparent. Gurney, Wanzer and Sawyer were among the hard-liners in the opposition to the 'nine hours' movement of the trade unionists.[57] Representative of the array of interests which could be mounted was the opposition which was formed in April 1888 to block the granting of a new tavern licence. The owner of a nearby factory said that it would be too close to his gates. A representative of the various temperance organisations objected because it would be in too close proximity to a local school, obliging children to walk past it. A petition for a general reduction in the number of licences which was submitted by the same coalition of interests contained the signatures of twenty-six manufacturers, as well as members of the WCTU, the Moral Reform Association, the Royal Templars and the Sons of Temperance.[58]

[213]

H

There were far fewer individuals and organisations willing to take to the public platform in defence of drink or the trade in it. Was this unwillingness not the realisation of the prohibitionists' hope that their ideas would become 'fashionable',[59] and that liquor dealers would rank with – as the famous Neal Dow of Maine put it at a conference in Montreal – the keepers of houses of ill repute and gambling dens?[60] Despite all this, there was an occasional public figure, unconnected with the trade, who put his reputation at risk. More than likely it would be someone from the Irish community; St Patrick's day could be an occasion for the praise of a dram or two. This occurred in 1875 when the journalist, James Fahey, despite the representatives on the platform of the Father Mathew Benevolent Association and various temperance societies, told of his pride in having Irish parents, although he admitted that he could take no more credit for the fact than if he were to drink when dry:

> and as a free confession is good for the soul I don't mind telling you, *sub rosa*, that I get dry sometimes and that I have drowned the shamrock this blessed day – with all due deference to our friends of the Temperance Society. (Laughter and cheers.)[61]

A perverse form of support for the rights of the drinker could also be expressed by the practice of creating disturbances during public meetings. Particularly harassed in this respect was D. B. Chisholm's Temperance Reform Club. In 1878 a newspaper referred to the 'unwarrantable noise' at such gatherings. On another occasion, when Chisholm was unable to pass the collection plate because there was such an uproar, charges were brought against three young men.[62] Much more important in the defence of the trade was organisation in the form of the Licensed Victuallers' Association. In 1876 delegates met in Toronto, where it was decided to encourage the formation of branches throughout the province. Adam Brown of Hamilton was selected as vice-president.[63] By the 1890s hotel keepers had some justification for thinking that they were a persecuted minority. In 1894 the Hamilton Hotelkeepers' Protective Association – the name tells a story – presented a petition to the police commissioners complaining that its members suffered unduly from police arbitrariness and officiousness.[64] Increasingly it was necessary to turn to local politics. In December 1894, according to one journalist, the liquor dealers were drawing up a slate of candidates who would uphold the maximum number of licences.[65] It was attitudes to such questions as licence numbers upon which elections now turned, but the liquor interest's candidates were unsuccessful in gaining a majority in January 1895.[66]

As the story with which this chapter opened illustrates, the provision of the law which had the greatest difficulty in gaining public acceptance was early Saturday and all-day Sunday closing. The law itself could be attributed to a combination of a strong Presbyterian tradition or sabbatarianism and Methodist attachment to teetotalism.[67] As the leading Methodist magazine put it, 'We cannot have the evils of a European Sunday in Canada, without inflicting a serious blow upon those religious principles, beliefs, and practices, which are essential to true national progress.'[68] Yet, in the early days of its existence, the law was observed more in the breach than otherwise. In 1878 *The Hamilton Spectator* could state that public opinion simply did not regard drinking after 7 p.m. on a Saturday as a crime. Nor if a man went drinking on a Sunday morning did he loose the good opinion of his neighbours. Even though regulation remained difficult, in the long run the attack on illegal establishments by both temperance and licensed forces did have an influence on public attitudes and behaviour. Just as the excesses connected with Saint Monday had died out by the 1880s, the demands of employers for a sober work force began to have greater effect. In addition, there were powerful temperance inpulses within workers' organisations such as the Knights of Labour.[69] All this, in combination with increasing religious and temperance pressure, meant that Sunday in Hamilton was not much different from Sunday in Toronto, the experience in which led one later observer to comment:

> It must be good to die in Toronto. The transition between life and death would be continuous, painless and scarcely noticeable in this silent town; I dreaded the Sundays and prayed to God that if he chose for me to die in Toronto he would let it be on a Saturday afternoon to save me from one more Toronto Sunday.[70]

Conclusion

If, at times, especially in the 1870s and 1880s, it seemed to temperance organisations that the police commissioners were reacting to infractions of the law with less than zealous pursuit, then one explanation might well be that they were responsive to the state of public opinion. The same cause may well explain why hotel keepers in the 1890s felt that they were unfairly treated. In this way the stricter laws had had an educative effect. Adam Crooks had been quite explicit about this role of the law when introducing his reforms.[71] One price which was paid, especially in the 1870s, was the thoroughgoing disrespect for certain parts of the law. But the signs were more favourable as time went on. Take, for instance, the number of charges and convictions for illegal selling. During the twelve-month period ending in April 1878 there were 108 cases brought to court, with seventy convictions and two cases unsettled.

Compare this with a similar period ending in July 1895, when, despite an increased population, there were only twenty-one charges and thirteen convictions.[72] Of course, it would be foolish to attribute this entire change to public attitudes as such, since it also resulted from an altered attitude on the part of the police. The trend in police thinking generally was towards penal control of overtly criminal behaviour and away from social control over a perceived 'dangerous class'.[73] Nevertheless the weight of contemporaneous opinion was so overwhelming in the view that public attitudes to drinking had undergone a transformation that it would seem perverse in the extreme to deny its effects.

Another manifestation of the change in the law and public opinion was the reduction in the number of licences combined with the raising of the fees. Again it was Crooks who set the whole matter in motion in a serious way by ordering that a strict ratio be observed between population and the number of licences. When the law came into effect, Hamilton had seventy-eight shops and 111 saloons and taverns. After May 1876 the number was cut back to sixty-one and sixty-eight.[74] In 1888 the number of shops suffered a further reduction to forty.[75] By 1894, while saloons and taverns remained at their former level, shop licences had been reduced by half.[76] Again, this was undoubtedly reflective of public opinion, which was increasingly condemnatory of licensed shops due to their encouragement of female and juvenile drinking, the distaste felt by teetotallers at having to buy their groceries in close proximity to the sight and smell of liquor and the persistent refusal of licensees to obey the law.

Buried within this analysis of changes were many gains and losses of a personal kind – all the way from the thankful woman who, as was told of the Glaswegian wife, could get her husband past seven pubs but not fifteen, to the aggrieved moderate drinker who could not share a glass of beer with his friends and workmates on a Saturday evening. Conviviality poured itself into other institutions or was sublimated into the exertions necessary for respectability and upward mobility. Material deprivation was suffered by those who lost their licence without compensation or who built premises in the often fruitless pursuit of one. Because the ultimate aim of temperance advocates was prohibition on a national scale, the reduced level of drinking in Canada, or its low consumption in comparison with Britain or the United States,[77] was not taken as any invitation to relax their grip. Far from it, for a social revolution was afoot in North America. The fault in its design was that it relied on the law for its complete realisation. That, as the experience of Hamilton showed, was a by no means futile but much less than perfect instrument of social change.

Notes

1 *Hamilton Spectator*, 12, 14 and 19 August 1878.
2 Jack S. Blocker Jr., *'Give to the Winds thy Fears': the women's temperance crusade, 1873–74* (London, 1985), p. 123.
3 See my 'Beer under pressure: the origins of Prohibition in Canada', *Bulletin of Canadian Studies*, VIII (1984), pp. 83–100.
4 MU 7270, Series A, Rev. John Linton Collection, 'The Dominion Alliance for the Total Legal Suppression of the Liquor Traffic', Proceedings 1882, p. 9, Public Archives of Ontario (PAO).
5 *Ibid.*, July 1899, p. 11.
6 *The Canadian Biographical Dictionary and Portrait Gallery of Eminent and Self-made Men*, Ontario volume (Toronto, 1880); *Hamilton Spectator*, 3 June and 14 September 1878. For Chisholm's short parliamentary career see Bryan Palmer, *A Culture in Conflict: skilled workers and industrial capitalism in Hamilton, Ontario, 1850–1914* (Montreal, 1979), pp. 146–8.
7 Principally relied on in this paragraph were: Marjorie Freeman Campbell, *A Mountain and a City: the story of Hamilton* (Toronto, 1966); John C. Weaver, *Hamilton: an illustrated history* (Toronto, 1982); Michael B. Katz *et al.*, *The Social Organisation of early Industrial Capitalism* (London, 1982); Michael J. Doucet, 'Working class housing in a small nineteenth century Canadian city: Hamilton, Ontario, 1852–1881', in Gregory S. Kealey and Peter Warrian (eds.), *Essays in Canadian Working Class History* (Toronto, 1979); Elizabeth Bloomfield, 'Manuscript industrial schedules of the 1871 census of Canada: a source for labour historians', *Labour/Le Travail*, 19 (1987), pp. 125–31.
8 Eric H. Monkkonen, *Police in Urban America, 1860–1920* (Cambridge, 1981), p. 53; RG10, Series S, *Board of Police Commissioners, Minutes, 1872–1913*, 16 November 1880, Hamilton Public Library, hereafter referred to as *Board*.
9 *Hamilton Spectator*, 6 January 1878; *Board*, 16 February 1892.
10 James F. Richardson, *Urban Police in the United States* (London, 1974), pp. 16–17; Nicholas Rogers, 'Serving Toronto the Good', in Victor L. Russell (ed.), *Forging a Consensus: historical essays on Toronto* (Toronto, 1984), pp. 122–5.
11 *Board*, 27 August 1885.
12 *Ibid.*, 27 February, and 16 March 1875; 27 March 1880.
13 *Legislative Assembly of Ontario*, 29 January 1868.
14 *Ibid.*, 19 March 1873, 25 February 1874, 20 January 1875, and 15 January 1876.
15 *Ibid.*, 20 January 1875.
16 P. B. Waite, *Arduous Destiny: Canada, 1874–1896* (Toronto, 1971), p. 90.
17 *Hamilton Spectator*, 7 and 9 May 1888.
18 *Mail and Empire* (Toronto), 1 August 1898.
19 *Hamilton Spectator*, 21 March 1889.
20 *Board*, 11 March, 15 April and 5 July 1884; 23 September, 23 October, 3 December 1886; 12 May 1891; 3 February 1892; 7 August, and 4 September 1894.
21 Clive Emsley, *Crime and Society in England, 1750–1900* (London, 1986), pp. 138 and 149.
22 *Hamilton Spectator*, 30 May 1876.
23 F. H. Armstrong, *The Forest City* (Canada, 1986), p. 107.
24 *Hamilton Spectator*, 31 October 1878.
25 RG 10, Series K, *Police Court Proceedings, 1875–78*, Hamilton Public Library; *Board*, 27 February 1875.
26 *Hamilton Spectator*, 12 November 1878.
27 *Police Register*, reel 61, 4 October, 7 December 1878, Hamilton Public Library.
28 *Hamilton Spectator*, 2 January 1879.
29 *Ibid.*, 10 January 1879.
30 *Ibid.*, 25 February 1879.
31 *Ibid.*, 11 November, 2 December 1879.

32 John C. Weaver, 'The modern city realized: Toronto civic affairs, 1880–1915', in A. F. J. Artibise and G. H. Stelter, *The Usable Urban Past: planning politics in the modern city* (Toronto, 1979), pp. 39–41.

33 Richardson, *Urban Police*, pp. 44 and 58.

34 Rev. John Linton Collection, MU 7277 (18), *Report: The Special Committee appointed to consider the Subject of the Unrestrained Sale of Intoxicating Liquors and the Regulation of Shop, Saloon and Tavern Licenses ...*, PAO.

35 Constance B. Backhouse, 'Nineteenth-century Canadian prostitution law: reflection of a discriminating society', *Histoire sociale/Social History*, 18 (1985), pp. 388–90.

36 *Board*, 4 January 1873 and 29 May 1879.

37 *Hamilton Spectator*, 17 and 18 January 1878.

38 *Board*, 15 November 1878.

39 *Ibid.*, 19 May 1884.

40 Campbell, *A Mountain and a City*, p. 173.

41 For a spate of such cases in Ontario see *Hamilton Spectator*, 12 September 1889.

42 C. S. Clark, *Of Toronto the Good* (Montreal, 1898), p. 16.

43 *Hamilton Spectator*, 30 March 1888.

44 *Board of Police Commissioners, Minutes, 1896–1913*, 29 January and 11 August 1909, Hamilton Public Library.

45 *Ibid.*, 30 January 1907.

46 *Board*, 22 October 1895.

47 Richardson, *Urban Police*, pp. 89 and 98.

48 Charles W. Humphries, *'Honest enough to be Bold': the Life and Times of Sir James Pliny Whitney* (London, 1985), p. 44.

49 *Board*, 11 March 1872.

50 *Ibid.*, 26 February 1875.

51 *Hamilton Spectator*, 11 January 1879.

52 *Board*, 26 January, 5 February 1884.

53 *Hamilton Spectator*, 2 March 1875.

54 *Board of Police Commissioners, Minutes, 1896–1913*, 4 October 1899.

55 *Hamilton Weekly Spectator*, 28 March 1898.

56 *Hamilton Spectator*, 19 February 1878.

57 Palmer, *A Culture in Conflict*, pp. 139–45.

58 *Hamilton Spectator*, 11 April 1888.

59 *Daily Advertiser* (London, Ont.), 31 March 1871.

60 *Christian Guardian*, 22 September 1875.

61 *Hamilton Spectator*, 18 March 1875. For Fahey's brief but interesting career see *Dictionary of Canadian Biography*, pp. 11, 307–8.

62 *Hamilton Spectator*, 21 January, 4 March 1878.

63 *Ibid.*, 12 May 1876.

64 *Board*, 12 February 1894.

65 *Hamilton Spectator*, 8 December 1894.

66 *Globe* (Toronto), 22 January 1895.

67 See J. R. Burnet, 'The urban Community and changing moral standards', in Michael Horn and Ronald Sabourin (eds.), *Studies in Canadian Social History* (Toronto, 1974), pp. 298–312.

68 *Christian Guardian*, 30 July 1879.

69 Palmer, *A Culture in Conflict*, pp. 21 and 181.

70 Burnet, 'The urban community', p. 314.

71 *Legislative Assembly of Ontario*, 20 January 1875.

72 *Police register*, 1894–95; *Hamilton Daily Spectator*, 30 April 1878.

73 Monkkonen, *Police in Urban America*, p. 147.

74 *Hamilton Spectator*, 1 May 1876.

75 *Ibid.*, 11 April 1888.

76 *Ibid.*, 17 December 1894.

77 Graeme Decarie, 'The Prohibition Movement in Ontario, 1894–1916', Ph.D. thesis, Queen's University, Kingston (1972), pp. 33–5.

CHAPTER THIRTEEN

Thieves, drunkards and vagrants: defining crime in colonial Mombasa, 1902–32

Justin Willis

In September 1911, in Mombasa Magistrates' Court, a woman was convicted on a charge of illegally selling palm wine. She was fined seventy-five rupees, a hefty sum when the monthly wage of most Africans was ten rupees or less. Commenting on the case, the local newspaper noted with satisfaction that 'the police are to be congratulated on securing a conviction'.[1] That the long-established trade in palm wine on Kenya's coast had been restricted by colonial legislation was not unusual, but that the police should have been congratulated for enforcing the law seems more so. The implied distinction, between the theoretical criminalisation of an activity by legislation and its effective criminalisation by consistent police action, sheds light on the problems of policing an African city, and on the very limited influence which the state was able to exert over the daily life of individual Africans in the town, despite its deployment of several different policing organisations.

In 1900 the administration of the East African Protectorate issued the Palm Wine Regulations, which initially applied only to the towns of Mombasa and Malindi but which within three years were extended to cover the whole coast.[2] These regulations allowed only persons licensed by the Collector (the then equivalent of a District Commissioner) to sell palm wine. The licence cost fifteen rupees a year, a fee shortly afterwards raised to twenty-five rupees.[3] The punishment for contravening these regulations was a fine of up to 500 rupees and up to three months in prison. Initially there was no limit on the number of licences issued, presumably since the more licences that were issued the greater would be the revenue. The Palm Wine Regulations, however, quickly stopped being seen as a source of revenue. Instead, their implementation became closely connected with the labour issue.

From the earliest years of British rule on the coast, administrators were uncomfortably aware that there was not sufficient local labour available to meet the rapidly growing demands of government and private

European employers.[4] People there were in abundance; but few were willing to take up employment for the wages and on the terms offered by most European employers. In particular, the population of Mombasa disliked and successfully avoided contracts of employment.[5] A large casual labour force existed in the town, working for a few days a month on the docks, as hawkers or boat men, in many other occupations outside the strict discipline of colonial labour controls. This labour force was housed not by employers or the state, but through a multitude of different arrangements with patrons, relatives, creditors and friends. Mombasa's growing casual labour force slept in spare rooms and stores, on verandahs and even in ceiling spaces of houses in the rapidly growing town. These men and women worked for a day or two at a time, when they chose, defying attempts to control their time.

The palm wine trade was soon identified by administrators as a major cause of the labour problem. On the one hand, it provided occasional employment and an income for numbers of tree owners, tree tappers and hawkers, in Mombasa and on the adjacent mainland: individuals supported by the trade who needed no other work.[6] On the other, the discipline and reliability of other prospective workers were undermined by their drinking, as the *East African Standard* declared in 1906:

> Our attention has been drawn to the evils of the drink trade and the unrestricted sale of palm wine among the natives. The word unrestricted is used, because the regulations relating to the sale are of so lenient a nature, that any person can deal in the stuff on payment of the sum of Rs 25 per annum ... to get a useful native population, that will serve the purpose for which the vast sum sunk in the country are partly expended, viz. to make them of use to the Empire ... the brute instincts must be eradicated.[7]

Increasing concern led to a number of different proposals for new legislation. The police were active in these demands for tighter laws:[8] the assistant district superintendent of police wrote in 1908:

> There have been 811 people convicted under the Police Ordinance, a great proportion being for drunk [*sic*]. This state of affairs is rather serious and I would respectfully suggest that the number of licences be curtailed, that the price be raised and that tembo [palm wine] be sold only on licensed premises.[9]

With these suggestions the police set the agenda for the tightening of the palm wine laws in the next few years. Township rules and the discretion given to the District Commissioner (DC) to refuse to issue licences were used, particularly in 1912–13, to limit drastically the number of sellers in Mombasa (and also in the hinterland). In 1912 there were seventy-four licensed sellers on the island, a number reduced to twelve by 1914.[10] Moreover, hawkers were denied licences; only sellers with established premises were to be allowed to sell. New legislation against the trade was passed in 1915, but never used, and was replaced by another ordinance in 1921.[11] This required the tappers and producers of palm wine, as well as its sellers, to be licensed, barred women entirely from the trade, allowed local authorities to impose restrictions on drinking hours, and gave permission for the establishment of municipal beer halls, a step finally taken in Mombasa in 1934.[12]

These restrictions on the palm wine trade were part of a wider assault on the easy access to the casual and informal labour markets that allowed so many Africans in Mombasa to avoid contract work, or to desert from contracted employ. The introduction of taxes, the punitive clauses against deserters under the 1906 Masters and Servants Ordinance, and in Mombasa specific legislation requiring the licensing of hawkers, porters, guides, boat men, and others, all were laws aimed at regularising and increasing the labour supply. Yet the palm wine laws were peculiar in one vital way – the police were instrumental in calling for these laws, and they enforced them in Mombasa.

The police and crime

A police force was created in 1902. The creation of this separate force caused some dissatisfaction amongst the Collectors, whose irregular force of retainers and 'messengers' had up to that time been the only force of law other than the army. In 1910 one coastal DC complained of:

> the tendency of militarism in the Police Department. Another factor which has considerably enhanced the military leanings of the Police has been the appointment of numerous officers who had served in the South African war. The outcome of this is a smart well-drilled force which is known as Police, but the members of which in their bearing as well as in their restricted duties are nothing but trained troops.[13]

This was not simply the griping of a disgruntled administrator. The military leanings of the police force, the reliance on ex-army officers and the concentration on drilling and marksmanship rather than on detective work were also noted by the official historian of the Kenya Police.[14] His own motives for joining the force in 1904 are revealing:

> I much liked the country and was strongly tempted to accept Captain McCaskill's offer, the more so as he stressed the fact that the Force was a semi-military one, often on active service with the KAR [King's African Rifles], and innumerable safaris would afford opportunities for big-game hunting.[15]

It was not, however, simply the military leanings of the police to which administrators objected. The Police Department did continue to emphasise their paramilitary role: the commissioner proudly noted in 1926 that policemen were taught 'bayonet fighting on lines adapted from the latest methods employed by the British army'.[16] But the increasing employment of officers with previous police service in India, or with RUC training, redirected the force towards a concern with investigable crimes against property and the person which, while 'police' work, was far from dealing with the totality of offences against the law. The DC's complaint of 'restricted duties' is crucial: DCs found that the police were unwilling to assist them in enforcing large numbers of laws.

Statistical evidence on crime in early colonial Mombasa is scanty, so that all comments on the nature and activities of the police must be to some extent impressionistic. Yet such evidence as there is suggests that the police and the administration were in dispute over the nature of 'crime'; over which activities constituted crime and should be combated by the police. For example, a hut tax, later a hut and poll tax, was introduced to force Africans into wage labour. District Commissioners began to collect this tax, using the police to enforce payment and round up defaulters, but were soon refused the use of police as tax collectors.[17] The Inspector General of Police made it clear in 1906 that he did not consider such work to be 'ordinary police duties'.[18] In Mombasa the police particularly avoided involvement with policing those laws which were directly associated with labour. After 1906 it was a criminal offence for an African to break a contract of employment, a law intended to force regular working upon Africans by binding them to their employers. Yet the police force in Mombasa made little effort to catch deserters, even when told where they were, as one irate plantation owner observed in 1909.[19] Foran's history of the Kenya Police is taken almost verbatim from police annual reports,[20] and its concentration on deeds of derring-do against bandits and tales of cat-burglars reveals how senior policemen saw crime: their prime concern was offences against property and the person.[21] Below the senior ranks of the force, the inclinations of individual policemen were naturally towards the policing of liquor and theft laws, rather than the labour laws. As the Commissioner and Police regretfully admitted in 1925, bribery and extortion were not uncommon in the Kenya police force,[22] and those engaged in more lucrative 'crimes' naturally had rather more ability to pay.[23] The policing of petty labour regulations was neither glamorous nor rewarding for the average officer.

As second-class magistrates DCs themselves had considerable powers of arrest, trial and sentencing, and it was they, rather than the police, who bore the burden of controlling the labour force in Mombasa. To do so, they reinforced their own messengers, after 1913, with ward headmen for the town under the terms of the Village Headmen Ordinance.[24]

According to later reports, the major function of these worthies was to roam the town in groups as tax collectors.[25]

The police, restricted by numbers and inclination, confined themselves to policing theft, brawls and murder, and the palm wine laws. These misdemeanours generally carried heavier sentences, putting them beyond the scope of the DC's powers as a magistrate, but, more important, they constituted a threat to property and order. While the administration pursued a campaign against the palm wine trade as part of labour policy, the police saw drunkenness as a cause of theft and disorder, offences which they were willing effectively to criminalise by policing.[26] Their struggle was against drunkenness, not idleness, and in their calls for tighter legislation they made no mention of the labour problems over which the local newspapers fulminated. Police patrols arrested Africans out at night after 10 p.m. without a light,[27] but Mombasa became notorious as a haven for deserters from contracts, who went undetected and unpunished. 'Mombasa affords a ready asylum to the professional contract breaker, who at Mombasa gets an advance on his engagements to work here, and returns without fulfilling it,' noted the disgruntled Assistant District Commissioner (ADC), at Takaungu in 1909.[28] In 1912 a European planter resorted to tracking down and charging for himself a number of deserters from his plantation.[29]

The relative operational independence of the police allowed them considerable latitude in defining their own duties. At any police station where there was an officer of the rank of inspector, Asian or European, the police were under the control of that officer, not of the local administration. One of the first priorities of the Police Department after its creation was to acquire more officers, for the Inspector General of Police noted in 1906 that the shortage of officers had allowed the control of the police in many areas to fall into the hands of the Collectors, so that 'it is impossible to say what duties the police are performing'.[30] The police sought to impose their view of what duties they should perform, wresting these detachments back from administrative control by the appointment of more inspectors. Though the DC had enormous powers as executive, one-man police force and judge, he could not tell the police what to do.

The results of one police attempt to enforce the administration's labour laws, in 1912, make clear why the police were reluctant to become involved, and illustrates how difficult and unrewarding intervention in the casual labour market was. There were at the time no deep-water berths in Mombasa harbour. Steamers anchored in the harbour, and their cargo was lightered to shore. Passengers were also taken ashore in boats, these being provided through small-scale private enterprise. There was intense competition between the boats for custom, for there were a number of owners, and each boat was crewed by by the owner's friends, relatives and dependants, who received a cut of the takings, not a wage. Not unnaturally, such competition, and the possibilities of fleecing newly arrived tourists and settlers, produced a rather chaotic situation. Fares could vary wildly, and touts from the boats boarded steamers to bargain, which might be accompanied by a judicious degree of physical force, not to mention kidnapping of luggage. There had for several years before 1912 been a regulation requiring the registration of boats and crews, and the charging of fixed tolls,[31] but no attempt was made to enforce it. In February 1912 the *East African Standard* began a campaign demanding action to improve the situation, and alleging incompetence on the part of the water police, a division of the Police Department without European officers.[32]

In May 1912 Inspector Bristow took command of the water police, and on 15 May a new set of boat regulations was issued, prohibiting the soliciting of custom.[33] On the arrival of an Italian steamer Bristow was rowed out to oversee disembarkation, and attempted to force the boatmen to form a queue, the vessels to approach the steamer one at a time when summoned. This suggestion proved unpopular, and when Bristow ordered his men to arrest the touts who were swarming on to the steamer in search of customers, the touts commandeered a rowing boat belonging to the Italian consul and made off to shore. Inspector Bristow's sturdy rowers set off in pursuit, but were thwarted, first by two lighters which became mysteriously becalmed directly in their path, and then by a large crowd on the shore which greeted the fugitives with considerable acclaim. Bristow did not attempt to land.[34]

When all the boat men were assembled, the inspector having summoned reinforcements, they refused to give the runaways up to the police; 'the strikers replied defiantly that they were all in the *shauri*'.[35] The matter had indeed become a strike, which, it was said, had 'spread to the town'.[36] The government withdrew all the boat mens' licences and organised a temporary passenger service, using the police boat. The newspaper noted optimistically that this system was working well.[37] Evidently not, for by June the boat men were back at work and causing trouble again, the government having apparently reissued licences. The government climb-down may have resulted from the realisation that all government boat men were similarly unregistered, unidentifiable and impossible to discipline – despite the law.[38] The effective registration of boat crews seems never to have occurred, although the amount of disruption they caused produced no further complaints after July 1912. The opening of the deep-water berths in the mid-1920s began to make these networks redundant, and to close this off as an area of casual labour; but some boats were still in use in the early 1930s, still crewed by casual, unregistered labour – the friends, relatives and clients of the boat owners.[39] The police, having contained the disorder that had been so upsetting to European opinion, made no further attempt to intervene in the organisation of labour on the boats. Inspector Bristow's experience had revealed that networks of casual and informal labour in Mombasa could protect very successfully the identity and the freedom of those breaking the labour laws, and that if the police wished to maintain order, a direct confrontation with casual labour was to be avoided.

The narrow definition of crime, and the avoidance of certain duties, that characterised the Police Department throughout Kenya was thus further encouraged in Mombasa by the near impossibility of policing certain forms of crime. There was no effective tradition of the police as an arm of the state in Mombasa, though the town had been in existence for centuries. The nineteenth-century Omani governors of Mombasa had a small force of Baluchi soldiers who occasionally intervened to impose the Governor's will, but the populace of the town were policed and judged by the heads of the large clans which made up its population, and by Islamic courts.[40] These clans and courts recognised the rule of the Omani Sultan of Zanzibar and his local governors, but they did not rely on the sultan for a legal code, or the physical means to enforce it.[41] The imposition of a new system of colonial laws in such a situation required a degree of control and coercion which was not easily sustainable. The colonial police force was, moreover, uniquely unsuited to the task; despite the knowledge that policemen from up-country were of limited use in Mombasa[42] the police force was unable to recruit significant numbers of coastal Africans.[43]

The administrative staff, by contrast, continued to try and enforce the laws, but with limited success. Complaints continued about the ease with which Africans could evade the labour laws by moving to Mombasa, particularly with reference to the Native Registration Ordinance. Passed during the first world war, this law was enforced in Kenya in 1920. Under the ordinance, Africans leaving the reserves to seek employment had to carry a card bearing a number and their personal details, on which a record of their employment status could be entered. Without it an African could not be employed, and it was an offence not to carry the card. It was intended to prevent just the sort of desertion, resort to casual labour and informality that characterised Mombasa's growing population. Yet early in 1924 a meeting of coast DCs agreed to suspend the operation of the ordinance on the coast.[44]

Several different justifications for this embarrassing admission of failure were offered. The first was that it was a goodwill gesture to the Wanyika (the Mijikenda of the hinderland), who had 'had rather a poor time during the war and afterwards'.[45] But very real labour difficulties and serious problems in administering the registration ordinance effectively on the coast seem to have been more important in shaping official opinion. The Resident Commissioner, Mombasa, suggested, more convincingly, that the decision reflected difficulties over the registration of members of the Swahili Twelve Tribes of Mombasa, numbers of whom claimed 'non-native' status and thus exemption from the ordinance.[46] The truth was, more simply, that the administration in Mombasa was failing effectively to enforce the ordinance, an accusation levelled by the Chief Registrar of Natives in 1922, who quoted the DC, Kilifi, as saying:

> It is useless for me to enforce the Ordinance in this district unless steps are taken to see that Mombasa comes into line. In every single instance where a Mombasa native comes to my office or into the district he leaves his certificate in Mombasa, as he states he never carries it in the town, and did not know it was obligatory elsewhere.[47]

Mr Wedderburn, a representative specially sent to Mombasa by the Chief Registrar to encourage registration, gave it as his opinion that it was impossible to enforce the carrying of certificates,[48] an attitude vigorously denounced by his superiors[49] but which prevailed in the 1924 decision. It is worthy of note that the police had withdrawn so far from the whole question that they took no part in this correspondence, nor in the decision to suspend the ordinance. The police in Mombasa quite simply had no wish to enforce the registration ordinance within the city.

The administration was as incapable of enforcing the labour laws as was the police force. In 1926 the Senior Commissioner at the Coast admitted that 'the position is somewhat irregular' but asked the Native Affairs Department for money to finance the extra staff that would be needed to attempt enforcement.[50] The money was not forthcoming.[51] There were only 543 registrations in 1926, all voluntary, this being a significant improvement on 1925, when none had been recorded, but well below the 1,983 who had registered in 1922. The Native Affairs Department finally gave way in 1927 and provided money to support the policing of the Ordinance; that year saw 6,582 registrations in the town.[52] Again, it was the administration that policed and enforced the legislation. In 1927 there was accordingly an enormous jump in the number of registration cases brought in the Resident Commissioner's court – 1,205, compared with the 348 in 1923.[53] Characteristically, the police report for the year mentioned nothing of this, noting only that the number of reported housebreakings and thefts in Mombasa had dropped from the previous year.[54]

Housebreaking was a major fixation of the Mombasa police. One commissioner of police called housebreaking 'perhaps the most definite criminal act of all'.[55] Considerable police energy was directed towards the suppression of housebreaking, particularly through the use of night patrols, and police reports devoted considerable space to graphs and tables plotting the progress of the struggle.[56] The commissioner was particularly happy to record that in only one of the forty-nine housebreakings in Mombasa in 1926 was the victim a European.[57] Yet housebreaking was one of the least common crimes in the city: there were fewer than fifty reported cases every year between 1926 and 1929.[58] Over the same period the number of criminal cases tried in the Resident Magistrate's court in Mombasa rose from 1,601 to 3,414.[59] This dramatic increase seems to have been entirely due to the administration's new resolve to enforce the Native Registration Ordinance: the police reports from 1925 to 1928 show a steady drop in reported cases of crimes against property and the person, while judicial reports of the same period reveal a dramatic rise in the number of criminal cases tried.[60] In 1929 the Police Department annual report still saw the major problem facing the police as the increasing sophistication of bank, house and shop robberies.[61] It is difficult to escape the conclusion that the police held their own priorities in defining, and acting against crime.

This period marked, in a sense, the height of the independence of the police in Kenya. In 1925 R. G. B. Spicer, previously of the Ceylon Police, was appointed Commissioner of Police for Kenya. He energetically continued the dispute over the definition of crime:

> The Commissioner considered that the standard of prevention and detection of crime was still too low. But he thought this fact was partly attributable to the Force being saddled with many extraneous duties – such as work being performed for other Departments, the requirements of the Registration of Natives Ordinance ... it was urged that the police be relieved of these duties.[62]

The commissioner was attempting to confirm for the whole police force the relief from these 'extraneous duties' that the police in Mombasa had effectively secured for themselves. The objection to the administration of the ordinance was partly a criticism of the 'criminalisation' of labour infractions beyond the Masters and Servants Ordinance. The administration's zeal for enforcing the registration laws in Mombasa resulted in many prosecutions but had only limited effect. Workers in Mombasa could still obtain casual work without registration certificates, avoiding contact with officialdom. Short of going through the entire town, house by house, there was no way of finding and punishing all those without certificates. The terms of the ordinance were, to all intents and purposes, unenforcible without the co-operation of employers.

There were other problems also. In 1923 one Mathma Kinanda was discovered to be in possession of two identities, and two registrations, and to have been theoretically in the employ of Mr Eckstein and Mr Jivanji, both of Mombasa, neither of whom saw very much of him.[63] In 1929, complaining of the ease with which Africans could evade the punitive effects of the labour laws by obtaining temporary registration in a different identity, the Native Affairs Department commented that the practice was particularly rife in Mombasa.[64] More than two-thirds of the Mombasan registrations in 1927 were temporary. In enforcing the Native Registration Ordinance the administration of Mombasa could make sure that registered large employers, who employed Africans on contract, employed only those with a registration certificate. It could not ensure that the certificates identified the workers correctly, nor could it make all those working as casuals, hawkers and the like obtain certificates.

Perhaps because of the attention being paid to the registration laws the ability of the administration to enforce other laws declined even further. The number of hut and poll tax cases dealt with by the Resident Commissioner's court dropped from 306 in 1923 to nine in 1927.[65] This was not due to any new-found enthusiasm for prompt payment of taxes among Mombasa's population. In 1929 the Mombasa District Commissioner noted that 'The population figures which are given every year are based on tax collections and are obviously quite unreliable, especially in respect of the native population'.[66] The implications of this remark were spelt out rather more clearly in the 1930 comment that it was 'obvious that there is a considerable evasion of Tax, in fact it is a common saying that Government does not require Tax from Up-country natives working on the Island'.[67] Africans in Mombasa believed that the Native Hut and Poll Tax Ordinance, like the Native Registration Ordinance, did not apply to them.

Vagrants in Mombasa

The ability of the police to set their own agenda, and to avoid policing some laws, was challenged in the late 1920s when they were again drawn into conflict with casual labour. Vagrancy had for some time defied official action, since the original legislation on the subject, the Vagrancy Regulations, was aimed at 'disreputable Europeans' and required that those imprisoned for vagrancy should be given waged work (a condition which was not considered suitable for Africans).[68] In 1927 the Mombasa Township Committee asked for the Governor's permission to apply in Mombasa the vagrancy rules recently introduced in Nairobi.[69] The township committee was a non-elected body composed of European and some Indian entrepreneurs, the Arab administrator of Mombasa, and the DC, who chaired its meetings. It could ask the

Governor for legislation but could not make its own. In 1929 it became the Mombasa Municipal Board, a body which could make by-laws. Breaches of these by-laws were, legally speaking, breaches of the ordinance which established the board and hence criminal offences, so that offenders could be arrested by the police.[70] In 1927, however, it still required the Governor's authority for action.

Under the vagrancy rules:

> The collection of natives or others in tents or outbuildings in the vicinity of shops or dwelling houses who are not the actual house or shop servants in the immediate employ of the owners or the occupiers of such houses or shops is prohibited.[71]

It was also an offence to be 'found lying, wandering or loitering in any highway, yard or other place during the night'.[72] Such restrictions instantly made illegal the living arrangements of thousands of Africans, housed in the yards, storerooms and verandas of friends or patrons, or sleeping in empty sheds around the Mwembe Tayari area. There was another section of the rules, though, even more threatening to the casual workers of Mombasa; it was an offence to 'remain within the Island of Mombasa for more than seven days without employment the proof whereof shall be on the native'.[73] This was indeed the real kernel of the rules, for the township committee asked at the same time for new casual labour rules, establishing a register of casual labour and a system of arm brassards to identify such labourers, who had to seek re-registration each month.[74] Registered labourers were required to work if offered a job. Africans seeking dock or portering casual labour would have to be registered to avoid being expelled under the vagrancy rules, but the DC could refuse to register those who did not work regularly, and thus cause their expulsion. Mombasa's army of informal workers, water carriers, hawkers and prostitutes would have to seek licensing and regulation to prove that they were employed, or be expelled.

The proposals represented a reconciliation, a compromise, between two groups of European employers, each represented on the Township Committee, but with rather opposed interests – the stevedoring and shorehandling companies, who relied on casual labour, and the railways, public works and plantation employers, who sought strict enforcement of existing labour laws. The shipping companies' casual labour was partly made up of Africans signed up to others who were moonlighting, or had absconded completely, tempted by the high daily wages offered for dock labour, and this was greatly resented by other employers.[75] The shipping companies employed labour in gangs, through headmen, and they had doggedly resisted earlier attempts to make them demand registration certificates of each individual worker, which would have disrupted the

J

system and cost a great deal of time and money.[76] On the other hand a scheme which would be enforced by someone else, somewhere else, and which would impose more regular discipline on their casuals, was entirely welcome. The resolution of the dispute between these two groups of employers would be at the expense of the administration and the police.

The police had initially taken a cool view of the rules, the Mombasa superintendent viewing them only as a measure to be held in reserve, against 'crime', which category did not include any of the activities which the measures sought to make criminal:

> Having regard to the acute housing shortage, large daily demands for casual labour at the docks and the fact that the temperature in Mombasa is conducive to natives sleeping out of doors at night, it is not proposed, in the absence of a crime epidemic, rigorously to enforce this legislation.[77]

Yet this attitude did not survive the year. Five months later, the superintendent was pressing for passage of the rules as an urgent measure.[78] In the event the Governor delayed the vagrancy rules, about which official unease had already been expressed, as he was alarmed about their effect on the population of Mombasa.[79] He also delayed the casual labour rules, claiming that the proposed badges were not yet ready.[80] In an interesting reversal, the administration was avoiding implementing labour laws which the police were demanding.

Though thwarted in 1927, the European employers of Mombasa were soon able to use the Municipal Board's new powers of legislation to create casual labour laws, and they informed the Governor that it preferred these methods to relying on the government to pass an ordinance.[81] Even more important, they were able to persuade the police to enforce laws against vagrancy – not, in this case, their own by-laws but the previously forgotten Vagrancy Ordinance of 1920, which allowed for the arrest and deportation to the reserves of anyone 'unable to show that he has visible and sufficient means of subsistence'.[82] This phrasing, while slightly less definite than that of the 1927 proposal, allowed a police campaign that led to numbers of convictions and expulsions in 1932.[83]

What caused this change in the attitude of the police, the extension of what constituted criminality in their eyes? In one sense it was not a reversal, for the superintendent called for the rules as a measure against a growing number of up-country thieves who were moving to Mombasa.[84] The same concern was expressed in the Police Department annual report for 1927, which referred to 'an influx of up-country natives who tend to oust the old law-abiding Arab, and to change for the worse the characteristics of the native population of the island'.[85] The population of Mombasa island, having stayed a little below 20,000 between 1913 and 1921,[86] grew dramatically in the 1920s to reach more than 40,000 by 1931.[87] The police force expanded nowhere nearly as rapidly; local figures are not available, but the total strength of the force in Kenya rose only from 1,941 in 1908 to 2,171 in 1929,[88] a miniscule increase over a period when the urban populations which the force policed were growing so dramatically. The police feared a resulting rise in the kinds of crime which they chose to police, and the vagrancy measures were originally referred to by the police as the 'Prevention of Crime Rules',[89] a name ironic in that they would have instantly created thousands of new criminals, but indicative of police attitudes.

Yet the attitude of the police was not simply the result of a chance convergence of their interest in preventing crime against property and the employers' interest in controlling labour. It was an acknowledgement of the new powers and influence acquired by employers through the creation of the Municipal Board, their new ability to make laws and to cause them to be enforced. The police did not come quietly, however. In 1930 a new Police Ordinance was passed, reaffirming the operational independence of the police and giving the commissioner almost complete control of discipline and promotion,[90] though this control was somewhat diminished by an amending ordinance in 1934. In Mombasa the police retained their opposition to the thankless and virtually impossible task of enforcing the labour laws. In 1934 the DC, Mombasa, remarked, without further comment, that 'during the year 1933 the African Police were instructed not to arrest people without registration certificates'.[91]

Conclusions

Employers continued to be troubled by labour shortages, unreliability and desertion throughout the 1930s. In 1940 the *Mombasa Times* editorialised, 'There are far too many idle natives running wild on this island.'[92] The problem could not be legislated away, for the enforcement of the law was impossible in a town where no effective attempt had been made to control the time and space of employees, where casual labour predominated and employers refused to provide accommodation or any kind of social security for their employees. Employers discovered that not until they themselves were willing to bear the burden of the costs involved could Mombasa's casual labourers be forced to register, or to work with the sort of regularity demanded of them.[93]

Colonial law made many activities theoretically illegal – trading without a licence, doing certain kinds of work without registration, breaking a contract to work, selling palm wine without a licence. In Mombasa some of these activities, like the palm wine trade, were

[231]

well established, and most were cherished, giving as they did the chance to survive outside the restrictive framework of the labour laws. Some of these activities also supported those employed within the framework of the labour laws, feeding, sheltering and caring for them. Despite this, such activities were generally seen by officials and European employers as against their interests, for their concern was to establish a regular supply of labour. It was this which caused the activities to be declared illegal. The laws did not prevent them, however, for the police did not enforce most of them, concentrating instead on what they saw as 'crime', theft and violence rather than on what had been defined as crime by law. The threat to public order that resulted when European opinion forced the police into an attempt to enforce the labour laws – the fight with the boat men – impressed upon them that the implementation of the law was not always conducive to the control of what they saw as crime.

The exception was the campaign against palm wine, seen by administrators as a part of labour policy, but by the police as an anti-'crime' measure, and one worthy of enforcement. The policing of labour and tax laws was left to the administration, officials of which had considerable legal powers, but which none the less proved unequal to the task. Historians of colonial Africa have recently come to a new appreciation of the weakness of the colonial state on the ground, and the accommodations and compromises which it made to survive. The reluctance to become involved and the jealous preservation of their own autonomy shown by the Kenya Police should be seen in this context, as part of the disaggregation of a colonial state which was in truth far from monolithic. From around 1930 the police found it more difficult to restrict their attention to those activities defined by themselves as 'crime'. The new political power given to non-official Europeans in municipal government allowed them to create new legal definitions of crime and to impose their definitions of crime on to the police force, which was impelled into kinds of policing it had hitherto avoided.

Notes

Items prefixed KNA are stored in the Kenya National Archives, Nairobi. Those prefixed PRO are in the Public Record Office, London. Items appearing in the form 'Int. 44a' refer to interviews carried out by the author in Mombasa.

1 *East African Standard*, weekly edition (W), 2 September 1911.
2 Palm Wine Regulations, 24 November 1900, KNA, AG/4/1579, and Tritton, Sub-commissioner, to HM Commissioner, 22 July 1903, KNA, PC, Coast 1/1/93.
3 Lane, Sub-commissioner, to Assistant Collector, Rabai, 28 April 1905, KNA, PC Coast 1/9/99.
4 Draft of Mombasa District Report, 1905–06, 8 May 1906, KNA, PC Coast 1/1/113; also *East African Standard* (W), 11 August 1906.

5 Hollis, Secretary for Native Affairs (SNA), *Evidence to Native Labour Commission of 1912–13* (Nairobi, 1913).
6 See, for example, Osborne, ADC, Rabai, to Acting PC, 16 October 1907, KNA, PC Coast 1/1/130; Hollis, SNA, to Secretary for Administration, 28 September 1907, KNA, PC Coast 1/1/130.
7 *East African Standard* (W), 24 February 1906.
8 See, for example, Reddie, DC, Mombasa, to Hobley, PC, 20 May 1913; DC, Mombasa, to PC, 20 November 1912, KNA, PC Coast 1/10/54.
9 Assistant District Superintendent of Police (ADSP) to Inspector General of Police (IGP), 2 April 1908, KNA, PC Coast 1/1/138.
10 DC, Mombasa, to PC, 20 November 1912; and DC, Mombasa, to PC, 4 January 1915, KNA, PC Coast 1/10/54.
11 PC to DC, Mombasa, 18 December 1912, KNA, PC Coast 1/10/54; 'Statement of objects and reasons', Lyall-Grant, Attorney General, 15 March 1921, KNA, AG/4/1523.
12 Mombasa District Annual Report, 1934, p. 3, KNA, DC MSA 1/4.
13 Skene, DC, Malindi, 'Memo on the Police Dept.', 1910, in KNA, PC Coast 1/1/138.
14 W. R. Foran, *The Kenya Police 1887–1960* (London, 1962), pp. 15, 26.
15 Foran, *The Kenya Police*, p. 17.
16 Kenya Police Annual Report, 1926, p. 10, PRO, CO 544/20.
17 Osborne, ADC, Rabai, to PC, 28 October 1907, KNA, PC Coast 1/12/42.
18 Kenya Police Annual Report, 1906, PRO, CO 533/14.
19 Brand to Collector, Mombasa, 29 January 1907, KNA, PC Coast 1/12/41.
20 Cf. Kenya Police Annual Report, 1926, pp. 14–17, PRO, CO 544/20, with Foran, *The Kenya Police*, pp. 68–71.
21 Foran, *The Kenya Police*, pp. 61 and 72–4.
22 See Spicer, Commissioner of Police, Circular No. 18, 30 September 1925, in PRO, CO 533/393/14.
23 Int. 43a.
24 Mombasa District Annual Report, 1913–14, KNA, PC Coast 1/1/213.
25 Mombasa District Annual Report, 1935, pp. 9–10, KNA, DC MSA 1/4.
26 See PC to IGP, 6 May 1908, KNA, PC Coast 1/1/138.
27 Tritton, Sub-commissioner, to HM Commissioner, 25 March 1903, KNA, PC Coast 1/1/93; *East African Standard* (W), 3 February 1906; *East African Standard* (daily), 20 February 1912.
28 Takaungu Sub-district Annual Report, 1909, section VIII, 'Labour', KNA, DC MSA 1/1.
29 *East African Standard* (daily), 20 April 1912.
30 Police Department Annual Report, 1906, PRO, CO 533/14.
31 'Registration of Boats', attached to Despatch No. 624, 28 November 1906, PRO, CO 533/18.
32 *East African Standard* (W), 24 February 1912.
33 *East African Standard* (daily), 22 May 1912.
34 *East African Standard* (daily), 21 May 1912.
35 *Ibid.*
36 *East African Standard* (W), 18 May 1912.
37 *East African Standard* (W), 29 May 1912; and *East African Standard* (daily), 21 June 1912.
38 Memo. of Minutes of Township Committee, 19 September 1912, KNA, PC Coast 1/11/377.
39 Int. 44a.
40 M. Swartz, 'Religious courts, community and ethnicity among the Swahili of Mombasa: an historical study of social boundaries', *Africa*, XLIX, 1 (1979), pp. 29–41.
41 F. J. Berg, 'Mombasa under the Busaidi Sultanate', Ph.D. thesis, University of Wisconsin (1971), p. 98.
42 Police Department Annual Report, 1926, p. 4, PRO, CO 544/20.
43 Police Department Annual Report, 1929, p. 5, PRO, CO 544/28.
44 Acting Senior Commissioner, Coast (SCC), to all DCs, 17 April 1926, KNA PC Coast 1/10/120B.
45 Watkins, SCC, to CNC, 18 December 1924, KNA, PC Coast 1/10/120B.

46 Mombasa District Annual Report, 1924, pp. 4–5, KNA, DC MSA 1/3.
47 Chief Registrar of Natives to SCC, 27 March 1922, KNA, PC Coast 1/10/120B.
48 Native Affairs Department (NAD) to SCC, 29 September 1924, KNA, PC Coast 1/10/120B.
49 Ibid.
50 Acting SCC to Chief Native Commissioner (CNC), 28 April 1926, KNA, PC Coast 1/10/120B.
51 CNC to SCC, 9 June 1926, KNA, PC Coast 1/10/120B.
52 Mombasa District Annual Report, 1927, KNA, PC Coast 1/1/110.
53 Mombasa District Annual Reports, 1923 and 1927, KNA, DC MSA 1/3.
54 Police Department Annual Report, 1927, p. 51, PRO, CO 533/380/10.
55 Police Department Annual Report, 1929, p. 15, PRO, CO 544/28.
56 Police Department Annual Report, 1926, pp. 23–25, PRO CO 544/20.
57 Police Department Annual Report, 1926, p. 38, PRO, CO 544/20.
58 Police Department Annual Report, 1929, p. 34, PRO, CO 544/28.
59 Justice Department Annual Report, 1926, p. 5, PRO, CO 544/20; and Justice Department Annual Report, 1929, p. 6, PRO, CO 544/28.
60 Justice Department Annual Report, 1929, p. 6, PRO, CO 544/28.
61 Police Department Annual Report, 1929, p. 34, PRO, CO 544/28.
62 Foran, The Kenya Police, p. 65.
63 Chief Registrar of Natives to Resident Commissioner, Mombasa, 31 October 1923, KNA, PC Coast 1/10/120B.
64 Native Affairs Department Annual Report, 1929, p. 78.
65 Mombasa District Annual Reports, 1923 and 1927, KNA, DC MSA 1/3.
66 Mombasa District Annual Report, 1928, p. 5, KNA, DC MSA 1/3.
67 'Report on Native Affairs in Mombasa', December 1930, p. 19, KNA, DC MSA 3/3.
68 HM Commissioner to HM Sub-commissioner Tritton, 5 November 1901, KNA, PC Coast 1/1/106.
69 Lambert, Commissioner for Local Government to Chair, Mombasa District Committee, 14 February 1928, KNA, AG/4/1319.
70 Local Government Ordinance of 1928, particularly sections 74, 75, 117, PRO, CO 533/328/2.
71 Lambert, Commissioner for Local Government, to Chair, Mombasa District Committee, 14 February 1928, KNA, AG/4/1319.
72 Ibid.
73 Ibid.
74 Ibid.
75 Minutes, Special Meeting, Port Advisory Board, 23 June 1924, KNA, AG/4/2968.
76 Frudd, Union Castle Mail Steamship Co. Ltd, Memo, 1924, KNA, AG/4/2968; Ainsworth-Dickson, Chair, District Committee, to Acting Colonial Secretary, 15 August 1926, KNA, AG/4/2968.
77 Superintendent of Police, quoted in Resident Commissioner, Mombasa, to Acting Colonial Secretary, 24 May 1927, KNA, AG/4/1319.
78 Vidal, Chair, Mombasa District Committee, to Colonial Secretary, 11 October 1927, KNA, AG/4/1319.
79 Lambert, Commissioner for Local Government, to Chair, Mombasa District Committee, 14 February 1928, KNA, AG/4/1319.
80 Ibid.
81 Minutes, Mombasa Municipality General Purposes Committee, 15 July 1930, in Mombasa Municipal Archives.
82 Memo on the Vagrancy Ordinance of 1920, in PRO, CO 533/389/9.
83 Mombasa District Annual Report, 1932, p. 13, KNA, DC MSA 1/4.
84 Vidal, Chair, Mombasa District Committee, to Attorney General, 11 October 1927, KNA, AG/4/1319.
85 Police Department Annual Report, 1927, p. 41, PRO, CO 533/380/10.
86 See Mombasa Political Record Book, p. 27, KNA, DC MSA 8/2; PC to Chairman, Famine Committee, 28 June 1918, KNA, PC Coast 1/2/6; Mombasa District Annual Report, 1922, p. 1, KNA, DC MSA 1/3.

87 Mombasa District Annual Report, 1931, p. 3, KNA, DC MSA 1/4.
88 East African Protectorate Annual Report, 1908–09, 'Police', PRO, CO 544/1; Police Department Annual Report, 1929, p. 2, PRO, CO 544/28.
89 Vidal, Chair, Mombasa District Committee, to Attorney General, 31 October 1927, KNA, AG/4/1319.
90 Governor to Secretary of State for the Colonies, 20 May 1930, PRO, CO 533/393/14.
91 Mombasa District Annual Report, 1933, p. 27, KNA, DC MSA 1/4.
92 *Mombasa Times*, 17 January 1940.
93 See F. Cooper, *On the African Waterfront: urban disorder and the transformation of work in colonial Mombasa* (New Haven, 1987).

CHAPTER FOURTEEN

Bobbies to Boers: police, people and social control in Cape Town

Bill Nasson

> Things are ever so different in the Transvaal from what they are at the Cape ... especially in regard to the treatment of natives. You see, there are so few aboriginal natives at the Cape that we are prepared to place them almost on an equality with the coloured folk. And because the coloured or Cape boy has a strain of European blood, he gets almost all the privileges of the white man, including a parliamentary vote. Now Transvaal ... holds other ideas.[1]

With these bluff words an Irish police sergeant named Maloney reportedly pointed out to a rural Afrikaner service recruit called Venter why the social experience and social categories awaiting policemen in early twentieth-century Cape Town were not of the same character as that confronted in the agrarian Transvaal or on the industrial Witwatersrand. Historical studies certainly seem to underline this. Self-evidently, the archetypal police force 'Zarps' of Johannesburg, drawn indiscriminately from the 'Rand's poor and uneducated Afrikaners',[2] would have been met with indignation and incredulity had they tried to dispense their everyday physical-force justice in the older 'Mother City'. Likewise, Cape Town did not share the bad reputation of an industrialising Kimberley where, in the later nineteenth century, the monstrous 'arbitrariness of law enforcement' and the capriciousness of 'mechanisms of worker control' permitted the police to create 'a climate of insecurity and fear'.[3]

The principal point was that Cape Town was different; police work there could not be grounded upon the unfettered bullying of 'barbarous' or 'still partly uncivilised' blacks. It was instead bound by more settled and congenially stable relations, and a social code marked by a kind of tactful paternalism and customary restraint. Accordingly, only men of 'better' or 'respectable' character would be able to exercise their duties effectively, according to Maloney.[4]

Such particularistic – and starry eyed – representations of the Cape

Town police, and popular understandings of their relations with lower-class inhabitants, are undoubtedly essential to any historical appreciation of the colonial locus and colonial texture of maintaining law and order in the city. For what one might term a colonial social consciousness obviously ran deep in Cape Town; after all, unlike, say, Johannesburg, it had the settled weight imparted by a considerable history of white settlement and settler hegemony. Moreover, its economy – trade and the social relations of small manufacturing production – was not the only key determinant of its formation and identity as a social unit. What Robert Ross has called 'the prime locus of power' in the city, as embodied in the 'legal monopoly of force and thus of life, death and corporal punishment', derived 'in the first instance from the strength of the Dutch and the British imperial systems'. It was in Cape Town, 'if not on the frontier', that vaulting imperial power was made a palpable reality.[5]

Yet, while Cape Town was emphatically not a South African frontier town, it still carried its frontier into the first half of the twentieth century; this was a permanently uneasy and intermittently fractious shadow line between what the social geographer John Western has called 'the colonial city of British imperialism'[6] and political and social forces seen as threatening the dissolution of this nineteenth-century inheritance. In an important sense, the conduct of Cape Town's policing can be usefully understood in this context. Conceptions over time of a reformation and transformation of the police from an old-timer 'British' force to a newcomer Afrikaner or 'Boer' force reflected the remoulding of social structure and institutions as a local state had its older segregationist traditions inflated into a more intense and contagious apartheid from the end of the 1940s. So, if in one respect the Cape Town experience offers an intriguing historical example of the development of a 'colonial' style police without the trauma of decolonisation, it is equally apparent that sensitivity to mid-twentieth-century changes in the social ethos of that colonial model was a notable feature of the popular expression of sentiment towards the city's policemen.

In establishing the basic outline of the police force in late Victorian and early Edwardian Cape Town, the first important fact is the alteration in the general structure of local policing which took place during the course of the nineteenth century. At the turn of the century, policing arrangements in the city consisted of a haphazard, unprofessional system of voluntary watchmen and nightwatchmen, and 'rounders' or constabulary *dienaars*; this parish-type organisation was manned by Dutch and British ex-soldiers but also included 'Malays' and Coloured men recruited from the labouring poor.[7] With the consolidation of British control after the second Cape occupation in 1806 came attempts to reform Cape Town's policing by dismembering its eighteenth-century structure, and reorganising the force as a uniformed, disciplined, and more impartial and professional instrument of law enforcement. This adaptation emerged in the context of increasing social fear about the growth of a 'dangerous class' in early nineteenth-century Cape Town, and the threat which this army of down-and-outs posed to urban stability and propertied Capetonians.

By the 1850s Cape Town had acquired a reformed 'New Police', modelled on the London Metropolitan Police; this salaried Cape Constabulary patrolled both the city and the residential areas and peripheral centres which spread out along the Cape peninsula railway line running from the town centre to Simonstown naval base. Police capacity was supplemented with a contingent of Water Police assigned to coastal and port duties to suppress smuggling and pilfering. The constabulary was now not only a more uniform and cohesive establishment but also increasingly an ethnically homogenous one; since the 1820 recruiting preference had been markedly for British policemen, who were expected to 'show greater loyalty to what was really a British institution'.[8] A more rational police force for an increasingly segregated city was necessarily 'exclusively white and predominantly British'.[9] There was little if any enthusiasm for the incorporation of anyone graded officially as 'Other than White'.

The hold of the racially inscribed, clubby conventions of the police could clearly be seen by the 1870s, when the town council, for example, affirmed its strongest 'objection to Coloured persons being employed on such important duties', extravagantly pledging 'an increased rate of pay to keep up the prestige of the Force, rather than have a single Coloured man enrolled in the Force'.[10] In fact police service in the city was anything but prestigious. Firstly, even in the closing decades of the nineteenth century the Cape Town force was still too small to combat urban crime and disorder effectively; much of its law enforcement action was slack and ill disciplined or amateurishly inept. In July 1880, for instance, a British visitor scoffed:

> Of course no one expects perfect protection, but that which is offered by the constabulary of these parts is really quite useless. Even when a uniformed man is on the scene, and gives pursuit after a criminal act, the cheeky miscreant simply runs in and out of a row of dwellings until the law tires of the chase. Dark and dangerous passages are not a feature likely to encourage the constable to remain and keep a vigilant watch. Wisely, he does not, as a rule, endeavour to summon assistance as this does not appear to exist. In truth, for bad characters it is an agreeable case of 'run well and fast and you won't get caught'.[11]

Secondly, by nearly all accounts there were other difficulties too, like sagging morale and short service inclinations. Long hours and poor pay and promotion prospects ensured that the calibre of recruits left much to be desired; senior officers were uncomfortably aware that police authorities were obliged to draw mostly upon indifferent unskilled or semi-skilled white workers. Even though a literacy entrance requirement was introduced early in the 1880s, the image of enlisting men changed little; the chief distinguishing features of Cape constables were that they were 'poor, unskilled, and often illiterate'.[12] Thirdly, apart from flat purses and flat feet, the late Victorian force had a miserable reputation for unreliability and drunkenness; detectives in particular were known for their stealthy addiction to the seaport haunts and pleasures of gambling and drinking, all the while hustling for protection perquisites or sharpening other practices of petty abuse. The ease with which corruptible men could be corrupted was amply exposed with the outbreak of the South African war in 1899. With the Rand in depression and further subject to unwelcome restrictions on prostitution, Cape Town acted as a magnet for those from Johannesburg and elsewhere who held no place in 'respectable' society, and who wished for none. Growing numbers of prostitutes, pimps, brothel keepers, receivers and con men adopted a territorial base over which the controls of the authorities, both physical and social, were weak. The response of the Cape Attorney General, T.L. Graham, was the introduction and passing in 1902 of a 'Morality Bill' in order to deal with the sex trade, especially those transactions which encouraged black men and white women to come together 'for the purposes of illicit sexual intercourse'.[13] The small squad of plain-clothes 'morality police' assigned to suppress such acts of criminal immorality was not entirely zealous, proving not at all averse to bribery; trial proceedings of men eventually unmasked suggested that bad housing, bad pay and other service grievances were important factors in police susceptibility to pay-offs and other corrupting influences.[14]

The policing picture, then, in the years leading up to Union, was of a generally low-status force operating under a considerable number of internal deficiencies and external constraints. While incremental improvements were made to manning levels, pay and standards of conduct in the 1900s, they were never sufficient to meet the needs and demands of crime control in a cosmopolitan city which was difficult to police tightly; crucially, the Cape Constabulary or Cape Peninsula Urban Force, as it was also termed, was incapable of substantively regulating urban life, of really *policing* colonial society in Cape Town. The organisation of this establishment was affected by the centralising rationalisation of local police forces which followed upon Union. The amalgamation of a new post-1910 Union force culminated in the launch of a single state police, the South African Police, in April 1913. Cape Town was henceforward to be policed within the Cape Western Division of the South

African Police; its old and undermanned transport branch, the Water Police, was also remodelled as a component of a national Railway Police.[15] The formation of the South African Police bore the stamp of bureaucratic rationale, a new disciplinarian ideology of efficiency and, perhaps most significantly, a distinct militarisation of drill and organisational hierarchy. Cape Town police were now an assimilated *national* police arm, attached to an increasingly militarised administrative body.

Yet, both before and after this phase of national structural reorganisation and expansion, it remains evident that Cape Town's policing history was still to be placed within the inherited structure of a local terrain, since it was mostly local imperatives and influences rather than national ones which continued to be important in shaping the social and cultural significance and role of the city police. It will have been apparent already that, since its colonial inception, Cape Town's 'new' urban constabulary was not only a force very much within the Victorian Metropolitan Police tradition, but one which had acquired an increasingly representative British inflexion. For instance, the direct recruitment of English-speaking colonial hands was fostered by conditions in the difficult South African War years in the early 1900s, when mounting urban law enforcement and peacekeeping calls caught the police on the hop. In the face of persistent local shortages and service irregularities, how best to fatten the thin police establishment was plain: the swift expansion of the Peninsula constabulary from 290 men in 1900 to almost 660 men by the end of 1903 was fed by a sizeable influx of Scottish (mostly ex-Glasgow police) and Irish (ex-Royal Irish Constabulary) foot constables.[16] They joined a 'bobby' force officered by old Peelite Englishmen like the Acting Chief of Police, G. C. Stanley-Foster, and containing Australians and even an anglicised Swede in the shape of Sub-inspector Thor Osberg.[17]

War demobilisation, beginning in 1902, brought a further batch of British job hunters as semi-skilled ex-servicemen looked to settling into a local livelihood. Some of these newly enlisting men had struck up relationships with Coloured women or had married them after being demobbed. In these cases, plebeian white British 'outsiders' became popularly assimilated by natives as known 'insiders'. A typical Scottish or Irish town constable would be either absorbed singly into predominantly Coloured residential localities or would find a comfortable place within Cape Town's tenuously surviving 'special tradition of multiracialism',[18] virtually a cocky lower-class sub-culture inside an increasingly corrosive segregationist milieu, a way of life in which, as Vivian Bickford-Smith has pointed out, in 'District Six and other predominantly working class areas, Whites, Coloureds and Africans ("illegally") lived in the same streets, the same houses, and with one another'.[19]

Even in fairly scruffy working-class neighbourhoods ordinarily marked by a generalised suspicion or dislike of the presence and attention of the police, socially integrated 'bobbies' like ex-Northumberland Fusilier Albert Thomas were able to lead lives underpinned by the resilience of family ties with workers and the social nexuses of neighbourhood, sport and religious affiliation. Accorded a mixture of respect and mock-deferential popularity for toughness, honesty and integrity, Thomas's policeman status was perhaps as potent a symbol of belonging as was his class. In certain circumstances, to be a Cape Town 'bobby' in the earlier decades of the twentieth century meant precisely this – to be recognised as someone who policed tolerantly and 'fairly' and had an entitlement to share in the associational life of a working community:

> British Bert he was called. He lived right in here, here with us. He was like the other Irish and those cockneys who were police – they came after the Boer War. Sergeant Thomas was fair, he never beat any person, he had a good name for himself. He used to walk so proud, with a tiny black baton which he kept in his jacket pocket. He was quite a visiting sort of chap, also, dropping and saying 'Morning, no trouble around here today, I hope.' Things like that. Then he'd even have a cup of tea. He wasn't all mighty and standoffish like he was European and he was Coloured. Man, in those days, I'm talking about even in the 'thirties and the war, there were *proper* police, they never carried guns.[20]

What men such as Albert Thomas surely embodied was the persistence in Cape Town of something of the ethos of a liberal policing tradition, centred on an awareness of local police autonomy, the hegemonic presence of municipal and local state authority, and modest police provision which in some contagious sense glossed 'social police' accountability with a powerfully resonant 'Britishness'. That conscientious upholder of such traditions, Acting Commissioner Colonel Robinson, clearly had the last element much in mind when in 1903 he voiced his disquiet that the immigration into Cape Town of vast hordes of 'alien' Europeans posed a potentially tricky crime problem, as they would 'hitherto have been subject to the rigid supervision of a military police, and it is to be feared that many may take some advantage of a milder control of the British police force'.[21]

Even allowing for a happy shortage of troublesome Fenians or Thuggee in the western Cape, this was a rather remarkable picture of restrained, consensual policing in the empire. What these Germans, French or Russians were entering was a colonial city with a police system apparently kid-gloved rather than iron-fisted in purpose, and reputedly quite unlike elsewhere in the empire, where, as in Ireland or India, for example, the police were customarily deployed in a more forceful and distressingly illiberal 'political' way.[22] Something of this quite beguiling order seems to have held good: exactly how much, and under what kind of durable local and popular conditions, is a large and intriguing historical question.

None of this is to say that those who guarded Cape Town's lingering liberal capitalist class and racial order against disagreeable levels of violent and malicious crime[23] did not have a coercive political function; nor is it to say that they did not play that imposing social control or class repressive role which more rootedly Marxist police historians unambiguously and exclusively allot to the police.[24] The more intrusive public order and public discipline work of the Cape Town police was a mandate obviously most acted upon either at times of economic crisis and widespread social distress or when a shifting political calculus produced urban upheaval and intensified tension.

In the 1880s, for instance, ethnic and religious frustrations within the city's Islamic population over social exclusion and roughshod intolerance of Muslim practices by bourgeois settlers boiled over into rowdy public demonstrations. When police waded in to disperse assemblies there were ugly clashes and some ferocious stone-throwing by enraged crowds, apparently baying, 'Kill the *dieners*'.[25] In these disorderly streets the thin lines of '*dieners*' or constables were certainly a considerable pro-vocation, aggravated by a prickly state of affairs in which, since the 1870s, they had also been moving in routinely to suppress the more exuberant forms of communal working-class recreation. The instabilities of the depression added further weight to these hostilities in the 1880s, fuelling the underlying character of community revolt; as living stan-dards in some of the poorest and most deprived parts of Cape Town deteriorated, angry Muslims and also the Coloured dispossessed hurled themselves at tiny, scattered clusters of monitoring police, whom they regarded as authoritarian petty despots. Engulfed by rioters, truncheon-bearing policemen found crowd control beyond their capacity, a number having to back off with cracked heads. It was only when the authorities fell back on the mobilisation of militia volunteers that demonstrators were overawed into dispersing.[26] In the sense of embattled, proletarian self-definition which came out of the slump, the police were, as Bickford-Smith has remarked, 'British and White, easily identified as protecting the interests of the dominant class'.[27] Yet if they did so, it was without themselves becoming a more visibly military kind of presence.

In the depressed years which followed the end of the South African war, the police invigilated what were construed to be seditious activities, kept a watch on labour unrest, and paid close attention to anything which threatened the maintenance of public peace. There was a spate of troubles, both through generally fragmentary working-class organisa-tion and through riot over this unsettled period, but undoubtedly the most convulsive moment of all was what the excitable Cape Town

[242]

newspaper, the *Cape Argus*, termed the 'Hooligan Riots' of August 1906. The immediate origin of this series of running disturbances was a mass demonstration of Cape Town's hungry unemployed organised by the avowedly Marxist Social Democratic Federation, a body founded by recent British immigrants of racial temper, including some ex-soldiers who would presumably not have found police employment to their liking. Egged on by an SDF orator who reminded listeners that 'law and order meant nothing more than the policeman and his club', a petitioning crowd, contemptuously described by police as 'low class people from the slums', attempted to march on parliament with a demand for work and a living wage.[28] It ran into a contingent of foot and mounted police which barred the way. But the SDF was persistent and well organised; demonstrators regrouped and on several successive days there were riots in which commercial property was attacked and there was some physical assault, including attacks on police by both men and women.

In response, careering mounted constables were deployed with some success to scatter a 'rabble tide' of marching gangs which were 'outside the pale of civilization'; in one tremulous incident, police who found themselves being manhandled drew firearms but fired into the air.[29] Sporadic police attempts at ritual crowd negotiation seemed generally to have got nowhere. British sub-inspectors spoke no Afrikaans/Dutch with which to try to parley with a hard core of non-respectable 'non-European' or 'European' men who were identified as ringleaders. Across a wall of resentment that now divided seething demonstrators and police they found no comprehensible vocabulary; there was probably none to find.

In the event, the turbulent and defiant reception the police received probably helped to tip the balance towards tougher measures of control: again, volunteer militia and regular troops were turned out as an aid to hard-pressed civil police. Beyond or beneath this was an unprofessional police intelligence system consisting of several dim private detectives hired to snoop on SDF and trade union political meetings and to report any insurrectionary plottings in the criminal maze of District Six, a disreputable locality which was to respectable Cape Town what 'Little Sodom' was to Liverpool or 'China' to Merthyr Tydfil. The level of trustworthiness and reliability displayed by these agents was very poor and regular Cape Town CID officers seem to have held them in low regard.[30]

The collapse of police authority during 'The Hooligan Riots' produced some interesting negotiation between colonial authority and the Cape Town-based African Peoples' Organisation, a body representative of skilled artisan and petty-bourgeois class interests, 'which sought to defend the franchise, residence and employment of "civilised"

Coloureds'.[31] Crewe, the Colonial Secretary, advised a dutiful APO-led delegation that in view of the need to pay greater attention to the means of anticipating future public order disturbances, 'it would be a wise thing ... that we should have certain numbers of your people employed in the police force who would be able to assist the Europeans who are now in the police.' Veldsman, the APO secretary, in turn assured Graham, the Attorney General, that the delegation favoured the swearing in of 'respectable' Coloured citizens; however, unless the terms of service were to be absolutely non-discriminatory, enlistment would not satisfactorily secure 'the full co-operation of the coloured people in the suppression of crime and the maintenance of law and order'. After some wrangling over wage scales and some toying with the remote alternative possibility of contracting African detectives from outside Cape Town, the authorities were able to move. Helped by a register of picked volunteers supplied by the Coloured delegation, the Attorney General authorised the discreet employment of several men on a monthly basis as undercover constables.[32] This co-operation and bounded integration may perhaps be seen as a testimony to an oscillating tradition of local liberalism; its moral category of respectability even drew some very slight adaptations in policing strategy into the sphere of paternal patronage and respectable independence.

The early twentieth century also saw Cape Town's over 10,000 African workers expelled from a tangle of cosmopolitan residential areas and segregated and disciplined with police repression. Clearly then, and also later, African dock and railway workers were wholly excluded from the dense cultural terrain of networks, motivations and values that appear to have been so important in constructing the Coloured working-class and petty-bourgeois view of the world of the 'bobby'. Instead, relations were expressed in invariably conflictual terms. The beginnings of enforced urban segregation in the city in 1901 – which saw Africans turfed out of District Six and other suburbs and lumped together in an outlying native location – was characterised by a rash of evaded and contested evictions. Police were charged with surveillance of compliance with removal orders, and empowered 'to use any force necessary to effect such removal' to the prescribed 'native reserve location' of Uitvlugt, renamed Ndabeni in 1902.[33] With mass African opposition taking the form of a location rent strike, provision was made for rents to be exacted under threat of criminal penalties;[34] police were directly involved in strikebreaking, hauling identified offenders off Cape Town-bound trains and arresting them. There was also regular police harassment of those who tried to organise public protest against removals and racial discrimination, typified by the breaking up of a meeting of Africans on Grand Parade in Cape Town and by other harsh interference with common rights of public meeting, assembly and movement.[35]

A massive influx of African labour into the city during and in the aftermath of the first world war produced another segregationist spasm in local municipal government and pressure groups representing white bourgeois interests. The early 1920s 'Underworld'[36] of Cape Town became a rather literal black legend. As the Ndabeni location collapsed under the pressure of continuous population inflow and continuing insecurity and disaffection Africans again installed themselves in the poorer terraces of the city. There they were watched by beady-eyed constables; but immediate action to enforce standing segregationist measures was at most half-hearted. Police activity was characterised by a token handful of arrests which failed to bring court prosecutions and by a bout of inertia, in which 'they let Africans live wherever they could find accommodation in Greater Cape Town'.[37] Some policemen openly confessed that they were reluctant to move against 'illegal' residents in the face of such large and stubbornly rooted numbers of offenders and of so much popular hostility. Outrage came not only from migrants themselves but also from neighbours partly united with them by common patterns of unskilled and casual work, and from those who collected rents by letting or sub-letting rooms or outside shacks to men commonly known in District Six as:

> the backyard people ... often they used to stay in people's yards, outside. They'd stay away until it was dark before they came back. Then, they had to be a bit careful, because the 'Irish' were checking on lots of native people who were staying in town.[38]

By 1923 there were increasingly shrill demands from civil leaders for the police to show less indifference to the degenerating 'human condition' of the town and attend to the need to expel Cape Town's alien underclass to the native location. An anticipated sweep failed, however, to materialise. There was no more than a desultory collection of drifters and others sleeping rough, some of whom were removed to Ndabeni by magistrates' order early in 1924. Furthermore, not all 'wandering natives' experienced arrest and the courts; some vagrants were given washing facilities, tea and bread, and lodged overnight in police stations before being sent off with homilies about respectable behaviour. Here is a classic example of Eric Monkkonen's argument that, whatever the founding historical purposes of uniformed police forces as instruments of class domination and control, 'managing' the 'dangerous classes' or the 'lawless classes' at times entailed the relative leniency of welfare service as well as repression.[39]

Finally, before any round-up, the police sought to ensure that additional location accommodation, hastily thrown up to cope with removals, had proper sanitation. 'Men of good character', like Colonel Gray or Inspector Kennedy, had the good sense to realise that dysentery ought not to be an additional penalty for those booted out to Ndabeni. And, as Christopher Saunders has pointed out, such officers were deplorably disinclined 'to act over the festive season, or while a visiting Naval Squadron was in Table Bay, fearing that Africans might resist being expelled from the town'. Several years later there were again clamorous protests from the Cape Town council that the police were being insufficiently dutiful in ensuring that affected Africans observed the oppressive Urban Areas Act by removing themselves to the new Langa location; the police shrugged that their regular force was undersized and not up to mass evictions.[40] In the inter-war years in general, while content to invigilate 'subversives' and to intervene selectively in demonstrations and labour disputes, the police were undoubtedly less than resolute in taking on the segregationist policing of Africans within the city.

Much the same was true of the second world war years when for large numbers of disembarking white imperial troops, particularly less disciplined Australian battalions, Cape Town's District Six 'China' became the promised land, as wide-eyed soldiers and deserters flooded in to savour the attractions offered by Coloured and African card-sharpers, prostitutes and illicit liquor outlets. Although there was great public pressure on the police to suppress the 'immorality' of unprecedented levels of interracial promiscuity, even with the considerable zeal of assisting military police they lacked the clout to make their law-enforcement presence effectively felt. Inhabitants soon learned that soldiers were 'warned about District Six', and when police tried to cordon off its boundary streets to troops they devised precarious rooftop entry and exit routes for randy brothel customers and those in search of drink. Within, the district was virtually a no-go area for the police, with the occasional intrepid and intruding constables hounded out 'by the Aussies, man, they just gave it to them ... it was such a rumpus. They were so wild'.[41]

Trading interests desperately petitioned the police to crack down on 'mad and drunken' Australians who indulged in wanton vandalism and intimidated shopkeepers and street traders into reducing the prices of foodstuffs and clothing for local girlfriends and the tribes of thin children who habitually followed them around, or who 'just helped themselves and encouraged the people to join them ... it was like Christmas'.[42] When, from time to time, the police did try to arrest offenders and to insist on better behaviour in the streets, they met with contempt and considerable intimidation themselves; as one District Six inhabitants remembers, 'You know what the Aussies did? Once the police did come and the Aussies just put them in the back of their own van, "like monkeys", and they just drove them around. But in those days the police was mild. Not like the *boere* that you have today.'[43] Here is a scrap of oral testimony also charged with significance for understanding popular historical definitions of a decisively changed police presence in Cape Town in the post-second world war period.

It also provides an appropriate point at which to return to the theme of 'bobbies' and 'boers' with which this chapter opened. Afrikaners were, of course, a far from negligible element in the ranks of Cape Town police in the earlier decades of the twentieth century. As successive post-war slumps and the 1930s depression intensified the mostly rural pauperisation of so-called 'poor whites', steadily growing numbers of 'Dutch/ Afrikaans-speaking policemen' sought security 'in the Cape Town SAP because they were unable to subsist in the impoverished rural areas'.[44] Responding to criticism of the recruitment of 'borderline cases', an official commission in 1919 also pointed out that a:

> real reason why recruits of this low standard of age and education are accepted is the fact that it was desired with the best intentions to afford a useful and honourable career to Europeans who belong to the Poor White and bijwoner class.[45]

For the most part, such men appear to have shaded into a force in which the hegemony of 'the hard core of older hands',[46] the intensely local beat of the 'Irish brigade', ran deep in people's social perceptions and social consciousness. Through this established milieu, Afrikaner constables also fell into a kind of 'bobby' identity; indeed, the social distance between them and those they policed could at times be close. With unmarried constables ineligible for barrack accommodation, a number of them were obliged to board cheaply in predominantly Coloured neighbourhoods because of wage levels which depressed their standard of living below that 'appropriate to a white policeman'.[47] For this they endured the racist sniggers of colleagues. Efforts to expand barrack places in the 1920s and 1930s may in fact be viewed more as a sign of concern about the need to prevent the 'contamination' or 'corruption' of impoverished constables than of any especially repressive intent towards the lower-class, racially jumbled areas in which such men were having to lodge.

Within the force, discontent over contract conditions and pay during the inflationary first world war years banded together Afrikaners and other constables in strike action in 1918; the brief stoppage, in which low-ranking Afrikaner strikers were prominent, drew quite appreciable popular support from both white and black workers, and a failed courtship from the Federation of Labour Unions.[48] Soldiers were drafted in to protect installations but, as with the 1918–19 Boston and London police

[247]

strikes, the Cape Town protest was almost inevitably regarded as more serious than it actually was.

Even as the Cape Western South African Police became more lower-class Afrikaner in origin, in Cape Town it retained its pervasive and legitimating 'traditional' communal identity through the 1920s to the 1940s. In the popular idiom of local beliefs and assumptions, there were differentiations between 'Irishmen' and 'Jewboys' in the force and 'Dutchmen', but the common attitude and temperament of policemen were viewed as somehow instinctively 'UP', or 'Hofmeyr-type people'.[49] In other words, in a variety of distinctive ways the Cape Town SAP was policing the social order and social discipline of the coalitionist United Party and its fragmentary liberal paternalist embodiment like the Cape parliamentarian J. H. Hofmeyr. The police were thus an integral part of an intensely local social and political environment in which a UP which endorsed 'the maintenance of white civilisation' and social, including residential, segregation between Coloureds and whites still had a conditional attachment to 'Coloureds' existing franchise rights and their inclusion with whites in the civilised labour policy'. Segregationalist zeal was still somewhat tempered by 'vague insinuations of special treatment' for Coloured citizens.[50]

While radical Coloured political organisations like the National Liberation League called for judicial investigation of police 'hooliganism' at anti-segregation protests at the end of the 1930s,[51] the police do not seem to have been particularly reviled or feared as *Afrikaners*. Police delegates were in fact welcomed to a 1942 NLL conference on violent crime in Cape Town, and were warmly applauded for bold promises of more rigorous action against the chronic street-gang menace centred in District Six, much of this rather an expression of Dutch courage. Sergeant Willem Nel, however, could not be accused of this; drafted in as 'a tough up-country policemen', his 1940s Special Squad virtually ran a personal war against criminal gangs, trying to contain disorder through heavy-handed apprehension of suspect inhabitants and through dealings with influential criminal power brokers like the almost legendary Globe Gang, overlooking their shady practices in return for Globe control of the more habitually murderous of their competitive gang rivals.[52]

Nel's campaign, often in the face of unnervingly violent street opposition, won not only the admiration of bourgeois and respectable working-class inhabitants but the apparent wary respect of his criminal opponents and collaborators. While he regarded the Globe Gang as 'very decent blokes', in many quarters he was clearly considered a similar sort of 'bloke' himself.[53] Memorably, he was perhaps Cape Town's last really conspicuous 'bobby'; a normally rowdy and fairly lawless working-class community not only knew him but where 'Oubaas' ('Old Boss') Nel lived. 'Oubaas Nel was half and half as they used to call him ... he had a Boer name but a character like the tough old Irish we used to have around here.'[54]

Change in the social identification, structure and significations of police behaviour is mirrored in the realignment of national politics after 1948, as an ascendant Afrikaner nationalism expanded the boundaries of juridico-legal state coercion. The shifting tendencies of crime control and class control became subsumed much more actively and directly as race control. It remains essential, and empirically accurate, for historians to pay attention to the way in which dominated black groups built an awareness in this period of a newly determinant *Boer* authority; its tribal cohesiveness and lacerating presence in the 1950s seemed to be fixing an ominous new future for a customarily 'British' city such as Cape Town. For within the context of the perceived experience that people drew from their own lives and traditions, and from the forces acting around and upon them, an Afrikaner nationalist government made a highly visible difference to modes of thought and behaviour.

The key element was quite clear. It was, as Jeffrey Butler has recently insisted, 'the exclusively *Afrikaner* character of post-1948 apartheid legislation, as distinct from South Africa's long-standing regime of white privilege and the segregation which secured it'.[55] For the city's identity it meant the imposition of the rationalising, 'regimented segregation of apartheid', brusquely eclipsing 'the more laissez-faire, rather haphazardly semi-segregated colonial city of British imperialism'.[56] For the city's police it meant a sharp accentuation of the role of Afrikaner 'outsiders' as the local captains of control; whatever the expansive recruitment tendencies of the preceding decades, it was the apartheid era which finally endowed Cape Town with 'basically an Afrikaans police force, nationally controlled and trained in Pretoria'.[57]

Moreover, it was the bloody-minded identity of those turned out to physically enforce new racist legislation, which weighed very heavily on the values and sensibilities of settled inner-city communities. For the local politics of the age of 'bobby' policing began to erode; a markedly more homogenous, newly recruited and inexperienced Afrikaans-speaking 'new police' nibbled through the controls of a popular civic liberalism of social contact and calculative deference. The rapid retirement of older men and their replacement by 'raw *Boere*, man, not the better kind of officer we were used to'[58] reflected the decomposition of the traditional and the familiar as upstart policemen no longer seemed to know their place.

Police enforcement of the most petty and odious imperatives of urban segregation turned what before 1948 had been a fairly 'badly managed drama' into a 'bitterly effective one'.[59] As the 'new' policing transcended

[249]

localism it left the indelible mark of apartheid humiliation on the lives
of growing numbers of black Capetonians. Those who sought autonomy
and to live as well as they could in the law-abiding, 'respectable' working-
class world they inhabited were sent scuttling back to the streets of
District Six, shocked and bemused at being hounded out of recreational
spots they had traditionally appropriated as their own:

> They even marked the benches! There was me and another girl and we just
> flopped down the bench and...God, these people. It was all *Boere*. 'Get up,
> bloody Hottentots, look where you sit. Stand up! Stand up!' Apartheid –
> we just got to know that. 'Hey – you know, watch where you're playing.'[60]

With unprecedented authoritarianism, law enforcers now reformed
custom.

There was also strong reaction within politicised, more bourgeois
Coloured neighbourhoods. Older schoolchildren sometimes engaged in
symbolic behaviour, activating cheeky cultural codes to assert identities
and allegiances intended to irritate or ridicule passing policemen. For
some the Union Jack was a natural symbol:

> We got a whole lot of little flags then, about 1949 [1947], I think, when
> the royal family came out ... Some days I used to take them to school.
> Well, one day we were hanging around after school, nothing to do. These
> two young *konstabels* came walking down. I said, 'Dare you, let's now show
> these *Boere* something.' So we waved our flags and chanted 'God save the
> Queen' when they came past. Hell, those Boere looked very cross.[61]

Other artful, and brazen, elements stopped policemen to ask for advice
or directions in artful and convoluted English, to the relish of com-
panions. These, and similar episodes, were part of a myriad of culturally
inflected responses to what was viewed as a malignant and illegitimate
Boer police presence.

This outlook also animated political organisation. The growth of
popular anti-apartheid agitation in Cape Town during the 1950s saw not
only an increase in intimidation by the security police but a significant
increase in the surveillance of 'agitators'. Like the police of Bombay
city, the security operations of Cape Town police mostly concentrated
on the quiet accumulation of political intelligence. Before the formation
of the feared Security Branch in the 1960s, 'political' policing does not
appear to have been seen as a serious physical threat. Those at gatherings
of radical groupings such as the Non-European Unity Movement knew
the identity of the podgy man with the fluttering notepaper as well as
he knew them. As one might expect, English-speaking orators were
quick to mock the presence and perseverance of known police spies,
regarded as feeble-minded 'Transvaal' or 'Free State' *Boere*:

That van Dyk, he was a terrible spy, it was so obvious. He was really an ignorant farm type, you could see it on his face, always confused. Well, on one occasion, one of our speakers stopped and said, 'Excuse me, sergeant, is this all too fast for you? Maybe you could spell it all better if I talked in block letters.' Man, he really brought the house down.[62]

Such asides naturally bore a more serious dimension. Taunting identifications eloquently underlined activists' increasing consciousness of themselves as preyed upon by a political police and, as the scorching rhetoric of the petty bourgeois-led NEUM reflected, their bitter social indignation at the racism and class inversion in relations with a discriminatory police:

recruited from the poorest layers of the Herrenvolk ... the semi-literacy and general coarseness of the majority of them is notorious ... in a country where possession of a white skin is an 'open sesame' to almost any walk of life, they have a particular grudge against all Non-Europeans ... they regard the educated non-European as someone who has risen at their expense.[63]

But for all the escalation of local feeling, for all that bobbies had become Boers, there were still some continuities with what was seen as an older, more nuanced style of policing. Something of the ambivalence could be seen in police repression of the Pan-Africanist Congress-led anti-pass law protest in the Cape Peninsula in 1960. In Gerald Gordon's novel *Four People*, a work which authentically embodies traces of that charged historical moment, representative experience of the police is captured by the character Philemon Zwelinzima Mfilu, who, exhausted after evading his uniformed pursuers, 'slept awhile, dreaming again of the hovering tongue, helmet and baton but now the figure had the face of a jackal, larger than he had ever seen and behind it he could hear the barks of other jackals'.[64] And yet, when some 30,000 Africans marched into the centre of Cape Town, the city's chief of police, Colonel I. B. S. Terreblanche, averted a head-on collision through receptive personal mediation with the march leader, Philip Kgosana, and attendant white liberals, negotiating a conditional disbanding of the march on the basis of police good faith and acceptance of the legitimacy of grievances. Terreblanche clearly had no 'appetite for confrontation'.[65] The police in Cape Town always acted as a social control apparatus: clearly, the terrain of compromise and coercion upon which they worked was politically complex and culturally dense.

Notes

1 J. G. van Alpen, *Jan Venter, S.A.P.* (Cape Town, n.d., c. 1900–20), pp. 29–30.
2 C. van Onselen, *Studies in the Social and Economic History of the Witwatersrand, 1886–1914*, 2, *New Nineveh* (London, 1982), p. 113.
3 W. H. Worger, *South Africa's City of Diamonds: mine workers and monopoly capitalism in Kimberley, 1867–1895* (New Haven, 1987), p. 123.
4 Van Alphen, *Jan Venter*, p. 31.
5 R. Ross, 'Structure and Culture in pre-industrial Cape Town', Western Cape 'Roots and Realities' conference paper, Centre for African Studies, University of Cape Town, July 1986.
6 J. Western, 'Undoing the Colonial City', African Studies Association conference paper, Los Angeles, October 1984.
7 P. W. Laidler, *A Tavern of the Ocean* (Cape Town, n.d.), pp. 105–6, 160; L. van Onselen, *A Rhapsody in Blue* (Cape Town, 1960), p. 12; K. D. Elks, 'The police and the people: Cape Town, 1825–1850', *Cabo*, 4, I (1986), p. 13; 'Crime, community and police in Cape Town, 1825–1850', M.A. thesis, University of Cape Town (1986), p. 22.
8 Elks, 'Police and the people', p. 15.
9 *Ibid.*, 'Crime, community and police', p. 36. For the conduct and standing of the police more generally in this earlier period see also Elks, 'Crime and social control in Cape Town, 1830–1850', in C. Saunders *et al.* (eds.), *Studies in the History of Cape Town*, 6 (Centre for African Studies, University of Cape Town, 1988), especially pp. 26, 32, 39.
10 Cape Archives (CA), I/CT 14/66, Resident Magistrate to Colonial Office, 27 April 1874.
11 *Cape Weekly Chronicle*, 17 July 1880.
12 S. Feast, 'The Policeman as Thief-taker, Street-cleaner and Domestic Missionary: Police and Policing in Cape Town in the 1860s and 1870s', B. A. Hons. dissertation, University of Cape Town (1988), p. 17.
13 R. Hallett, 'Policemen, pimps and prostitutes – public morality and police corruption in Cape Town, 1902–1904', in Saunders (ed.), *Studies*, 1 (1979), p. 9.
14 *Ibid.*, pp. 9, 35.
15 Van Onselen, *Rhapsody*, p. 7.
16 *Cape Parliamentary Papers (CPP)*, G.42–1901, Cape Town Police Force, Report for 1900; G.22–1904, Cape Police No. 3 District, Report for 1903.
17 Hallett, 'Public morality and police corruption', pp. 9–10; A. Bank, 'Crime in Cape Town, 1890 to 1900', B.A. Hons. dissertation, University of Cape Town (1988), p. 18.
18 The phrase is G. M. Fredrickson's: *White Supremacy: a comparative study on American and South African history* (New York, 1981), p. 260.
19 V. Bickford-Smith, 'Commerce, Class and Ethnicity in Cape Town, 1875 to 1902', Ph.D. thesis, University of Cambridge (1989), p. 447.
20 Interview, February 1988, Mrs A. H., b. 1898, Cape Town; father, storeman; mother, seamstress. Dressmaker.
21 *CPP*, G.22–1904, Cape Police No. 3 District, Report for 1903.
22 For India see David Arnold, *Police Power and Colonial Rule: Madras, 1859–1947* (Delhi, 1985), and also B. Porter, *The Origins of the Vigilant State: the London Metropolitan Police Special Branch before the first world war* (London, 1987), p. 17.
23 See Hallett, 'Violence and social life in Cape Town in the 1900s', in Saunders (ed.), *Studies*, 2 (1979), pp. 126–76.
24 For which see, for example, S. L. Harring, *Policing a Class Society: the experience of American cities, 1865–1915* (New Brunswick, 1983).
25 *Cape Times*, 20 January 1886; *Cape Argus*, 19 January 1886. See also I. Goldin, *Making Race: the politics and economics of coloured identity in South Africa* (Cape Town, 1987), p. 29.
26 *Cape Times*, 21 January 1886.
27 Bickford-Smith, 'Class and ethnicity', p. 356.
28 *Cape Times*, 3 August 1906.

29 *Cape Argus*, 9 August 1906.
30 *Cape Times*, 18 August 1906.
31 Goldin, *Making Race*, p. 32.
32 CA, AG 1709, folio I, Papers relating to the 1906 Disturbances; more generally, R. Hallett, 'The Hooligan Riots, Cape Town: August 1906', in Saunders (ed.), *Studies*, 1 (1979), pp. 42–87.
33 Saunders, 'The creation of Ndabeni: urban segregation and African resistance in Cape Town', in *Studies*, 1, p. 172.
34 M. W. Swanson, 'The sanitation syndrome: bubonic plague and urban native policy in the Cape Colony, 1900–1909', *Journal of African History*, 18, 3 (1977), p. 397.
35 *Cape Times*, 15 March 1901.
36 *Ibid.*, 6 February 1922.
37 Saunders, 'From Ndabeni to Langa', in *Studies*, 1, p. 196.
38 Interview, January 1989, Mr S.C., b. 1927, Cape Town; father, waiter; mother, laundress. Schoolteacher.
39 E. H. Monkkonen, *Police in Urban America, 1860–1920* (New York, 1981), pp. 86–92; 'From cop history to social history: the significance of the police in American history', *Journal of Social History*, 15, 2 (1982), p. 580.
40 Saunders, 'Langa', pp. 199, 209.
41 Interview, March 1986, Mrs B.J., b. 1915, Cape Town; father, dockworker; mother, domestic worker. Domestic worker.
42 *Cape Times*, 22 August 1942; interview, December 1985, Mrs G.J., b. 1919, Stellenbosch; father, factory worker; mother, factory worker. Factory worker.
43 Interview, Mrs G.J.
44 D. Lombaard, 'The Cape Town police strike of 1918', in Saunders *et al.* (eds.), *Studies*, 5 (1984), p. 172.
45 Union Government, *UG. 49–1919, Third Report of the Public Service Commission of Inquiry*, p. 14; Lombaard, 'The Cape Town Police Strike of 1918', B.A. Hons. dissertation, University of Cape Town (1982), p. 50.
46 Van Alphen, *Jan Venter*, p. 159.
47 *Cape Times*, 19 February 1919.
48 For the strike generally see Lombaard, 'Police Strike'.
49 Interview, January 1989, Mrs V.L., b. 1918, Cape Town; father, artisan; mother, dressmaker. Shopworker.
50 G. Lewis, *Between the Wire and the Wall: a history of South African 'Coloured' politics* (Cape Town, 1987), pp. 193, 247.
51 *Cape Times*, 29 March 1939.
52 On Nel and the suppression of street gangsterism see D. Pinnock, 'From Argie Boys to Skolly Gangsters: the lumpen-proletarian challenge of the street-corner armies in district six, 1900–1951', in Saunders and H. Phillips (eds.), *Studies*, 3 (1980), p. 163; *The Brotherhoods: street gangs and state control in Cape Town* (Cape Town, 1984), pp. 24–30; 'Stone's boys and the making of a Cape Flats Mafia', in B. Bozzoli (ed.), *Class, Community and Conflict: South African perspectives* (Johannesburg, 1987), pp. 420–1.
53 *Ibid.*, 'Stone's boys', p. 420.
54 Interview, November 1987, Mr P.D., b. 1923, Cape Town; father, street vendor; mother, factory worker. Printworker.
55 In his review of S. Marks and S. Trapido (eds.), *The Politics of Race, Class and Nationalism in Twentieth Century South Africa* (1987), *Journal of Imperial and Commonwealth History*, 17, 1 (1988), p. 133.
56 Western, 'Colonial city'; see also his *Outcast Cape Town* (Cape Town and Pretoria, 1981), pp. 31–58.
57 K. Albert, 'The Police and their Image: a comparative study of the American and Cape Town policeman', M.Soc.Sci. thesis, University of Cape Town (1978), p. 6.
58 Interview, Mr P.D.
59 G. H. Pirie and D. M. Hart, 'The transformation of Johannesburg's black western areas', *Journal of Urban History*, II, 4 (1985), p. 406.

60 Nasson, ' "She preferred living in a cave with Harry the snake-catcher": towards an oral history of popular leisure and class expression in District Six, Cape Town, ca. 1920s–1950s', in P. Bonner *et al.* (eds.), *Holding their Ground* (Johannesburg, 1990).

61 Interview, Mr H.J., b. 1938, Cape Town; father, shop owner; mother, clerical worker. Schoolteacher.

62 Interview, March 1989, Mrs H.G., b. 1917, Cape Town; father, businessman; mother, teacher. Schoolteacher.

63 *Torch*, 20 May 1956.

64 G. Gordon, *Four People: a novel of South Africa* (Cape Town, 1964), p. 205.

65 Terreblanche had, however, overplayed his hand and was reprimanded by government Ministers for having been too 'soft'. For the incident see T. Lodge, 'The Cape Town troubles, March–April 1960', *Journal of Southern African Studies*, 4, 2 (1978), p. 238; *Black Politics in South Africa since 1945* (Johannesburg, 1983), pp. 222–3.

INDEX

Note: Page references in italics indicate tables and illustrations.

INDEX